HOW TO SUCCEED IN LAW SCHOOL

Fourth Edition

Professor Gary A. Munneke
Pace University School of Law

BARRON'S

Copyright © 2008, 2001, 1994, 1989
by Barron's Educational Series, Inc.

All inquiries should be addressed to:
Barron's Educational Series, Inc.
250 Wireless Boulevard
Hauppauge, New York 11788
www.barronseduc.com

ISBN-13: 978-0-7641-3979-6
ISBN-10: 0-7641-3979-7

Library of Congress Catalog Card No. 2008009059

Library of Congress Cataloging-in-Publication Data
Munneke, Gary A.
How to succeed in law school / Gary A. Munneke.—4th ed.
    p. cm.
Includes bibliographical references and index.
ISBN-13: 978-0-7641-3979-6
ISBN-10: 0-7641-3979-7
1. Law—Study and teaching—United States. 2. Law students—
United States—Handbooks, manuals, etc. I. Title.

KF283 .M86 2008
340.071'173—dc22   2008009059

PRINTED IN THE UNITED STATES OF AMERICA

9 8 7 6 5 4 3 2 1

Acknowledgments

I wish to thank law students beyond count who have contributed their insights to my understanding of the law school experience, but especially my wife, Sharon. I also wish to thank the many professional colleagues who contributed diverse perspectives during the preparation of this text. Finally, I acknowledge the thinking of Brian Siegel, whose thoughts have been incorporated in this edition.

—Professor Gary A. Munneke, J.D.

The author gratefully acknowledges the following sources:

Legalines; Torts, Adaptable to Materials by Prosser. Copyright © 1988 by Harcourt Brace Legal & Professional Publications, Inc. Reprinted with permission of the publisher.

Gilbert Law Summaries: Torts by Marc A. Franklin, Twenty-first Edition. Copyright © 1997 by Harcourt Legal & Professional Publications, Inc. Reprinted with permission of the publisher.

Torts in a Nutshell: Injuries to Persons and Property, 1977 by Edward J. Kionka. Reprinted with permission of the West Publishing Company, St. Paul, Minnesota.

"Intentional Interference with the Person," reprinted from *Prosser & Keeton on Torts,* Fifth edition, 1984, with permission of the West Publishing Company, St. Paul, Minnesota.

Sample Multiple Choice Exam Questions reprinted with permission of Professor Richard Walck, Williamsburg, Virginia.

Restatement of the Law, 2nd, Torts, copyright © 1964 by the American Law Institute. Reprinted with the permission of The American Law Institute.

Table of Contents

About the Author   x

Chapter 1. What Is Success?   1

   A. Introduction   1
   B. How You Define Success   2
   C. Everyone Is Unique   4
   D. Something Different   5

Chapter 2. Choosing a Law School   7

   A. The Right School for You   7
   B. Your Law School   8
   C. Setting   10
   D. Day Versus Evening School   10
   E. Curriculum   11

Chapter 3. Understanding the Law School Experience   12

   A. The Law School Calendar   12
      1. Orientation   12
      2. First Classes   13
      3. Routine   16
      4. The Wall   17
      5. Panic   18
      6. First Semester Finals   18
      7. Semester Break   18
      8. Renewed Hope   19
      9. The January Blues   19
      10. Falling Behind   19
      11. The Mad Rush   19
      12. Finals Again   20

   B. Law School Courses   20
      1. Torts   21
      2. Property   21
      3. Contracts   21
      4. Civil Procedure   22

5. Constitutional Law   22
6. Criminal Law   23
7. Professional Responsibility   23
8. Legal Writing   23

C. The Professors   24

D. The Students   26
1. Classmates   26
2. Upperclass Students   29

E. The Law School Culture   30
1. Rules and Procedures   30
2. Relaxation and Breaks   32
3. Competition   33

Chapter 4. Studying the Law   34

A. The Classroom Experience   34
1. Class Preparation   34
2. Briefing Cases   48
3. Classroom Routine   54
4. Note Taking   63

B. After Class   66
1. After Class Review   66
2. Talking to Professors   67
3. Outside Reading   68
4. Synthesizing   70
5. Outlines   71
6. Checklists   76

C. Other Concerns   76
1. Memorization Versus the Big Picture   76
2. Study Groups   77
3. Computers   78

D. Using the Library   78

Chapter 5. Taking Exams   80

A. The Role of Ongoing Study   80

B. Review for Exams   81
   1. By the Professor   81
   2. By Yourself   81
   3. With Your Study Group   82
   4. Practice Exams   83

C. What Kind of Exam?   83
   1. Essay Exams   83
   2. Short Answer Exams   86
   3. Multiple-Choice Exams   88
   4. Combined Formats   90
   5. Other Testing Options   91

D. The Examination   92
   1. Beforehand   93
   2. Instructions   93
   3. Read the Question   94
   4. Organize   95
   5. IRAC   103
   6. Logic   105

E. Writing   107
   1. Grammar and Style   107
   2. Legibility   108

F. Time   110

G. Test Anxiety   112

H. Practice Questions   113
   1. Problem 1—Sally Westchester   113
   2. Problem 2—Ronnie and Nancy   121
   3. Problem 3—Sam Student   125

I. Conclusion   127

Chapter 6. Managing Technology in Law School   128

A. Electronic Learning   128
B. Legal Research   129
C. Computers   130

Chapter 7. Avoiding the Pitfalls of Law School   132

A. Time Management   132
  1. Common Difficulties   133
  2. A Time Management Model   133
  3. Establish a Schedule   134
  4. The Daily List   135
  5. A Tickler System   135

B. Money Management   136
  1. Financial Planning   136
  2. Financial Aid   136
  3. State Versus Private Schools   137
  4. Working   137
  5. Scholarships   138
  6. Budgeting   139

C. Stress Management   140
  1. Responsibility   140
  2. Commitment   140
  3. Little Aggravations   141
  4. Signs of Stress   141
  5. Stoicism   142
  6. Causes   142
  7. Coping   142
  8. Exercise   143
  9. Diet   143
  10. R & R   143
  11. Meditate   144
  12. Help   144

D. Sex, Drugs, and Rock-and-Roll   145
  1. Life in the Fast Lane   145
  2. Prognosis for Type A's   146
  3. A Nonreligious Argument for Slowing Down   146

E. The Job Market   146

Chapter 8. Diverse Students   149

A. Women   149
B. Racial and Ethnic Minorities   150

C. Second Career Students   151
D. Physically Challenged Students   151

Chapter 9. After the First Year   152

A. Academics   152
  1. Class Rank   152
  2. Classroom   153
  3. Course Selections   154

B. Student Activities   155
  1. Law Review   155
  2. Moot Court   156
  3. Student Government   156
  4. Special Interest Groups   157

C. Other Learning Experiences   157
  1. Scholarly Writing   158
  2. Research Assistants   158
  3. Nonlaw Courses   158
  4. Clinical Education   159
  5. Skills Training   159
  6. Summer School   159
  7. Foreign Study   160
  8. Specialized Curricula   160
  9. Work Experience   160

D. Problems   161
  1. Waning Interest   161
  2. Self-fulfilling Prophecy   162
  3. Jobs   162

Chapter 10. Conclusions—What Is Success?   163

APPENDICES

A. Suggested Reading   166
B. Resource Materials on Intent and Battery   169
C. More Torts Questions   193
D. More Long Essay Questions   204
E. More Short Answer Questions   217

INDEX   228

About the Author

Gary A. Munneke is a Professor of Law at Pace University School of Law in White Plains, New York. He is the author of numerous books and articles on the legal profession and legal education, including the areas of career planning and placement, as well as lawyer recruitment and training. These publications include: *The Legal Career Guide, Careers in Law, Opportunities in Law Careers, Your New Lawyer, Non-Legal Careers for Lawyers,* and *Materials and Cases on Law Practice Management.* Since 1988, he has prepared the introductory section of *Barron's Guide to Law Schools.* He has spoken at numerous programs for lawyers, law students, and prelaw students, and conducts specialized training for entering law students on how to succeed in law school.

Professor Munneke is a member of the Texas and Pennsylvania bars, and is active in the American Bar Association where he serves as a member of the ABA Board of Governors and House of Delegates.* He has served as chair of the ABA Law Practice Management Section, and as chair of the Law Practice Management Publishing Board, on the editorial boards of *Legal Economics* and *Barrister* magazines, as a member of the Task Force on the Role of the Lawyer in the 1980s, Standing Committee on Publishing Oversight, and as president and research chair of the National Association for Law Placement. He has been recognized as a fellow of the American Bar Foundation and the College of Law Practice Management, and by *Who's Who in American Law.* Before coming to Pace, where he teaches Torts, Professional Responsibility and Law Practice Management, Professor Munneke was a member of the faculty at Widener University School of Law and assistant dean at the University of Texas School of Law where he received his J.D. in 1973.

---

*The opinions expressed in this book represent the views of the author and do not reflect the policy of the American Bar Association or its Board of Governors.

CHAPTER 1

What Is Success?

A. Introduction

A good starting point in addressing the topic of how to succeed in law school might be to try to define success. How you define that elusive term may well determine whether or not you achieve it in law school, in your career, and in life. Whereas much of this book addresses the nuts and bolts of maximizing your potential in the legal education process, before you take the time to look at the specifics, consider briefly the bigger picture.

In 2007, there were over 1,100,000 lawyers in the United States. Of these, slightly over half are engaged in the private practice of law. They provide legal services for individual and institutional clients. All the rest work in a wide variety of roles in corporations, government agencies, education, private associations, the military, and entrepreneurial activities. Their work is as varied as human endeavor itself, because legal issues impact every aspect of modern society. While the lawyer population is concentrated most heavily in large urban and metropolitan areas, lawyers live and work almost everywhere.

Most readers will have heard or read that the United States today has more lawyers than any society in history. Many will have heard somewhere that all these lawyers represent a colossal waste of intellectual talent, or that our country is "overlawyered" already. Such views ignore the reality that the institutions of a complex, pluralistic, rights-oriented society require lawyers in order to function. Whether or not society benefits from so many lawyers, those who enter the legal profession cannot escape the consequences of these numbers. Law practice is extremely competitive, and many lawyers at some point in their careers will not practice law. For someone just starting law school, the range of opportunities after graduation is heavily influenced by law school performance.

B. How You Define Success

Take a few minutes to create a fantasy of your perfect job. Imagine yourself at that point in your career where you have achieved all the goals you have set for yourself by undertaking a legal education. What kind of work will you be doing? For whom will you work? What services will you provide? In what kind of organization will you work? What will be your role? Where will you be? What will your lifestyle be like? When you look back over your life, what will you tell people were your accomplishments? When you die, what will they say at your funeral?

Although you may not be able to know with certainty where life's crooked road will take you, you can and should imagine where you would like it to go. Store your fantasy in a pocket in your mind. Pull it out when times get tough. Change it when times change. Run with it when time flies. Implicit in this fantasy should be your own definition of success. That definition will determine your perception of success in law school as well as life. There are several predominant views on law school success, and it may help you to look at those now.

Will you consider yourself a success in law school if you graduate at the top of your class? If this is the criterion, then there is little hope for most entering law students. With 200 law schools there can be only 200 valedictorians. If there are 45,000 annual law school graduates, only 4,500 can graduate in the top 10 percent of their class. Many people who choose to go to law school are competitive by nature. For them it is the race that counts. Like an Olympic gold medalist, there is no point in aspiring to attain second place. These students often have pursued life as a series of competitions with winning as the ultimate objective. They will pursue their careers with the same ardor, seeking victory in every case, and defining success as a win-loss record.

If you must win every battle in every war to consider yourself successful, the chances are good that you will be doomed to failure, in law as well as life. In this profession, victory is seldom total or defeat ultimate. You will win some, lose some, and settle some on the courthouse steps. Your competitive nature can help you if you maintain some perspective.

Do you define success as finishing law school? Perhaps you are just thankful to have been accepted. Maybe school has always been a struggle for you, and you have fought and clawed every step of the way against formidable odds and slim probabilities. You might be the first in your family to attend law school, or even college. English may be a second language for you. Your resources may be so limited that you have had to work and scrape to put yourself through school. You may have a family to support and pressure at work. You may have personal or family problems that get in the way of accomplishing what you might without these impediments. For you, simply graduating may be the fulfillment of your dream.

If you define success as this sort of uphill battle, you should remember not to set your sights too low. You cannot let your problems become your excuse. And you cannot let graduation become the culmination of your search for success.

Do you define success as getting the job you want when law school is over? Frequently, people in this group place too much of their identity on one outcome. They set themselves up for failure by establishing goals based on vague, ill-considered perceptions of what lawyers do or how much money they make. Sometimes these students are seeking shortcuts to material goals; sometimes their interests are defined by a political, social, or moral agenda for which law is a vehicle.

These students need to keep an open mind. They need to realize that opportunities other than those they perceived when they entered law school may ultimately serve them better. They need to have alternatives if their first choices fail to materialize.

Do you define success as learning? In many respects, this is a sensible approach to law school because it places success in the context of developing the professional skills and obtaining the legal knowledge to become a competent lawyer. Here, too, lie pitfalls for the unwary.

In the most extreme form, you may adopt learning itself as your goal and become a professional student. If you are lucky, you will get a job as a law professor and be paid for your study. If you are unlucky, you simply may be considered a dilettante by friends and colleagues. In the less extreme form, you may find practice frustrating, never having time to fully research any subject or keep up with changes in the law or reflect about what the law ought to be. If you define success in this way, you will need to let your pragmatic side prevail from time to time.

Do you define success in terms of personal happiness? Perhaps law school and a legal career are vehicles for financing or creating the lifestyle you want. It is clear that a career in law can provide a vehicle for attaining a good lifestyle, and that it can afford in the long run great personal and professional satisfaction.

Although in one sense all of us want to be happy, some people confuse long-term satisfaction with short-term gratification. For them, happiness means having fun. Unfortunately, some people never learn to delay gratification. They want the best of everything; they want it all; they want it now. They forget that law school is not always fun, and practice is frequently not easy. Having a good time can stand in the way of doing what you have to do. On the other end of the spectrum are those individuals who seek happiness but forestall satisfaction forever. For these puritans, the good life is always just around the corner. Balancing professional work and personal life is not easy, but for those who try career satisfaction and happiness are not incompatible.

Do you define success in terms of recognition? You may have relied upon pats on the back and the encouragement of friends and loved ones to let you know that you have done a good job. Your wall may be covered with certificates and awards that demonstrate your success. Your quest for such tangible acknowledgments of your efforts may have become the dominant, motivating force in your life.

Unfortunately, in law school the pats on the back are all too few. And after graduation, you may find that fame is frequently fickle and elusive. In the practice of law, you may labor long in the vineyards without being recognized for the quality of your wine. If you have always relied on others for validation, you will need to find ways to appreciate and reward yourself.

C. Everyone Is Unique

You can help yourself in law school by defining success in a way that is consistent with your goals in life, flexible enough to bend with the winds of change, and realistic enough to let you feel good about yourself for what you accomplish.

The purpose of presenting these scenarios is not to discourage or depress you. It is rather to demonstrate that there are many ways to define success, and that each has inherent dangers. Successful people possess a battery of skills that help them achieve their goals, and many "successful" individuals refer to their good fortune as "being in the right place at the right time." Maybe being in the right place at the right time involves more than luck. This book proceeds on the assumption that success is not a matter of fate, but a complex and imprecise commodity involving specific skills that can be learned. Whereas success is ultimately subjective, and never total, it can be achieved if you know how to go about it.

This book contains ten chapters. Chapter 2 discusses important considerations in choosing a law school. Chapter 3 provides an overview of the law school experience. It will help you to know what to expect and how to cope. Chapter 4 deals with the study of law. It will help you to manage the learning process. Chapter 5 addresses the examination process, including both studying and taking tests. It will help you to maximize your performance on these instruments. Chapter 6 describes a number of practical tools you can utilize to make law school more manageable. It will help you to derive all the benefit you can from your legal education. Chapter 7 addresses some of the common pitfalls law students encounter. It could help you avoid disaster. Chapter 8 offers some specific advice to women, students of color, and physically challenged students, who represent student populations with unique concerns. Chapter 9 examines legal education after the first year, and offers insights into ways to maximize success in the upper class years. If these problems apply to you, the chapter will include suggestions on how to overcome them. Chapter 10 looks beyond law school to your career as a lawyer. It will return again to the issue of success, and offer some parting thoughts to abide you on your journey. Throughout the text, you will find specific examples and hints to help you to deal with the practicalities and uncertainties of law school.

D. Something Different

The very fact that you have picked up this book suggests that you are entering law school with at least a mild degree of trepidation. You probably have been inundated with horror stories from family, friends, prelaw advisors, and newspaper articles. You may have been warned that law school is "unlike anything you have ever done before." This unsettling pronouncement implies that a law school is like some impenetrable swamp, pocked with quicksand and populated by vile creatures lying in wait to devour the hapless traveler.

Remember: over 40,000 of us every year come out alive and well on the other side. It may help to look back on some of the other barriers in your educational life.

When your mom bundled you off to kindergarten, she admonished you, "This is school. It's different from anything you have ever done before." And when you left elementary school to go to junior high, she reminded you, "This year you have to change classes every period. It's going to be different from anything you have ever done before." Then you went away to college, and if you can think back to that eventful day, your car was packed to capacity with all your earthly belongings and whatever else you could sneak out of the house. Remember mom and dad on the porch waving, as they told you once again, "You're on your own now. Nobody to tell you what to do; nobody to wake you up. This is different from anything you have ever done before." Surprisingly, miraculously, you survived college, just as you did all those previous experiences. Those of you who have worked, gone to graduate school, served in the military, or gotten married could cite other experiences different from anything you have ever done before.

The point of all this is that you survived those other transitions in life, and you can survive this one. In fact, one of the reasons you will succeed in law school is that you have learned how to handle things you have never done before. You bring with you to law school a unique set of skills and abilities that have helped you to succeed before. When you understand how law school works and what you need to do, you can succeed here, too.

CHAPTER 2
Choosing a Law School

A. The Right School for You

It is axiomatic to say that every law school applicant should strive to choose the best possible law school for him or her. Many readers will have spent much of the past year applying to law schools and trying to make the "right" decision. Even casual reflection should confirm the obvious—there is no single best choice for every person. As individuals we are diverse and heterogeneous, and our needs vary considerably.

Many applicants do not stop to think that success in law school starts long before they actually enroll; success may be influenced dramatically by their choice of school. Some, perhaps on the assumption that law schools are basically interchangeable, simply select the most prestigious school (based on some magazine survey). The quality of the educational program and the reputation of the institution are definitely factors to consider, but they are not the only factors. Even among superficially similar law schools, a closer look will indicate that each has its own personality. If you have ever spent time around identical twins, you probably learned that they are not all that identical. It is the same with law schools.

Your decision about which law school to attend should focus on your own unique needs as a student. If you can find a good fit for your personality, study habits, competitiveness, interests, and values, you will be a happier law student. And if you are a happy law student, you will probably be a good law student.

How many unhappy law students are dissatisfied with law school itself, and how many are dissatisfied with the law school they chose to attend? Who knows? It is very likely, however, that at least some of the discontented students would have fared better in a different environment.

If you discover that you are not satisfied with your choice of law schools, think about changing schools before changing careers. Almost all schools accept a small number of transfer students after their first year; many schools accept visiting students (who graduate from their "home" school) for up to one year of study. A few schools offer foreign study programs (see p. 160) that could provide respite from an uncomfortable situation.

Competition for transfer seats is generally intense. Since law schools usually admit no more transfer students than the number they have lost from the previous year's first year class, and since the number of applicants is often much greater than the number of available seats, academic excellence is often a prerequisite for acceptance as a transfer student.

The downside of transferring is that transfer students walk into a situation where friendships among classmates have been made, law reviews and moot court teams have been selected, and adjustment to law school has been completed. Transfer students may feel isolated; they may lose academic credit; they may have difficulty explaining the change when they go to job interviews.

This is not a decision to be made lightly, but for some students transferring or visiting at another school may be a viable option. It is undoubtedly easier to make a choice you can live with at the outset than to undo a bad choice later. Analogies to marriage immediately come to mind.

B. Your Law School

What factors contribute to making your law school unique? Although it is easy to make generalizations about the law school experience, based upon similarities in legal education throughout the United States, there are some important differences among law schools also. Your law school may have special traditions, rules, and other elements that make it different from the prototypical law school described here.

One issue that tends to have a disparate impact on law schools is prestige. This factor tends to be perpetuated by U.S. News "rankings." Although the ABA, LSAC, and most legal educators decry such rankings, they persist because they give students and law firms an easy answer. The U.S. News tiers, however, are basically meaningless, and usually confusing. There are between 15 and 20 genuinely "elite" law schools that are widely recognized as most prestigious. There are probably 20 to 30 other law schools that think of themselves as, and are considered in some circles to be, comparable to those in the first group.

A third group of one hundred or more schools have either not attained or do not aspire to the inner circle. These include many newer schools, state law schools whose primary mission is serving the population of their state, established law schools whose resources limit their objectives, and law schools where internal considerations (e.g., disputes with a central university administration, faculty infighting) have held back the school's development.

In many larger cities, there are two or more law schools. Within the area, there is probably a pecking order of prestige, influencing each school's ability to attract students. New schools, and older schools with checkered histories in the legal community, may not receive the recognition that the quality of their educational programs merit.

A few schools comprise a fourth group whose institutions provide a minimal quality of education. They lack adequate resources to do more than train lawyers for a purely local practice. These schools barely meet American Bar Association accreditation standards and, sometimes exist under the cloud of losing ABA approval. Fortunately, only a handful of accredited schools fall into this category. You should understand, however, that every school accredited by the ABA must meet rigorous standards enforced through regular inspections.

A fifth group of schools includes those that lack national ABA accreditation and are approved only in the state where they operate. The graduates of these schools usually can sit for the bar examination only in the state where they went to school, significantly limiting the geographic mobility of graduates. These institutions tend to be the least prestigious in the law school world.

Prestige generally is not a matter of discrete categories, but rather a fuzzy continuum that varies considerably depending upon the source. The relative prestige of the school, as perceived by those within the law school itself, has an impact on perceptions and attitudes within the law school community. Students at the most elite law schools may be rather smug; all others carry with them inferiority complexes of varying degrees. Your success in law school will depend in part upon your ability to maintain a positive attitude about yourself and your school, regardless of where you might be.

C. Setting

Another differentiating characteristic among law schools is the law school setting. As stated previously, the nation's largest metropolitan areas have several law schools, and these law schools vary from purely urban settings to suburban ones. Other law schools may be found in smaller cities, including many state capitals. Still other schools are located in small towns outside any major population center. These differences in environment have significant impact on the individual school's culture. For instance, urban campuses tend to attract more diverse student bodies than do suburban schools. The availability of legal employers to provide part-time jobs for law students may vary considerably. For instance, law schools located in seats of government or banking centers will have access to more employment positions in the public sector.

D. Day Versus Evening School

Another differentiation is between schools that have part-time or evening programs and those that do not. Part-time students usually work during the day at full-time jobs and go to law school at night. Evening students fall into two basic groups: those who must work full-time in order to attend school, and students returning to school as part of a mid-career adjustment. Generally, evening students are older than day students by virtue of their various experiences between college and law school. This does not mean that day students have not taken time away from school to work, play, have children, or con-template life. Many day students do these things, but as a rule, more of the part-time students have been out of school for a longer period of time. Thus, the backgrounds, interests, needs, and attitudes of evening students often differ from their full-time counterparts and, therefore, law schools with day and evening programs possess two distinct subcultures.

E. Curriculum

Although there are many curricular similarities, especially during the first year, among American law schools, there are differences as well. Schools strive to attain some degree of uniqueness in their course offerings that may not be apparent immediately. Some schools offer specialized curricular programs, advanced degree programs, and other activities that support a particular substantive area of practice. Some schools offer a single course taught by a well-known professor that is not available anywhere else. Some schools are more theoretical in their approach, whereas others focus on practical applications for learning. Many schools are influenced in the composition of their course offerings by the geographic locale of the law school or the mix of business and industry in the area.

What this means is that all law schools provide slightly different educational opportunities as well as philosophies. You can address this question during the admissions process by doing research on the schools you are considering. After you start law school, you may find that your school does not offer some courses you would like to take, in which case you may want to consider options for taking a limited number of courses at other law schools.

There may be other differences in law schools as well. Is your school state supported or private? Does the school have special course concentrations or programs? Does the faculty view the school's mission as a broad educational one, preparing its graduates for the practice of law, or teaching students enough law to pass the bar exam? What internship, externship, and clinical opportunities are offered? What percentage of the curriculum is taught by full-time, as opposed to adjunct, faculty? Although legal education may be similar wherever you are, every institution is unique. For more information, see *Barron's Guide to Law Schools*.

In order to succeed in law school, you should understand the unique setting of your particular school. Take some time to learn its strengths, weaknesses, and educational eccentricities. Find out what you need to do to benefit personally from your school's educational program.

CHAPTER **3**

Understanding the Law School Experience

A. The Law School Calendar

No two people are the same. A key to your success will be your ability to channel the skills you already have into a new educational program, while building new skills that will serve you in the future as a lawyer. It may help you to understand what is happening during the first year of law school by looking at the law school calendar. Although every law school is slightly different from all the others, in many respects they are all much the same. Virtually every law school in the United States models its curriculum, particularly in the first year, after the Socratic system promulgated at Harvard Law School in the 1870s. Although legal education has evolved in the past century, the general comments in this chapter will be substantially descriptive of your law school experience regardless of where you go to school.

1. Orientation

Law school starts with orientation. Orientation is designed to introduce you to the law school community (and some would say to lull you into a false sense of security about the upcoming ten months). The first step is check-in. Check-in is run by the Admissions Office, and you will be greeted by the smiling countenance of the admissions officer who recruited you or dealt with you during the admissions process. The Admissions Office will want to make sure that you have paid your tuition, that your financial aid is in order, and that your registration is complete. If it is not, the Admissions Office may send you to Financial Aid, the Registrar, or some other office for help. Depending on how check-in is organized, you may or may not have to wait in a long line. If the line is long, it generally portends three to four years of the same thing.

After checking in, and grabbing a cup of hot coffee, you will proceed to an auditorium where you will be subjected to a series of speeches you will not remember. You will hear from the dean, some associate deans, assistant deans, the financial aid officer, career services director, student bar president, law review editor, moot court board chair, head of security, and other administrators and students too numerous to name. They will all tell you how glad they are to see you, how talented you all are, and how their doors will always be open. You will never see most of them again. Although most schools have abandoned the tactic, a few of them may still use the old "Look to the right of you; look to the left of you; one of you won't be here next August." The truth is that 90–95 percent of those who enter law school eventually will graduate.

After this convocation, you may be given a tour of the facilities, including the law library, by engaging upperclass students just dying to tell you what law school is "really like." They will claim to know which professors are easy, difficult, arrogant, like women/men better, and what you will need to read in order to ace/pass their classes. You also may be solicited by various student organizations; they will all be around and still anxious for your membership after the first year.

One of your first lessons in law school will be to separate the wheat from the chaff. Learn where to find your assignments; how you can sign up for a locker; and where to get a parking permit. Learn to recognize The Dean by sight. (There are many deans, but only one Dean.)

At many schools, class assignments for the first day are posted prior to orientation online. An assignment page for each class will also tell you what books to buy for the course so you can go to the law school bookstore and pick up your books before the crowds arrive. You may also be able to order your books through any number of web sites. Don't wait until school has started to obtain your books and start reading. For a checklist of what to do orientation day, see Orientation Checklist on page 14.

2. First Classes

Unlike in undergraduate school, the first classes in law school are generally real classes. The professor may simply walk in and call on a

Orientation Checklist

____ Admissions

    ____ College transcripts (if needed)

    ____ Identification

____ Financial aid (if applicable)

____ Registrar — class schedule

____ Bursar — bring checkbook if not prepaid

____ Course assignments

____ Bookstore

____ Parking sticker

____ Locker

____ ID photo

____ Law school tour

____ Find out who "The Dean" is

____ Nearby food

____ Library carrel (if available)

____ Laptop configuration (if necessary)

Notes:

student for the first case. She may give a short speech on what will be expected of you in her course before turning to the cases. Or she may provide a background lecture for most of the first hour. It is likely that the professor will not simply say, "Hello, I'm Professor Jones. Your assignment for Tuesday will be to read the first 30 pages in the book. I'll see you Tuesday." During the first class, the professor may present certain special rules such as the maximum number of class cuts you are allowed, the number of times you may be unprepared before being dropped from the course, what the final exam will be like, what her office hours will be, what outside materials (hornbooks, treatises, etc.) you should read. Such information is important to know.

Anecdotal books about the law school experience such as *One L* and *The Paper Chase* may have instilled a sense of fear in the minds of many beginning law students. In reality, not all law professors are as foreboding and intimidating as Professor Kingsfield, the quintessential Contracts professor in *The Paper Chase*, although the terror and alienation described there is very accurate.

You will find yourself in a lecture hall with roughly one hundred more or less equally frightened souls. Although many law schools strive to keep first year classes to a manageable size, you may find that law school classes are larger than upper-level college or graduate school classes. Your sense of anonymity and privacy will be invaded by the seemingly all-knowing professor, armed with a seating chart and an uncanny ability to identify the least prepared student in the class to discuss the case at hand.

During the first week of classes, you will learn the ground rules. Let there be no doubt about it: this is the lions versus the Christians, and regardless of your religious affiliation, you and your classmates are the Christians.

Also, during the first week, you will be introduced to the subject matter to be covered in each course, the professor's unique philosophy of legal education, a new language called legalese, and those ponderous, pictureless tomes called casebooks.

You will also begin to get acquainted with your fellow law students. You may meet a few individuals whom you come to know as real people. Most of your classmates will fall into one of two groups: the nameless faces who fill the classroom and the ones who, by virtue of having been called on or volunteered to speak in class, are identified by name (as in "Mr. Klingbaum, who sits in the first row in Torts"). Custom dictates that you use last names to identify students (as in "Ms. Estela" or "Mr. D'Amico") and you refer to the teacher as "Professor" or "Dean" as appropriate.

You may encounter some upperclass students who offer with a certain patronizing smugness to teach you the tricks of the trade. A healthy sense of skepticism about the value or motives of such advice is a good sign that you will eventually become a successful lawyer.

3. Routine

After the first week of classes, you will begin to establish a pattern in each course, and a timetable for your entire life. The reading will average between 10 and 30 pages per night, per class. You may find that the progress in some of the classes is painfully slow, with the professor covering only a portion of the assigned reading each time. Some classes may move along at an almost military clip of three to four cases per class, no matter what. During the first few weeks, you will find yourself spending an inordinate amount of time "briefing" cases (see Chapter 4), attempting to fathom the classroom discussion, and wondering secretly if someone in the admissions office hadn't screwed up sending you an acceptance letter. You will wonder with increasing frequency whether you screwed up in deciding to come to law school. During this phase of school, you may wonder why everyone else in the class but you seems to know what is going on.

When I was in law school, there was a guy named Holtzman, and although Holtzman was only 3 or 4 years older than most of the rest of us, it seemed that in every class he had some personal experience relating to the case. If the case involved shoes, he had been in the shoe business; if the case involved clothes, he had been in the clothing business; if the case involved doctors, he had been in the medical business.

Other students will amaze you with their seeming ability to converse freely with the professor in legalese, whereas you find yourself stuck at the "Bonjour, Jean" stage. But you will derive hope from the fact that some students' comments will seem totally inane to you, reassuring you that you must be smarter than *someone* in the class. And you will find a wicked satisfaction in seeing a handful of students whose hands are always in the air given their comeuppance by the professor. In every class, there will be at least one individual who, no matter how bloodied by the fray, will keep coming back for more. A pack psychology will come to dominate the class and seek to drive out the weak or the deviant. By mid-semester, the fear of embarrassment in front of the class will inhibit all but the most fearless souls from making rash statements. This mentality is typified by graffito on a bathroom stall at one law school: "After the sixth week of class, if you don't know who the class jerk is, it's you."

These pressures to conform may dissuade some students from ever participating in class discussions unless specifically required to do so by the professor. By laughing at a fellow student, you help to create an environment where one day others may laugh at you.

As the semester wears on, the professor comes to be viewed not so much as a god, but as a common enemy. You learn that the classroom routine is a game the teacher always wins. You learn that the stupidest answers have some value, and you begin to recognize that even the most articulate students really don't know much more than you do. When you come to this realization, you will have reached another milestone in your law school journey.

4. The Wall

Somewhere between the tenth and twelfth week of classes you will "hit the wall." It is during this period that some students actually drop out of school; virtually every student at least contemplates that possibility. By this time in the semester, your work is piling up, final exams are just around the corner, and you still don't have a clue what you need to know. At this point, when your psychological and physical resources are drained, you will wonder if you can possibly survive for two and a half or three and a half more years. It is critical when you "hit the wall" to press on. It may help during this period to talk to a sympathetic professor, mentor, or counselor. Family and loved ones, who up until now have been totally supportive, will seem to become part of the problem. Prelaw school friends may find that you have changed, and you may find yourself increasingly irritated that they never "see the issue."

5. Panic

By about the thirteenth week of the semester, you will have no time to worry about such self-indulgent psychological concerns, because finals will be upon you. Some professors, in what is variously perceived as a last-minute attempt to catch up with the syllabus or a final effort to break your backs, will increase the reading assignments to two or three times what they were at the beginning of the semester. A full-scale panic attack may threaten to debilitate you before the first test. Somehow, you will survive.

6. First Semester Finals

At last, final examinations will arrive. As a rule, law school exams average one hour of exam for each credit hour of class, and in many cases count for 100% of your course grade (one exam—all the marbles!). The amount of material you will have to study will be immense (see Chapter 5). Whole parts of some courses may be incomprehensible when you go back to review them. When you walk out of these exams, your head will feel like someone used it as a piñata. You will have no idea how well you did, but if you thought the test was easy, you probably missed something really big.

7. Semester Break

Semester break is the time when you regroup. Immediately after your last exam, your impulse will be to engage in the most hedonistic activity possible. Many will actually succumb to this impulse. Next, you will sleep for two days. Then, you will engage in mindless activity such as watching soap operas or football games, reading trashy novels, attending holiday parties, or "vegging out" with your family. If you are an evening student, you may not have the luxury of all of this R & R. However, to the extent possible, you should try to get away from both school and work for a while.

Toward the end of semester break, you will begin to think about law school again. You may do some reading for class. You may reflect about how you will avoid making the same mistakes you did the first semester. You will rush madly to clear up loose ends in your personal life, in order to give yourself time to devote your full attention to law school.

8. Renewed Hope

The second semester is better in some ways, and worse in others, than the first semester. It is better in that you now know the ropes. You have a better picture of what to expect. You have a clearer idea of what it will take to succeed. On the other hand, the work load will pick up even more. The professors will take off at the same pace they ended the previous semester. In addition, at many schools a required moot court problem will swallow the bulk of your free time.

9. The January Blues

During January (and sometimes February or March) first semester grades will be posted. The wait for grades may be agonizing. The actual knowledge of your grades may be worse. Most students are disappointed in some or all of their marks. In order to get into law school you had to be at the top of your undergraduate class; now in law school you may find yourself no longer at the top of the heap. Unfortunately, many students do not handle this experience well. They go into a depression they do not escape until after the bar exam. Although there is no grade for it, your grade point average may depend on your ability to bounce back psychologically and to learn from this experience.

10. Falling Behind

In all but the warmest climates, the arrival of spring will bring the last great temptation of the school year. When the flowers begin to bloom, and warm winds touch the land, sitting in a law school classroom will not be your first choice of activities. Spring break may help, but chances are good that you will fall behind in your reading and studying. If you are not careful you could find yourself in the proverbial hot water.

11. The Mad Rush

As March dissolves into April, you will once again find yourself staring at final exams. If you have been diligent you will simply experience anxiety about finishing the year on a high note; if you find yourself hopelessly behind your schedule, you will be working feverishly to catch up. The last weeks of school will pass quickly, and your first year will be almost over.

12. Finals Again

Final exams in the spring probably will not seem as daunting. The experience will be the same as in the fall, but this time you will be more prepared for it mentally. The amount of work you cover in these exams will be more prodigious than in the fall, in part, because the spring semester cases build upon what you studied in the fall. But the skills you have developed during the course of the year will make the load seem more manageable. This time, when finals are over, you will just go home, have dinner with friends, and go on about your business.

Over a period of 36 weeks, more or less, you will have been transformed from an ordinary person into a budding lawyer. Whether you want it or not, like it or not, or need it or not, you will never be the same again. The process is in some ways like marine boot camp, taking apart whatever you were before you arrived and rebuilding it into a new person.

Whatever other criticisms of law school one might make, it certainly cannot be said that the program does not work. The purpose of this book is not to debate the merits of our system of legal education. It is to help you to deal with the process as it exists.

B. Law School Courses

The curriculum at most American law schools is similar. In fact, the first year law school curriculum has not changed appreciably in the past one hundred thirty years, although many schools are tinkering around the edges of first year curricular reform. At the same time, there are minor variations in course offerings from school to school, reflecting differences in educational philosophy and institutional tradition.

Most law school subjects are offered as 2-, 3-, or 4-semester-hour courses (based on the number of hours the class meets each week). Full-time first year students take 5 or 6 courses for a total of 14–16 credit hours each semester; part-time students generally take 1 or 2 fewer courses for 10–11 hours. At some schools, grades are based on an entire year's work for 4- to 6-hour courses. You will study some, if not all, of the courses described below during the first year of law school. Some schools will defer certain courses until the second year or not require them at all.

1. Torts

The word tort comes from an old French term meaning wrong. Torts as a law school subject area refers to a series of legal actions and remedies against wrongdoers for injuries sustained. Torts fall into three broad groups: *intentional torts* where an actor intends conduct that causes injury to another; *negligent torts* where an actor owing a duty to act with reasonable care toward another breaches that duty and causes injury resulting in damages; and *strict liability torts* where an actor causes injury to another without fault or intent but is held liable for policy reasons. You will study a number of distinct tort actions, including assault, battery, false imprisonment, and intentional infliction of emotional distress; negligence actions; misrepresentation; defamation; products liability; and privacy. Most of the examples presented in this book are taken from tort cases.

2. Property

The Property course deals with the rights associated with the ownership of property. In the beginning of the course you will probably discuss the origins of property rights in Anglo-American law. You will study such tantalizing questions as who owns the rights to a meteorite: the farmer in whose field it fell or the guy walking down the road who saw it fall? Some of us are still trying to figure that one out. A small portion of the course is devoted to the law of personal property, but the bulk of the year will involve issues relating to real property, or land. You will devote considerable time to basic concepts such as estates in land, transferability of land, and title. Some time during the year you will learn about future interests, those medieval devices for controlling the ownership of land beyond the life of the owner. You will also deal with more modern concepts such as easements, zoning, and land use planning.

3. Contracts

Contracts involves the study of the body of law governing the making and breaking of agreements. You will learn what it takes to create a binding contract with another party. You will spend considerable time discussing what happens when one of the contracting parties breaks its promises, or breaches the contract. You will learn about liquidated damages, specific performance, express and implied warranties, and unilateral contracts. Much of the course will deal with the development of contracts in the commercial setting, including the "battle of forms" and substitution of statutory law in the form of the Uniform Commercial Code for the common law in many situations.

4. Civil Procedure

Civil Procedure refers to the rules by which the civil courts operate. Most Civ Pro instructors utilize the Federal Rules of Civil Procedure in teaching their courses. Some of the course may touch upon historical material, such as the evolution of the English forms of action into the rules of procedure of today. Most of your time will be spent looking at such concepts as jurisdiction (including subject matter, personal, and diversity), standing, discovery, pleading, appeal, summary judgment, and numerous other provisions of the Rules. A substantial part of the course will address the "Erie problem." The case of *Erie Railroad v. Tompkins* held that the federal courts, while applying federal procedural rules, must apply the substantive common law of the state. The ripples from this seemingly simple rule have extended far beyond the original case and have engrossed generations of judges, law professors, legal writers, and students (perhaps "engrossed" is too strong a word for the student response).

5. Constitutional Law

Many law schools require Constitutional Law during the first year. As the name suggests, Con Law deals with the enforcement of rights and duties established under the United States Constitution. Because there are so many constitutional issues, no two professors will emphasize exactly the same topics. You will look at some fundamental problems such as jurisdiction and standing, separation of powers, the commerce clause, and the privileges and immunities clause. You will deal with cases arising under the first, fifth and fourteenth amendments, as well as others. Perhaps most importantly, you will study the decision-making process in the United States Supreme Court from Chief Justice Marshall's power grab of judicial review in *Marbury v. Madison* to Chief Justice Rehnquist's reshaping the direction of the Court in the 1980s and 1990s.

6. Criminal Law

Criminal Law is the law of crimes. For a good portion of this course, you will grapple with concepts such as intent, mens rea, and lesser included offenses. You will learn the basic elements of crimes you have known about all your life, and a few you have never heard of before. You will study such issues as the right to trial by jury, double jeopardy, the state's burden of proof, and conspiracy.

7. Professional Responsibility

Although most law schools offer Professional Responsibility during the last year of law school, some require it during the second year, and a few the first. Professional Responsibility deals with the ethical obligations of the lawyer in representing clients. A few of the subjects you will cover in this course are: lawyer/client confidentiality, conflicts of interest, legal fees, advertising and solicitation of business, fitness to practice law, lawyer discipline, and candor to the tribunal. In a broader sense, however, professional responsibility addresses the role of the legal profession in society. What is a lawyer anyway? Should there be limits on his or her conduct? Is law a business, a profession, or both? What is the role of the bar association? Can one be a good lawyer and a good person at the same time?

8. Legal Writing

At every law school, there is a course known by a variety of names, but with a general aim of teaching you how to conduct legal research, draft legal briefs and memoranda, prepare and make oral arguments, and gain an understanding of the legal system. These courses are often much maligned by first year students, but revered by lawyers who come to know the value of the skills they learned in that course. Legal Writing frequently requires a time commitment out of proportion with the amount of credit received. An important consideration during the course of the school year will be your ability to allocate time to Legal Writing in accordance with its relative importance and credit weight, and not to set aside work in other classes for research, writing, and advocacy projects.

C. The Professors

Law students develop a special relationship with their first year teachers. It is not uncommon to experience a love/hate relationship with these professors. Later in law school you will wonder how you placed some of these individuals on such high pedestals. During the first semester of law school they will be like gods: not necessarily in their perfection of appearance, but in their seeming knowledge and omnipotence.

Many of those who become law teachers attained their positions by having done very well academically in law school. Additionally, many of them enter the profession after having served as judicial clerks for the United States Supreme Court or other prestigious tribunals. Increasingly, today, law teachers have some experience in the practice of law. They come from large law firms, corporations, and government agencies. All of them have made an affirmative decision to pursue a career in education, rather than one in a traditional area of law practice. Professors who worked in large law firms or possess more than a few years of experience probably have taken a considerable cut in pay to enter the teaching field. Although law professors as a group have a higher median income than the average of all lawyers, they probably could make more money doing something else.

Law professors come in all sizes and shapes. It is difficult and somewhat risky to generalize about any diverse group of individuals. However, anyone who has attended law school will recognize the following few basic types:

Old School—The Old School professor believes in applying the Socratic method the way Dean Langdell must have intended. This professor thinks the only thing unrealistic about Professor Kingsfield in *The Paper Chase* is that Kingsfield was just too soft. My own Contracts professor was from the Old School. The only affirmative statement he made the entire year was, "Hello, my name is Professor Loisieux." He genuinely believed that it is necessary to reduce you to a quivering mound of jelly in order to strip away the last vestiges of non-legal thinking before inculcating that elusive commodity, the ability to "think like a lawyer."

The Sadist—This variation of the Old School professor reduces you to a blithering idiot because it's fun. Having been beaten up by neighborhood bullies as a child, the Sadist now wreaks revenge on unsuspecting law students by brutalizing them into submission. It may be difficult to distinguish between these two professors while you are in school, but, in later years, Old School will turn out to be a truly nice person.

Your Buddy—This professor wants to be everybody's friend. She doesn't want to be on a pedestal, but to party with you, hang out with you, and talk law with you. It is easy to forget that Your Buddy will not be sitting in the exam room with you, sweating out grades with you, or going through job interviews with you.

The Liberal—You may encounter some professors who went to law school in the '60s and '70s. They protested against the war in Vietnam, fought for free speech and free love, marched for civil rights, and listened to the Beatles. In some ways, they never quite escaped those heady days, finding the Supreme Court today a pale pretender to the Warren court, George W. Bush a cruel joke on the nation, and law school a place to relive those thrilling days of yesteryear.

The Legal Economist—The law and economics movement evolved in law schools emerged as a major theoretical school of thought in the 1980s and gained mainstream status in the '90s. The Economist approaches a case by analyzing the relative economic costs of different solutions to the problem in reaching a decision. This professor serves as the intellectual counterbalance to the Liberal in the law school world.

The Philosopher—Although most of your professors will be grounded somewhere in reality, occasionally you may encounter an instructor who talks more about Camus and Kant than he does Cardozo and Learned Hand. The philosopher will seem to float in and out of touch with the class as his cerebral meanderings take him to increasingly sophisticated strata of understanding. Unless you were a philosophy major, you quickly will conclude either that you are stupid or the prof is nuts.

The Novice—You may be given the rare treat of a law professor in his first effort in teaching. Teaching in a law school requires skill that is developed over a period of years, and it may be said of your Novice that no matter how enthusiastic, his or her best years are still in the future.

The Writing Professor—In many schools, special instructors are retained to teach the Legal Writing course. These teachers are often young lawyers who aspire to enter the teaching profession, practicing lawyers who are interested in dabbling in education, or graduate law students at your school. The Writing Professor may not be accorded the same status as regular faculty members, despite the demands of the job. The grades, however, count the same on your transcript.

No matter what their type, professors can serve as mentors, allies, cheerleaders, and advisors, in addition to teachers. Law school professors are remarkably accessible compared to professors in other graduate disciplines. You should make it a point to know at least one professor personally during your stay in law school. Reach out to them, and you will discover a valuable guide.

D. The Students

1. Classmates

Your classmates can be allies as well as foes during your struggle to master the first year of law school. They can help you to cope in a number of different ways. First, they can help you with assignments. If you happen to miss a class, you need to find someone whose notes you can review. If your own notes have gaps, you may be able to fill them with the help of someone else. If reading assignments or case citations are unclear, you should identify one or more people to call. Even though law school is a competitive environment, most students are willing to help out in this way, as long as their generosity is not abused.

You may study with one or more other students from time to time. Formal study groups will be covered more thoroughly in Chapter 4; informal small group discussions are common even among students who do not organize formal study groups. In law school, a great amount of learning takes place outside the classroom, and to the extent that your out-of-class conversations are discussions begun during class, the learning process will continue.

If you have ever been to the zoo, you may recall watching a pride of lions or other large cats. The young ones will tussle and play endlessly. Sometimes Mom or Dad will play too, letting the kittens attack and snarl and slap. You know that the older cat can send the kittens flying with a flick of the paw, but the parents play along until they get bored. You know that the kittens are learning skills they will need as adults in the wild, and the big cats are helping in the process. You also know that the kittens learn from their mock battles with each other just as they do from Mom and Dad. In law school, the professors take on the role of the big cats, and you as kittens should learn from them. However, you should remember that you learn from the rest of the litter as well.

Your classmates can provide an outlet from the pressures of law school. Whether it involves coffee in the morning, eating lunch or dinner, exercising or working out, or partying, you need to socialize from time to time. Those of you who are married to people unconnected with the legal profession and those who have jobs in nonlegal settings may find it less difficult to break away from law school psychologically. On the other hand, it may be more difficult to find the time to get to know your classmates socially. If you don't want your families and coworkers to despise you because you talk about law all the time, you should try to make some time to get to know your fellow law students in a social setting.

There is an insidious downside to developing relationships with your classmates. Several caveats are in order. Law school is very competitive. Some students will help no one. Some students will promise help, but fail to deliver. Some will take far more than they give. Always remember that the admissions committee did not pick the first year class on the basis of integrity. Although you will meet some of the most honest and honorable people you could hope to know, you may also encounter others who would stoop to any depth to get ahead and use any means to reach a desired end. Most of you will conclude that you are unwilling to lie, cheat, and steal in order to succeed in law school. Do not be so naïve as to believe that everyone feels the same. Beware of the snakes in the grass, and pick your friends carefully.

Your classmates can exert considerable pressure not to succeed. A collective striving for mediocrity may seem to be the norm. Those who study too much, talk too often in class, or don't get into the law school social scene may be branded as outsiders. You have had to deal with similar peer pressure since grade school. Even more insidious, some students try to give the impression that they are not working hard, while in reality they are putting in more hours than anyone. The point here is that the pressure to conform does not end in law school. You may have seen the gopher game at the boardwalk or midway. In this game, the gopher pops his head out of one of the number of round holes while the player, wielding a mallet, tries to knock him back into the hole again. If you imagine that the class is the midway player ready to knock down any gopher who has the audacity to stick his head up above the crowd, you get the picture.

One way the group may push you toward mediocrity is by encouraging you to socialize. Although occasional social activity is beneficial, too much can be the kiss of death. When study sessions deteriorate into bull sessions like you had when you were a freshman in college, when quick lunches extend into afternoon shopping trips, when an occasional class party becomes an evening ritual, then you will know you have exceeded the bounds of moderation.

Some semblance of self-discipline in the area of time management is absolutely essential. Time management will be covered in more detail in Chapter 7; at this time you should note that you must decide how much time you are willing to devote to personal and social activities, and live with that decision.

Socializing with other students can take on a more serious note: emotional involvement through love and dependency. Guess what? Law students fall in love. They fall in love with each other and with nonlaw students. It would be futile to say: "Don't fall in love." However, if you do, you will find yourself in turmoil. When you fall in love, your lover tends to become (at least during early stages of infatuation) all-important in your life. Unfortunately, so does law school. Justice Holmes once remarked that the law is a jealous mistress. This conflict appears in the novel *Phantom of the Opera*. Christine, the heroine, is torn between her physical relationship with the Viscompte de Chegny and her passion to excel in her career represented by her relationship with the Phantom. It is interesting to note that the author of the book, Gaston Laroux, was himself a lawyer, and may have understood the conflict in terms of the law.

A second dangerous emotional involvement is to buy into someone else's problems to the detriment of your own studies. Law students are not immune from the vagaries of life. Some of your friends will have serious problems while they are in school. The stress of law school may compound their anxiety. Some may turn to you to serve as an emotional crutch. In fact, some students are like magnets for those with problems. Lest your friend's difficulties drag you down, the best thing you can do is to get them to go to someone who can really help.

2. Upperclass Students

When you arrive at law school, you will find a place already populated by students who have gone before you. These upperclass students will be ready and willing to regale you with tales of their own experiences in the first year, to give you the inside scoop on all the profs, and to share the definitive answers on what you need to do to get ahead. Some of them will want you to join their organizations, come to their parties, or buy their old books. They may seem like the smug but grizzled veterans joined in the field by some new recruits in the standard war movie: "Don't worry, kid; I'll show you what you need to do to get out of this place alive." Of course, in the movies, the guy who says that always seems to get killed.

The lesson to learn is to take everything you hear with a grain of salt. You will find out information that is useful. Every law school has a grapevine, and the news, if not always accurate, is at least entertaining. Some of your sources may prove better than others. So use what you can and discard the rest.

Consider the motivation of the upperclass student who offers advice. Is this someone who just likes being a big shot? Someone who needs reaffirmation for his or her own decisions in law school (even if those choices have produced a record of mediocrity)? Someone who would like to ask you out? (Yes, this goes on in law school like everywhere else!) Someone who wants to sell you something (bar reviews, books, bar association memberships)? You do not have to shun all these people, just remember that they want something in return for their information. (In the words of Hannibal Lecter from *The Silence of the Lambs*, "Quid pro quo, Clarice.")

While casual advice should be approached with skepticism, it might be valuable to look for an upperclass mentor. Such a person might well be someone who has similar interests, career aspirations, problems, or background. For example, a first year student with young children at home might encounter an upperclass student who has gone through the same experience and survived. A mentor might be someone you happen to meet and become friendly with during the course of the year. Some schools even offer programs that assign upperclass mentors to first year students. However it occurs that a true mentoring relationship develops, take advantage of it.

A mentor can help to guide you through the law school maze, talk to you when you are down, share your joy when you are flush with success, and set an example for you to follow. Mentoring relationships are built upon a foundation of common interest, molded by walls of trust, and covered by a protective roof of the experience of the mentor for the student. Mentoring relationships are common in the legal profession, not only in law school but in practice as well. To the extent that you find a good mentor, you will discover that the law school experience is a more palatable one.

E. The Law School Culture

1. Rules and Procedures

Law school culture is unique, created in part by the intense experience of those involved, and in part by the insular setting of the law school itself. Because most law students did not attend undergraduate school at the university where they attend law school, they tend to have limited interaction with the university community generally. The law school on many campuses is set apart on the edge of campus or on a separate campus altogether. Some law schools are not connected with an undergraduate university at all. There are advantages and disadvantages to attending an "independent" law school. Such a school can devote all its resources to the law students, but may lack the rich culture of a university setting.

There may be other differences about the physical location or layout of the law building(s) that make the law school environment unique. Does the law school share its campus with undergrads or graduate students? Does the law school share space with other departments? Are law school facilities located in one building or several? The presence or absence of a nonlegal academic community affects not only the type and extent of extracurricular programs and activities, but also the sense of the law school as an insular institution.

In one sense, every law school is different (see Chapter 2), but in another sense, every law school is the same. Regardless of the idiosyncrasies of different law schools, the process of legal education is similar everywhere. In this environment, a distinct law school culture has evolved. Law schools have their own student government (the Student Bar Association, or SBA), activities (law reviews and moot court), social events, intramurals, and newspapers. Some law schools even have their own yearbooks. At many law schools, the students put on an annual comedy show, generally making fun of the faculty in a singular effort to even the score for a year's worth of abuse.

Within the law school culture, there are several common elements worth noting. First, rules and procedures take on a distinctly legal flavor. Announcements and information may be posted online or at a designated location by the registrar, the Dean's Office, Career Services, or teachers. You will be deemed to know what is in these notices by virtue of the doctrine of constructive notice. The upshot of this concept is that you have to watch out for announcements that pertain to you. The first example of constructive notice during your law school tenure will be the posting of class assignments on a bulletin board or Internet web site prior to the beginning of classes. You will find very little hand-holding by law school teachers and administrators. Students who graduated from small intimate colleges may find this somewhat of a shock.

A second concept that permeates the rules and procedures is the notion of due process. Lawyers, more than those who are not trained in the law, tend to be aware of individual rights to hearings, representation, confrontation of accusers, and appeal. Most law schools operate under some code of conduct for dealing with academic dishonesty, as well as a code of academic standards to cover issues involving academic performance. Both sets of rules tend to focus heavily on due process and protection of the individual.

Another aspect of the law school culture is that it is a small world. The largest law school in the country has fewer than 2,000 students; at most law schools the enrollment is no more than several hundred. The small size of the student body, combined with the nature of the educational process, means that students know much more about each other, law school affairs, and their professors than they did in all but the smallest undergraduate schools. Unlike your high school or college acquaintances, you will tend to maintain contact with many of your law school classmates throughout your career. At every law school there is a student grapevine, laden with information about everything from what courses to take, at which firms to interview, and who is sleeping with whom. The old adage, "Believe a tenth of what you hear and half of what you see," is apropos.

2. Relaxation and Breaks

You will find an abundance of opportunities for escape from law school studies in the form of parties and school-sponsored social events. During the year, there will be several receptions, mixers, picnics, and other social activities sponsored by the SBA. Many student organizations offer periodic events for their members. And informal groups of students organize their own parties as a break from the grind of law school or meet at a local bar for drinks after class.

In fact, if you are interested, you can find a party almost every night. Unfortunately, partying leads you down a certain path of self-destruction in law school. Everyone needs an occasional break from study; however, the occasional break can easily become a regular habit. The party scene can become an escape from law school pressures generally, and may shift your values away from learning.

If you were a party animal in college, it may be difficult to break out of old patterns. Unfortunately, most of us cannot get by with the same antics we did in undergraduate school. In law school, one all-nighter will not save a semester of neglect. For additional thoughts on this topic, see Chapter 7, which deals with time management and related subjects.

Law school provides abundant breaks between and during semesters. You will probably have two weeks or more between the end of first semester exams and the start of spring semester classes. Most schools provide a spring break midway through the second semester. And, of course, summers are open.

Students usually use breaks during the year either to get away for a vacation or to get ahead in their work. Sometimes you may not have a choice. If you decide to vacation, leave your guilt at home. If you take your books with you, plan and make time to study. If you have no time to study, do not make a pretense of it by surrounding yourself with symbols of law school while doing nothing to further your cause.

Summer vacation is another matter. Here are 12 to 14 weeks that you can utilize in a variety of different ways. How you choose to spend your summer vacation will have an impact, one way or the other, on your legal education.

A large percentage of law students work for legal employers during the summer. Although it is harder for them to find positions, many first year students take this option, even if they have to work for free. For some students, it is necessary to work in high paying nonlegal jobs in order to earn enough to come back to school the next year.

Many students go to summer school, at their institution, or abroad (see Chapter 9, page 160). You may find, however, that you are so burned out that you simply want to relax. And some students do just that after the first year. If you want to travel, this might be the time to do it, before you take your first job.

3. Competition

A final note about the law school culture is that it is competitive. Entrance to law school was competitive; law school itself competitive; and law practice by its nature is competitive. Your relationships with other students will be colored by competition. Ironically, many students try to deny the competitive nature of the process. They will say to each other that grades don't matter. They will ostracize fellow students who appear too competitive. They may deny to other students that they study as much as they do. On the other hand, competitiveness can go too far. In all likelihood, before you graduate from law school, you will hear about at least one cheating incident at your school. You will see other examples, such as library books being misshelved by unscrupulous students. If you are similarly tempted, don't give in; it's not worth it. Look at the problems President Clinton heaped upon himself by not honestly answering grand jury questions about his relationship with Monica Lewinsky.

CHAPTER 4

Studying the Law

A. The Classroom Experience

The most memorable part of the upcoming year will be the time you spend in class. Assuming that you spend 15 hours per week in class over the next 30 weeks, you can plan on 450 or more classroom hours of instruction during your first year of law school. Whereas other parts in this book deal with subjects such as outlining, synthesizing, and exam taking, this section deals with succeeding in the classroom. Maximizing the amount you can learn should be your fundamental objective, and a measure of your success. This section is subdivided into a number of discrete topics: preparation, class discussions, note taking, and follow-up.

One preliminary suggestion is that you attend class. Some professors permit a certain number of absences; others say they do not care about attendance at all. There are students who seem to consider it a moral obligation to take the maximum number of cuts allowed. My experience is that there is a high correlation between class attendance and first year grades. If you had a job, you wouldn't plan to miss the maximum number of allowable sick days and personal days just because your employer permitted it. To maintain a professional approach to law school, you will want to attend class without fail, stay up with your reading, and put in the same number of hours as a student that you plan to devote to your work as an attorney. Law firms expect associate lawyers to bill 1,800 to 2,000 hours, or more, to client matters each year, and to actually bill 2,000 hours you will have to work about 3,000 hours, or 60 hours per week—hardly a 9 to 5 schedule!

1. Class Preparation

You just cannot succeed in law school by going to class and showing up for the exams. Apocryphal stories abound in law school lore about students who never go to class, read someone's outline once before the exam, and invariably get the highest grade in the class. Even if such a stellar performance is possible, the chances are incredibly great that you will not be the performer. The truth is that you will work your tail off just trying to stay even. At most law schools, virtually everyone has a comparable history of academic success, but you undoubtedly will encounter some individuals who appear to run on different octane from everyone else. In most cases, these students simply work harder and more efficiently than their classmates. Thus, even if you are at the top of your class intellectually, the best assurance of academic success is hard work. Much of the effort occurs before class through reading and briefing the cases assigned.

To begin with, you must know how to read cases and other legal material. Your prior educational experience will have given you the fundamental skills, but those need to be adapted to the educational demands of law school.

In order to help you become familiar with the process of reading and briefing cases, we are going to examine a case from first year Torts involving one of the most memorable characters you will encounter: little Brian Dailey. The case, *Garratt v. Dailey,* appears in several first year casebooks.

Although we will be using this particular case as an example, the methodology can (and will) be applied countless more times throughout law school in all your classes, and, indeed, throughout your legal career. It will be well worth your time to think through the approach to dissecting this case, and thereafter to practice the technique until you master it, the sooner the better.

During the first weeks of law school you will find the case method to be cumbersome, time consuming, and confusing. You may feel that you are not studying efficiently, that your education would proceed much more smoothly if someone would just give you the answers and not expect you to decipher them from the hieroglyphic-like readings of appellate cases. The more cases you read, the more facile you will become with the format, the language, the analysis, and the style. The more cases you brief, the more quickly you will be able to do it. So, just do it.

To read the case critically, skim it to get an idea of what it is about. Note that this case appears in the contents of the casebook under the topic "Intent." A threshold question is: Why did the authors include this case? A quick overview of the *Garratt* case might bring to your attention some basic information.

1. INTENT
GARRATT v. DAILEY
Supreme Court of Washington, 1955.
46 Wash.2d 197, 279 P.2d 1091.

HILL, Justice. The liability of an infant for an alleged battery is presented to this court for the first time. Brian Dailey (age five years, nine months) was visiting with Naomi Garratt, an adult and a sister of the plaintiff, Ruth Garratt, likewise an adult, in the back yard of the plaintiff's home, on July 16, 1951. It is plaintiff's contention that she came out into the back yard to talk with Naomi and that, as she started to sit down in a wood and canvas lawn chair, Brian deliberately pulled it out from under her. The only one of the three present so testifying was Naomi Garratt. (Ruth Garratt, the plaintiff did not testify as to how or why she fell.) The trial court, unwilling to accept this testimony, adopted instead Brian Dailey's version of what happened, and made the following findings:

"III. * * * that while Naomi Garratt and Brian Dailey were in the back yard the plaintiff, Ruth Garratt, came out of her house into the back yard. Some time subsequent thereto defendant, Brian Dailey, picked up a lightly built wood and canvas lawn chair which was then and there located in the back yard of the above described premises, moved it sideways a few feet and seated himself therein, at which time he discovered the plaintiff, Ruth Garratt, about to sit down at the place where the lawn chair had formerly been, at which time he hurriedly got up from the chair and attempted to move it toward Ruth Garratt to aid her in sitting down in the chair; that due to the defendant's small size and lack of dexterity he was unable to get the lawn chair under the plaintiff in time to prevent her from falling to the ground. That plaintiff fell to the ground and sustained a fracture of her hip, and other injuries and damages as hereinafter set forth.

"IV. That the preponderance of the evidence in this case establishes that when the defendant, Brian Dailey moved the chair in question *he did not have any wilful or unlawful purpose* in doing so; that *he did not have any intent to injure the plaintiff, or any intent to bring about any unauthorized or offensive contact Pwith her person* or any objects appurtenant thereto; that the circumstances which immediately preceded the fall of the plaintiff established that the defendant, *Brian Dailey, did not have purpose, intent or design to perform a prank or to effect an assault and battery upon the person of the plaintiff.*" (Italics ours, for a purpose hereinafter indicated.)

It is conceded that Ruth Garratt's fall resulted in a fractured hip and other painful and serious injuries. To obviate the necessity of a retrial in the event this court determines that she was entitled to a judgment against Brian Dailey, the amount of her damage was found to be $11,000. Plaintiff appeals from a judgment dismissing the action and asks for the entry of a judgment in that amount or a new trial.

The authorities generally, but with certain notable exceptions, [citation] state that when a minor has committed a tort with force he is liable to be proceeded against as any other person would be. * * *

In our analysis of the applicable law, we start with the basic premise that Brian, whether five or fifty-five, must have committed some wrongful act before he could be liable for appellant's injuries. * * *

It is urged that Brian's action in moving the chair constituted a battery. A definition (not all-inclusive but sufficient for our purpose) of a battery is the intentional infliction of a harmful bodily contact upon another. * * *

We have in this case no question of consent or privilege. We therefore proceed to an immediate consideration of intent and its place in the law of battery. In the comment on clause (a) of § 13, the Restatement says:

"*Character of Actor's Intention.* In order that an act may be done with the intention of bringing about a harmful or offensive contact or an apprehension thereof to a particular person, either the other or a third person, the act must be done for the purpose of causing the contact or apprehension or with knowledge on the part of the actor that such contact or apprehension is substantially certain to be produced." [Citation]

We have here the conceded volitional act of Brian, i.e., the moving of a chair. Had the plaintiff proved to the satisfaction of the trial court that Brian moved the chair while she was in the act of sitting down, Brian's action would patently have been for the purpose or with the intent of causing the plaintiff's bodily contact with the ground, and she would be entitled to a judgment against him for the resulting damages. [Citations]

The plaintiff based her case on that theory, and the trial court held that she failed in her proof and accepted Brian's version of the facts rather than that given by the eyewitness who testified for the plaintiff. After the trial court determined that the plaintiff had not established her theory of a battery (i.e., that Brian had pulled the chair out from under the plaintiff while she was in the act of sitting down), it then became concerned with whether a battery was established under the facts as it found them to be.

In this connection, we quote another portion of the comment on the "Character of actor's intention," relating to clause (a) of the rule from [1 Restatement, Torts, 29, § 13]:

"It is not enough that the act itself is intentionally done and this, even though the actor realizes or should realize that it contains a very grave risk of bringing about the contact or apprehension. Such realization may make the actor's conduct negligent or even reckless but unless he realizes that to a substantial certainty, the contact or apprehension will result, the actor has not that intention which is necessary to make him liable under the rule stated in this section."

A battery would be established if, in addition to plaintiff's fall, it was proved that, when Brian moved the chair, he knew with substantial certainty that the plaintiff would attempt to sit down where the chair had been. If Brian had any of the intents which the trial court found, in the italicized portions of the findings of fact quoted above, that he did not have, he would of course have had the knowledge to which we have referred. The mere absence of any intent to injure the plaintiff or to play a prank on her or to embarrass her, or to commit an assault and battery on her would not absolve him from liability if in fact he had such knowledge. [Citation] Without such knowledge, there would be nothing wrongful about Brian's act in moving the chair and, there being no wrongful act, there would be no liability.

While a finding that Brian had no such knowledge can be inferred from the findings made, we believe that before the plaintiff's action in such a case should be dismissed there should be no question but that the trial court had passed upon that issue; hence, the case should be remanded for clarification of the findings to specifically cover the question of Brian's knowledge, because intent could be inferred therefrom. If the court finds that he had such knowledge the necessary intent will be established and the plaintiff will be entitled to recover, even though there was no purpose to injure or embarrass the plaintiff. [Citation] If Brian did not have such knowledge, there was no wrongful act by him and the basic premise of liability on the theory of a battery was not established.

It will be noted that the law of battery as we have discussed it is the law applicable to adults, and no significance has been attached to the fact that Brian was a child less than six years of age when the alleged battery occurred. The only circumstance where Brian's age is of any consequence is in determining what he knew, and there his experience, capacity, and understanding are of course material.

From what has been said, it is clear that we find no merit in plaintiff's contention that we can direct the entry of a judgment for $11,000 in her favor on the record now before us.

Nor do we find any error in the record that warrants a new trial. * * *

The cause is remanded for clarification, with instructions to make definite findings on the issue of whether Brian Dailey knew with substantial certainty that the plaintiff would attempt to sit down where the chair which he moved had been, and to change the judgment if the findings warrant it. * * *

Remanded for clarification.

[On remand, the trial judge concluded that it was necessary for him to consider carefully the time sequence, as he had not done before; and this resulted in his finding "that the arthritic woman had begun the slow process of being seated when the defendant quickly removed the chair and seated himself upon it, and that he knew, with substantial certainty, at that time that she would attempt to sit in the place where the chair had been." He entered judgment for the plaintiff in the amount of $11,000, which was affirmed on a second appeal in Garratt v. Dailey (1956) 49 Wash.2d 499, 304 P.2d 681.]

---

1. Can a child five years and nine months old have an intent to do harm to another? And if so, how can that intent be "fault"? Suppose that a boy of seven, playing with a bow and arrow, aims at a girl of five and hits her, and she is injured. Is he liable? Weisbart v. Flohr (1968) 260 Cal.App.2d 281, 67 Cal.Rptr. 114. See Weisiger, Tort Liability of Minors and Incompetents, 1951 U.Ill.L.F. 227.

What did you get out of this overview? First, you probably noticed the caption, which tells us about the judicial history and citation of the case. Here, we are looking at a 1955 decision of the Supreme Court of Washington (the state, not D.C.). Different casebooks will utilize slightly different formats, but they will all provide similar information about the case. Next, you must have noticed "HILL, Justice." This tells us who wrote the opinion. Some names appear again and again in the casebooks, so the fact that a certain name, such as Cardozo, appears may provide insights into the court's reasoning. Right after Hill's name is a statement of the facts. Basically, five-year-old Brian Dailey pulled a chair out from under Ruth Garratt, causing her to fall and fracture her hip. Garratt sued Dailey, and the trial court held that the kid did not intend to injure the victim. Now on appeal, we get to the real nut of the case: what exactly does "intent to do something" mean?

At this point, you probably are curious about the outcome, so you flip to the end where you discover the case was "Remanded for clarification." It was sent back to the trial court, but it was not affirmed or reversed. A note from the casebook editors in brackets says that upon reflection and using the appellate court's definition of intent, "knowledge with substantial certainty," the trial judge found for the plaintiff Garratt to the tune of $11,000, which was affirmed on a second appeal.

A question following the case asks, can a five-year-old intend to harm another? Based on the outcome of this case the answer must be yes. Then the editor sneaks in the question, "how can that intent be 'fault'?" That can lead to an interesting classroom discussion about whether fault and liability are necessarily co-extensive, and whether the standard ought to be the same for intentional torts and negligence torts.

By now you have a pretty good idea of what is going on, but to understand the court's decision, you have to tackle the heart of the opinion. The best way to do this is to go back to the start and read the case through one time without stopping, to see if you understand it. Some cases will seem clear to you after one careful reading. Many cases will include language, terms, or concepts that are confusing. You may finish reading some cases and have no idea what you read.

You cannot read a case, in which every word is important, as you would a trashy novel. Speed-reading will not help you to dissect the words in a case. Distractions may cause you to lose totally your train of thought. With a little discipline, however, you will pick up the main ideas of the case. Try to get a sense of what the dispute is about. Why did the parties fail to resolve their differences without resorting to the judicial process? Here, Mrs. Garratt was injured as a result of Brian's action—but should Brian (through his parents) be responsible for compensating Mrs. Garratt for her injuries? And remember: no matter what your first impression might be, both sides have made a strong enough argument to take the case all the way to this appeal.

During your first reading of the case you should not write anything. Before going further, take the time to define terminology that is new to you, using both a regular dictionary and a law dictionary. Highlight or underline key phrases and make notes in the margin. One reason not to buy used books in law school is the burden of following the previous owner's notations.

A more careful reading of the case leads to several observations. After summarizing the facts, Justice Hill quotes salient factual findings of the trial court AND italicizes certain words, to the effect that Brian did not intend to harm the arthritic lady or to play a prank. Generations of law students and, perhaps Justice Hill, may have suspected otherwise. The problem is that the Supreme Court can't overturn the trial court's findings of fact, only its application of the law.

After quickly dispensing with the preliminary issue of whether a minor who commits a tort with force can be held liable (he can), the court turns to a statement of the law on intent. First, the court cites the Restatement of Torts. Although persuasive and not binding, restatements are often cited by courts because they are clear and well thought out. In other cases, the court might turn to statutory provisions or prior cases in the jurisdiction or elsewhere. As in *Garratt*, at some point in the case—most often after the statement of facts—there will be an explication of the relevant legal principles.

To be found liable, the court says, Brian "must have committed some wrongful act…," and that a battery would constitute such an act. A battery is defined in the opinion as "the intentional infliction of a harmful bodily contact upon another," and the question boils down to intent. Notice how the court narrows its consideration from wrong to battery to intent, which it defines as an "act…done for the purpose of causing the contact or…with knowledge…that such contact…is substantially certain to be produced."

Thus armed with the law, the court proceeds to apply the law to the facts in this case. This deductive process is repeated in some form in virtually all legal reasoning. Logically, the statement of the law is the major premise, the critical facts present a minor premise, and the conclusion follows by applying the former to the latter.

In this case, after looking at the positions of both plaintiff and defendant, and acknowledging that the lower court found no intention to harm, the court concluded that the decision was not dispositive on the key issue of whether Brian knew to a substantial certainty that if he pulled the chair out from under Ruth Garratt, the consequence of contact with the ground was substantially certain to follow. Now we know that if the court had found in the trial court opinion facts to support an inference or legal conclusion that Brian had such knowledge, it would have reversed; as it is, the case must be remanded.

The decision or holding is the part of the case that articulates the court's conclusion. Sometimes the court will telegraph the holding by saying, "We hold…" or "It is our decision…" Often, as here, the holding is not set off in any obvious way. Can you find the holding here? Look six paragraphs up from where the court remands the case, to the paragraph beginning, "A battery would be established if…." In the following paragraph the appellate court directs the lower court how to apply the law on remand.

In the end, the student takes away an understanding of intent that is different from the concept of the term she brought with her to law school. The class in which *Garratt* is discussed (and perhaps the final exam) will present other fact situations applying the definition of intent as knowledge with substantial certainty that a consequence will follow an act.

If the case is fairly straightforward and/or comprehensible to you at this time, you may be able to prepare your brief (see page 48). Frequently, you will have to reread the case a third or fourth time to fully appreciate what it is all about. The process is a painstaking and time-consuming one. Over the course of your first year in law school, you may read over 1,000 cases, all of which employ the same structure and analytical process. At the beginning of the year, it will take much longer to read and understand these cases. You will often miss the issue, salient facts, or aspects of the court's reasoning. By approaching case preparation as suggested here, however, you can significantly improve your chances of understanding the cases. As you gain facility reading cases, you will be able to dissect them more quickly and efficiently, but this skill takes time to develop. By the time you complete the first year of law school, you will become much more skilled at reading cases, and by the time you graduate this activity will be second nature to you.

When you think you understand the case, you will want to reflect critically about how the case fits into the course material. The notes at the end of the case contain questions for further consideration. Sometimes these questions are designed to help you understand the case or think about the legal principle involved. Sometimes they raise policy issues or question the court's position. The notes will contain short excerpts of other cases. Although you probably will not have time to look up all these note cases, it would be a mistake to ignore them. The note cases often suggest contrary results and ask you to distinguish them from the principal case. Sometimes these distinctions will be based on factual differences or on differences in law among jurisdictions; sometimes the conflicts will seem to defy explanation.

Class preparation entails reading thoroughly, thinking about issues, and attempting to come to grips with thorny problems. You will find it helpful to develop your own hypotheses about the cases you read and test these theories in class.

Now that you know how to read an appellate case, it may be useful to try another one on your own. Remember to skim the case quickly to garner key information that will help you work your way through a more in-depth reading. Beginning law students often get bogged down in the verbiage or sidetracked by what turns out to be the court's digression from the central issue. After skimming the case, read it carefully, noting important facts, statements about the applicable law, and the analysis, applying the law to the facts in the case. Do not be afraid to highlight or underline passages or to make notes in the margin. Read the case again until you feel you comprehend not only the result but also the reasons for the result.

The following case is taken from the same section of the casebook as the *Garratt* case:

McGUIRE v. ALMY

Supreme Judicial Court of Massachusetts, 1937.
297 Mass. 323, 8 N.E.2d 760.

QUA, JUSTICE. This is an action of tort for assault and battery. The only question of law reported is whether the judge should have directed a verdict for the defendant.

The following facts are established by the plaintiff's own evidence: In August, 1930, the plaintiff was employed to take care of the defendant. The plaintiff was a registered nurse and was a graduate of a training school for nurses. The defendant was an insane person. Before the plaintiff was hired she learned that the defendant was a "mental case and was in good physical condition," and that for some time two nurses had been taking care of her. The plaintiff was on "24 hour duty." The plaintiff slept in the room next to the defendant's room. Except when the plaintiff was with the defendant, the plaintiff kept the defendant locked in the defendant's room. * * *

On April 19, 1932, the defendant, while locked in her room, had violent attack. The plaintiff heard a crashing of furniture and then knew that the defendant was ugly, violent and dangerous. The defendant told the plaintiff and a Miss Maroney, "the maid," who was with the plaintiff in the adjoining room, that if they came into the defendant's room, she would kill them. The plaintiff and Miss Maroney looked into the defendant's room, "saw what the defendant had done," and "thought it best to take the broken stuff away before she did any harm to herself with it." They sent for a Mr.

Emerton, the defendant's brother-in-law. When he arrived the defendant was in the middle of her room about ten feet from the door, holding upraised the leg of a low-boy as if she were going to strike. The plaintiff stepped into the room and walked toward the defendant, while Mr. Emerton and Miss Maroney remained in the doorway. As the plaintiff approached the defendant and tried to take hold of the defendant's hand which held the leg, the defendant struck the plaintiff's head with it, causing the injuries for which the action was brought.

The extent to which an insane person is liable for torts has not been fully defined in this Commonwealth. * * *

Turning to authorities elsewhere, we find that courts in this country almost invariably say in the broadest terms that an insane person is liable for his torts. As a rule no distinction is made between those torts which would ordinarily be classed as intentional and those which would ordinarily be classed as negligent, nor do the courts discuss the effect of different kinds of insanity or of varying degrees of capacity as bearing upon the ability of the defendant to understand the particular act in question or to make a reasoned decision with respect to it, although it is sometimes said that an insane person is not liable for torts requiring malice of which he is incapable. Defamation and malicious prosecution are the torts more commonly mentioned in this connection. * * * These decisions are rested more upon grounds of public policy and upon what might be called a popular view of the requirements of essential justice than upon any attempt to apply logically the underlying principles of civil liability to the special instance of the mentally deranged. Thus it is said that a rule imposing liability tends to make more watchful those persons who have charge of the defendant and who may be supposed to have some interest in preserving his property; that as an insane person must pay for his support, if he is financially able, so he ought also to pay for the damage which he does; that an insane person with abundant wealth ought not to continue in unimpaired enjoyment of the comfort which it brings while his victim bears the burden unaided; and there is also a suggestion that courts are loath to introduce into the great body of civil litigation the difficulties in determining mental capacity which it has been found impossible to avoid in the criminal field.

The rule established in these cases has been criticized severely by certain eminent text writers both in this country and in England, principally on the ground that it is an archaic survival of the rigid and formal mediaeval conception of liability for acts done, without regard to fault, as opposed to what is said to be the general modern theory that liability in tort should rest upon fault. Notwithstanding these criticisms, we think, that as a practical matter, there is strong force in the reasons underlying these decisions. They are consistent with the general statements found in the cases dealing with the liability of infants for torts, [cc] including a few cases in which the child was so young as to render his capacity for fault comparable to that of many insane persons, [cc]. Fault is by no means at the present day a universal prerequisite to liability, and the theory that it should be such has been obliged very recently to yield at several points to what have been thought to be paramount considerations of public good. Finally, it would be difficult not to recognize the persuasive weight of so much authority so widely extended.

But the present occasion does not require us either to accept or to reject the prevailing doctrine in its entirety. For this case it is enough to say that where an insane person by his act does intentional damage to the person or property of another he is liable for that damage in the same circumstances in which a normal person would be liable. This means that in so far as a particular intent would be necessary in order to render a normal person liable, the insane person, in order to be liable, must have been capable of entertaining that same intent and must have entertained it in fact. But the law will not inquire further into his peculiar mental condition with a view to excusing him if it should appear that delusion or other consequence of his affliction has caused him to entertain that intent or that a normal person would not have entertained it. * * *

Coming now to the application of the rule to the facts of this case, it is apparent that the jury could find that the defendant was capable of entertaining and that she did entertain an intent to strike and to injure the plaintiff and that she acted upon that intent. See American Law Institute Restatement, Torts, §§ 13, 14. We think this was enough. * * *

[The rest of the opinion holds that whether the plaintiff consented to the attack or assumed the risk of it is an issue to be left to the jury. There was no evidence that the defendant had previously attacked any one or made any serious threat to do so. The plaintiff had taken care of the defendant for fourteen months without being attacked. When the plaintiff entered the room the defendant was breaking up the furniture, and it could be found that the plaintiff reasonably feared that the defendant would do harm to herself. Under such circumstances it cannot be ruled as a matter of law that the plaintiff assumed the risk.]

Judgment for the plaintiff on the verdict.

———————

1. Can an insane person have an intent to do harm to another? And if so, how can such an intent be "fault"? How does the lunatic differ from the automobile driver who suffers a heart attack, in Cohen v. Petty, supra, page 11?

2. The American decisions are unanimous in their agreement with the principal case. The result has, however, been much criticized. See, e.g., Bohlen, Liability in Tort of Infants and Insane Persons, 23 Mich.L.Rev. 9 (1924); Curran, Tort Liability of the Mentally Ill and Mentally Deficient, 21 Ohio St. L.J. 52 (1960). Good, recent discussions of the whole problem include Fridman, Mental Incompetency, 79 Law Q.Rev. 502 (1963), 80 Law Q.Rev. 84 (1964); and Note, Insanity as a Defense, 54 Marq.L.Rev. 245 (1971).

3. It has been held, however, that the insanity may prevent the specific kind of intent necessary for certain torts, such as deceit, when the defendant is to be held liable only if he knows that he is not speaking the truth. See Irvine v. Gibson, 117 Ky. 306, 77 S.W. 1106 (1904); Chaddock v. Chaddock, 130 Misc. 900, 226 N.Y.S. 152 (1927); Beaubeauf v. Reed, 4 La.App. 344 (1926).

4. Even if an insane person lacks the ability to form the intent to commit a tort, an action may lie against persons responsible for controlling the insane person, based on negligent supervision. See Rausch v. McVeigh, 105 Misc.2d 163, 431 N.Y.S.2d 887 (1980).

2. Briefing Cases

In law school, you are asked to read and brief legal cases. The basic action in your classes is a question and answer dialogue led by the professor. Briefing is a mechanism that helps you play the game.

There is nothing mystical about briefing cases. The technique simply permits lawyers and law students to get a thumbnail sketch of a sometimes long appellate opinion. It should tell you quickly and accurately what you need to remember about the case.

In private practice, the busy partner may ask an associate to brief several cases. A judge may ask her law clerk to brief cases relating to an upcoming decision. Your law professors ask you to brief cases for a variety of reasons. The first reason is to teach you an approach to legal analysis that will in time become second nature to you. The second reason is to provide focus for classroom discussions. A third reason is to teach you a skill that you will always be able to utilize.

Whatever reasons there may be for the seeming drudgery of briefing cases, accept the fact that this activity will take up a substantial part of your time for the next three to four years, and beyond. So it makes sense to learn to do it well as soon as possible.

There are shortcuts to be sure. These shortcuts have certain risks that you should know when you consider whether or not to employ them. The first shortcut is the canned brief. For many of the more popular law school casebooks, you may buy a book or disk that contains briefs of all the cases in the book. Your professors will inveigh, some vociferously, against the use of canned briefs. You will have to weigh the risks. The simple truth is that learning the law involves learning how to attack legal questions. When you brief a case, you develop the analytical skill you need as a lawyer; when you read a brief written by someone else, you learn only information, and that really doesn't help you to understand the case.

A case brief should be utilized contextually. The case might be briefed with an eye toward its ultimate use in an appellate argument, a trial, a speech for the bar association, and so on. The brief is a shorthand statement of what the case means in a particular setting, rather than an objective statement of facts and law for all times. In classroom terms, this means that your brief should be a device to help you understand the case in light of your professor's approach to the subject matter and your own comprehension of the material.

There may be times you stay out too late the night before class; you don't hear the assignment; your mother dies and you just don't feel right about reading Contracts at the funeral. At times like these canned briefs can be useful to compare to your actual briefs. However, these applications for canned briefs should be for extraordinary situations rather than everyday practice. You will not understand *Garratt v. Dailey* by using canned briefs any better than you did *Moby Dick* by reading Cliff Notes in high school.

A second shortcut is to split up the briefing duties among several people in the study group, photocopying and passing out the work product to all. This system, although less expensive than buying commercial briefs, suffers from all the same drawbacks of canned briefs with the added disadvantage that the quality is no better than the students in the group. Assuming that you are not the dullest person in your study group, this means that some or all of the briefs you get will be inferior to the ones you would produce yourself.

A third shortcut is the technique of book briefing. With a highlighter to mark major points in a case and a pen to make notations and comments in the margin, you can avoid a lot of writing. After you have become experienced in reading and dissecting cases, you may find book briefing to be a useful tool. During the first year of law school, however, you need the discipline of going through the drill. I remember playing basketball in high school, and spending what seemed to me needless hours on what the coach called "fundamentals." Looking back on both basketball and law school, learning the fundamentals was necessary to success.

Let's look at the briefing process. The first thing to remember is that the operative word is "brief." (They do not call it, after all, a "long.") At least early in your first year of law school, you may notice that your briefs are longer than some of the cases. In your compulsion to cover everything and your inability to discern what is important, you can defeat the purpose of doing the brief. You must learn to distinguish what is significant and what is not. In one sense, this is complicated by the fact that most cases have been edited for inclusion in the casebook, meaning that almost everything can be important, especially if the professor chooses to make it so. Some students have an instinct for what is important; others must learn by trial and error. One way you can test your briefing skills is to listen when other students are called to recite in class. When someone else states the issue exactly as you did and gets shot down immediately, there is a message. When someone sees the case completely differently than you, you should think again about your analysis.

First of all, there is no one way to prepare a brief. Ultimately, the brief is a tool for you to use. If it accomplishes that objective, it is a good brief. Every professor will have his or her own thoughts on how to write a brief, and if you look at your classmates, you will see almost as many styles as there are people.

Generally, briefs include the following elements:

Case Description—This includes the name of the case, the court and date, and a general statement of the procedural posture (e.g., Who is suing whom, and why? How did the case get to where it is?). This information is usually quite straightforward, although in the early months of law school you might have some difficulty tracing the history of a particular case. One reason for this is that all courts do not use the same designations for the parties. You may see the terms petitioner and respondent, plaintiff and defendant, appellant and appellee, as well as other terms. To make matters worse, sometimes the names of the parties are reversed from trial to appeal (e.g., *Smith v. Jones* becomes *Jones v. Smith* if Jones is the party appealing). Despite the tediousness of figuring out these relationships, your understanding of the cases will be immensely aided if you comprehend this background information.

The Facts—One of the tricks of briefing is to learn which facts are important and which are not. Professors sometimes seem to take the position that every fact is equally important. This may move you to write statements of the facts as long as those in the casebook. This obviously doesn't work. You need to learn how to recognize the important facts. Draft a single sentence that includes as many factual points as possible. Include all those facts that the court will need in order to make its decision. After distilling these salient facts, supplement your first sentence with other information you think the court will need to know. If you read a book, a friend might ask you what the book was about. You could answer the question by retelling the story, but then your friend wouldn't have to read the book. You could say: "The book was about a mad sea captain named Ahab and his obsessive desire to kill a great white whale named Moby Dick. After some time at sea, and much whaling, the confrontation between Ahab and the whale ends in the destruction of the ship and its crew."

Another way to look at the facts in your brief is to think of them as a shorthand reminder about the more detailed facts you have read. In other words, if the words you write can trigger your memory as to other facts in the case, you don't have to write out all the information.

The Issue—As difficult as distilling the facts may be, identifying the issue in a case can be much more difficult. A good bit of the first semester in law school is spent developing the skills of spotting and articulating issues. To start with, there are usually many ways to view the issue. The parties may see the issue differently. It may be stated broadly or narrowly, depending on whether the author wants it to cover the facts in the particular case or not. Normally, however, the issue is stated as a question that can be answered yes or no.

The issue as stated should contain enough information to articulate the difference between the positions of the parties. When looking for the issue, ask yourself why these parties are in court. Because this is probably an appellate case, there is some reason the parties couldn't settle it before. What are they fighting about? What is the gulf between them?

The Holding—The holding is usually a one-sentence statement of the legal principle upon which the court's decision rests. The holding answers the question raised by the issue. It is a statement of law that you can read standing alone or in the context of the case. In some cases, the holding can be lifted verbatim from the case; in others, you will have to rephrase the words in the opinion. For purposes of later study do not state the issue by simply noting "yes" or "no" in answer to the question asked in the issue. Some complex cases may contain multiple issues requiring more than one statement of holding. But usually you can distill the court's decision into one sentence.

The Rationale—This step outlines the logical steps in the court's reasoning process. The purpose of this part of the brief is to help you understand how the court reached its decision (as opposed to what it decided). Judicial decisions are based on rational arguments. Depending on the case, these arguments may be simple or complex. You should read the case critically, to see if the court's reasoning is faulty or if you agree with the assumptions. Remember that the brief contains a summary of the court's reasoning, not a restatement of the opinion.

The Disposition—Although many brief formats do not include this item, it makes sense to mention somewhere in your brief who actually won or lost, and what will happen to the case after this decision.

Sometimes the disposition is clear from reading the case, whereas sometimes it is not.

Concurring and/or Dissenting Opinions—Sometimes the case will include concurring opinions where one of the judges on the bench agrees with the disposition of the case, but disagrees in part with the reasoning of the majority. In a dissenting opinion, the judge disagrees with the outcome of the case. When the casebook includes these opinions, the authors usually want to demonstrate that there are different ways to look at the problem. You may find that you agree with the majority opinion after reading it, and then find yourself persuaded by the dissent as well. Depending on the case, you can either summarize the reasoning of the concurring or dissenting opinion as you did in the rationale above, or you can summarize the critical differences between the reasoning in these opinions and the majority.

There is no magic in the format for preparing a written case brief. Everyone eventually settles on an organization that makes sense to them. It is important, however, to prepare each brief the same way; the same information should appear in the same place in every brief. This permits easy access to the information when you need it quickly, for example, when you are called on during class.

The format on page 53 is one that you can use or modify. You will note that there is general information about the case at the top, followed by the facts, issue(s), holding, and reasoning, as well as dissenting and/or concurring opinions at the end.

This format also leaves considerable space in the lefthand margin for class notes; many students leave space following the case for notes. It may be easier to follow the class discussion if you are working from one notebook instead of two. Sometimes class notes will require more space than you have provided next to the brief, so you may also want to allow extra space for them. One possibility is to leave the back of every page blank for overflow notes. (Hint: use the page facing the case you are discussing, that is, the back of the previous case, for overflow notes.) The topic of note taking is discussed more fully in a later section in this chapter. Before turning to that subject, let's try to do a few briefs utilizing the cases presented earlier in this chapter.

It should be apparent to you that the information you gleaned from these cases fits neatly into the brief format described above. Looking at the *Garratt* case, you recall that you identified basic information about the jurisdictional history and procedural setting of the case, the

Model Brief Format

Notes

Name of case
Court/date
Procedural setting
Disposition
Facts

Issue(s)
Holding
Analysis

Dissent

salient facts, the law on intent, the court's reasoning, and the disposition of the case. In fact, the brief is practically written for us. Transcribing this information to paper using the brief format just given, the result might look something like the brief that appears on page 55.

Now, you try your hand at briefing, using the *McGuire* case that you read. Remember: the key is to be brief. Your brief should be a shorthand guide to the opinion, and not simply a condensed version of it.

As your first year of law school progresses, you will build a greater facility for reading and dissecting cases. You will learn to recognize facts, identify issues, and appreciate legal reasoning. You will analyze cases in a fraction of the time it takes you now. Since you will always use this skill, the investment of time and energy now is worthwhile in the end.

3. Classroom Routine

During the first year of law school most classes will be run by the professor using some form of Socratic dialogue. Despite the wide variation in teaching styles, the Socratic method operates on a few basic principles. The first and most obvious is that the professor asks the questions and you give the answers. Some students may fake participation by posing questions to the professor. These students may find the tables turned against them when the professor says, "That's an interesting question, Mr. Jones. You've obviously thought about it. What do you think the answer is?" Or they may find their question twisted into one even more bizarre hypothetical and lobbed back into their court.

The second rule is that the professor is always in control. Because he controls all the questions, he also controls the course of the discussion. This situation is compounded by the fact that the professor knows the law and you don't. The scene is reminiscent of the old county fair where the professional boxer takes on all local comers with the prize going to anyone who can last a round. Needless to say, few of the amateurs win the prize. Perhaps an even better illustration would be the chess grand master who simultaneously plays 50 amateurs in a local tournament. The master, who locks horns intellectually with each contestant, ultimately prevails against all of them.

The third rule is that the student never wins. Even if it were a fair fight, you wouldn't win. But it's not, because the professor is both

Notes:

Garratt v Dailey
SC Wash 1955
Appeal of J for D

F: Dailey - 5- pulled chair out
from under Garratt-elderly -
causing broken hip. G sues D.
D says he intended no
harm - couldn't get chair
back when G started to sit
Tr.Ct. finds damages = $11,000

I: Did Dailey intend the act
which caused Garratt's injury?
(Can a 5-yr. old have intent?)

H: Intent may be defined as
knowledge with substantial
certainty that consequences
will follow, and if lower
ct finds such intent, D is liable

A: If child understand his act
may bring about a particular
consequence, he may be liable.
Different from intent to harm.

D: On remand, Ct. holds for P(G)

contestant and referee. Whatever you say is wrong, or at least questionable. If you say a case is correctly decided, the professor suggests that maybe a case with a contradictory result is better law. Or maybe the facts in the case should be distinguished from the rule of law you cited. If the rule is right, the policy may be bad. Or if you say the case is wrong, the professor may say the case is right. It may seem like a perpetual shell game. You have to pick which one of three shells is hiding the pea, and no matter which one you pick, the pea is always under a different shell.

The purpose of this drill is basically twofold: first, it aims to teach you to take a position and defend it logically, even in the face of hostile questioning; second, it forces you to question your own thinking. It attempts to demonstrate that there are different sides to almost any question. In time, you learn that given any set of assumptions, you can construct a logical argument to support the position. And you learn to hold your ground. In the classroom, it is more honorable to defend a position that is ultimately wrong (although few positions are truly, ultimately wrong) than to waffle at the professor's first probing question. By picking apart the flaws in your logic, while simultaneously forcing you to question and defend your position, the professor helps you to approach problems analytically, which is an important part of the learning process.

Many of us react badly to this criticism. We come to law school with an intellectual smugness, brought about in part by past educational successes, and in part by a deep-seated need to avoid being proven wrong in public. Some students experience terrible anxiety concerning classroom participation; a few become obsessed with the fear of being called upon in class. Some students become so traumatized by their perceived humiliation at the hands of the professor that they literally never recover, and throughout law school barely speak in class when spoken to. Some students withdraw from class itself by talking, doing other things in class, cracking jokes, or not reading class assignments. By doing these things the student, in effect, rejects the validity of the classroom experience. If the Socratic method has no worth, then their self-confidence is not undermined.

The truth is that the Socratic method does teach you valuable skills. You will reconfigure the way you approach and solve problems. No matter what you do after this, you will always "think like a lawyer." How then do you succeed in class? You must accept from the start that this is a learning experience. Whatever doubts you may have, keep in mind that you can learn from everything that goes on around you; from the professor's jibes, classmates' quips, and your own foibles. Don't worry if you don't look good. Everyone has a day in the spotlight, and almost everyone leaves feeling more or less inadequate. Your success here does not depend on performance at all.

Your classmates and professor don't hold up cards like judges in the Olympics: "Very good, Mr. Jones. That's about a 9.4; excellent technique. That answer would have scored higher but the difficulty level of the question was low." "Ms. Smith is really going to have to come up with a perfect answer here in order to stay even with the Germans."

There is nothing wrong with joining the fray; you learn by participating. The more you talk, the easier it is, and the better you get at making arguments. Although you can learn the skill by observing others, you can't beat experience as a teacher.

When I was in law school, there was one fellow who answered all the time. And the professors literally brutalized him. At a party, some of us asked our Torts professor how this guy could get knocked down so much and keep coming back for more. The professor said, "He's learning." And sure enough, at the end of the year, this guy was right up at the top of the class. Remember that your grades are based upon what you assimilate, not what you say in class. (Some schools, though, allow professors to adjust the grades upward or downward for outstanding classroom participation.)

The key to learning in the classroom is preparation. When you have read and briefed the cases, and considered the issues beforehand, you have a better chance to grasp what is going on in the classroom discussion. If you read the cases for each day's class before you go to class, you have won half the battle (see pages 34–35).

Law school professors often employ electronic tools, using either the TWEN or Blackboard system. Both permit online posting of materials, electronic discussion boards, submission of assignments, and live chats. The effect of this development is to extend the scope of the class beyond the classroom, and in some cases to provide additional work beyond a single exam as a basis for evaluating students.

In order to get a flavor of the classroom experience, take a look at another case on intent. Read it and brief it as you did the other two cases in this chapter. Think about how the three cases might fit

together in a discussion of intent. Look at the note cases and questions following the case to get a sense of where the classroom discussion might be going. These notes sometimes, but not always,
offer a preview of the professor's game plan. This case involves a
1970s look at a very current issue: sexual harassment.

SPIVEY v. BATTAGLIA
Supreme Court of Florida, 1972.
258 So.2d 815.

DEKLE, JUSTICE. * * * Petitioner (plaintiff in the trial court)
and respondent (defendant) were employees of Battaglia Fruit Co.
on January 21, 1965. During the lunch hour several employees of
Battaglia Fruit Co., including petitioner and respondent, were
seated on a work table in the plant of the company. Respondent, in
an effort to tease petitioner, whom he knew to be shy, intentionally
put his arm around petitioner and pulled her head toward him.
Immediately after this "friendly unsolicited hug," petitioner suffered
a sharp pain in the back of her neck and ear, and sharp pains into the
base of her skull. As a result, petitioner was paralyzed on the left side
of her face and mouth.

An action was commenced in the Circuit Court of Orange
County, Florida, wherein the petitioners, Mr. and Mrs. Spivey,
brought suit against respondent for, (1) negligence, and (2) assault
and battery. Respondent, Mr. Battaglia, filed his answer raising as a
defense the claim that his "friendly unsolicited hug" was an assault
and battery as a matter of law and was barred by the running of the
two-year statute of limitations on assault and battery. Respondent's
motion for summary judgment was granted by the trial court on this
basis. The district court affirmed on the authority of McDonald v.
Ford, [223 So.2d 553 (Fla.App.1969)].

The question presented for our determination is whether petitioner's action could be maintained on the negligence count, or
whether respondent's conduct amounted to an assault and battery
as a matter of law, which would bar the suit under the two-year
statute (which had run).

In *McDonald* the incident complained of occurred in the early morning hours in a home owned by the defendant. While the plaintiff was looking through some records, the defendant came up behind her, laughingly embraced her and, though she resisted, kissed her hard. As the defendant was hurting the plaintiff physically by his embrace, the plaintiff continued to struggle violently and the defendant continued to laugh and pursue his love-making attempts. In the process, plaintiff struck her face hard upon an object that she was unable to identify specifically. With those facts before it, the district court held that what actually occurred was an assault and battery, and not negligence. The court quoted with approval from the Court of Appeals of Ohio in Williams v. Pressman, 113 N.E.2d 395, at 396 (Ohio App.1953):

"* * * an assault and battery is not negligence, for such action is intentional, while negligence connotes an unintentional act."

The intent with which such a tort liability as assault is concerned is not necessarily a hostile intent, or a desire to do harm. Where a reasonable man would believe that a particular result was *substantially certain* to follow, he will be held in the eyes of the law as though he had intended it. It would thus be an assault (intentional). However, the knowledge and appreciation of a *risk*, short of substantial certainty, is not the equivalent of intent. Thus, the distinction between intent and negligence boils down to a matter of degree. "Apparently the line has been drawn by the courts at the point where the known danger ceases to be only a foreseeable risk which a reasonable man would avoid (negligence), and becomes a substantial certainty." In the latter case, the intent is legally implied and becomes an assault rather than unintentional negligence.

The distinction between the unsolicited kisses in *McDonald*, supra, and the unsolicited hug in the present case turns upon this question of intent. In *McDonald*, the court, finding an assault and battery, necessarily had to find initially that the results of the defendant's acts were "intentional." This is a rational conclusion in view of the struggling involved there. In the instant case, the DCA must have found the same intent. But we cannot agree with that finding in these circumstances. It cannot be said that a reasonable man in this defendant's position would believe that the bizarre results herein were "substantially certain" to follow. This is an unreasonable conclusion and is a misapplication of the rule in *McDonald*. This does not mean that he does not become liable for such unanticipated results, however. The settled law is that a defendant becomes liable for reasonably foreseeable consequences, though the exact results and damages were not contemplated.

Acts that might be considered prudent in one case might be negligent in another. Negligence is a relative term and its existence must depend in each case upon the particular circumstances which surrounded the parties at the time and place of the events upon which the controversy is based.

The trial judge committed error when he granted summary final judgment in favor of the defendant. The cause should have been submitted to the jury with appropriate instructions regarding the elements of negligence. Accordingly, certiorari is granted; the decision of the district court is hereby quashed and the cause is remanded with directions to reverse the summary final judgment.

It is so ordered.

————

1. Distinguish:

A. The intent to do an act. The defendant fires a rifle, or drives an automobile in excess of the speed limit.

B. The intent to bring about the consequences—the bullet, or the car, hits a man. It is this that is always important in determining whether there is an intentional tort. See Etcher v. Blitch, 381 So.2d 1119 (Fla.App.1979), cert. denied, 386 So.2d 636 (1980).

2. Distinguish:

A. The defendant does not act. He is carried onto plaintiff's land against his will. Smith v. Stone, Style 65, 82 Eng.Rep. 533 (1647).

B. He acts intentionally, but under fear or threats. Twelve armed men compel him to enter plaintiff's land and steal a horse. Gilbert v. Stone, Style 72, 82 Eng.Rep. 539 (1648).

C. He acts intentionally, but without any desire to affect the plaintiff, or any certainty that he will do so. He rides a horse, which runs away with him and runs the plaintiff down. Gibbons v. Pepper, 1 Ld.Raym. 38, 91 Eng.Rep. 922 (1695).

D. He acts with the desire to affect the plaintiff, but for an entirely permissible or laudable purpose. He shoots the plaintiff in self-defense, or as a soldier defending his country.

In which of these is there an intent to do harm?

3. In some cases it may not seem important to distinguish between negligent and intentionally wrongful conduct: the defendant will be held liable in either situation. Nevertheless, the distinction may be legally significant. Thus:

A. Will defendant be liable for punitive damages? See infra, Chapter 10, Section 3.

B. Will the defense of contributory negligence be available to defendant? See infra page 569, note 10.

C. Will defendant's employer be liable under the doctrine of *respondeat superior*? See infra page 649.

D. How far will the law trace the consequences of defendants' wrongful act? See Tate v. Canonica, 180 Cal.App.2d 898, 5 Cal.Rptr. 28 (1960) (liability for causing suicide).

E. Will the defendant be protected under a liability insurance policy? See Allstate Ins. Co. v. Hiseley, 465 F.2d 1243 (10th Cir.1972). Cloud v. Shelby Mut. Ins. Co., 248 So.2d 217 (Fla.App.1971).

F. Has the state statute of limitations run? See the principal case.

G. Will an employer be subject to liability to an employee in spite of a general worker compensation immunity shield?

An exception is sometimes permitted for intentional wrongdoing. Does an employer's intentional failure to train an employee to perform a dangerous task supply the requisite intent to injure under the workers' compensation intentional injury exception? See Reed Tool Co. v. Copelin, 689 S.W.2d 404 (Tex. 1985). What about an employer's deliberate exposure of employees to dangerous products? See Millison v. E.I. du Pont de Nemours & Co., 101 N.J. 161, 501 A.2d 505 (1985). In Blankenship v. Cincinnati Milacron Chemicals, Inc., 69 Ohio St.2d 608, 433 N.E.2d 572 (1982), cert.

denied, 459 U.S. 857 (1982), the court held that the relevant workers' compensation statute did not expressly prohibit lawsuits based on intentional torts and harm caused by an employer's intentional conduct was not an injury arising out of the "normal course" of employment. Note, however, that not all jurisdictions hearing suits for intentional torts have gone as far as Ohio in broadening their concept of "intentional." But compare Bardere v. Zafir, 102 A.D.2d 422, 477 N.Y.S.2d 131 (1984), aff'd, 63 N.Y.2d 850, 472 N.E.2d 37, 482 N.Y.S.2d 261 (1984), holding that in the absence of a showing of "specific acts [by the employer] directed at causing harm to particular employees" the doctrine will not apply.

4. Does this mean that a court's characterization of a defendant's conduct as "negligent" or "intentional" is influenced by the legal effect of its finding? Cf. Lambertson v. United States, 528 F.2d 441 (2d Cir.1976), cert. denied, 426 U.S. 921 (1976).

Imagine that you are sitting in Torts class, and the professor says, "Let's talk about the *Spivey* case." He pauses to look at the seating chart in order to create a dramatic effect. His eyes scan the room methodically, stopping at you. "What happened in this case?" You look at your brief and your casebook, and you try to explain how the plaintiff was hugged by the defendant, causing her injuries. "Did he hug her hard? Is that what caused the harm?" You explain that you don't know how hard the hug was, but you do know that the harm was unforeseeable. "What is unforeseeable?" You mumble something about knowledge of the risk, but before you are finished, the professor has shot back, "How would you say that this knowledge of a risk is different from knowledge that consequences are certain to follow?" The former, you say, has to do with negligence, the latter, with intent. "Is there some line that divides intent from knowledge about a risk?" Before you can answer, the professor is asking you hypotheticals, some you recall vaguely from the notes, and others whose source you wouldn't begin to guess.

The hypothetical game works like this: if you answer five times that the plaintiff wins and the sixth time that the defendant wins, the professor wants to know why the defendant wins in the last case but not the others. If you answer that the plaintiff wins all six times, the professor will want to know what the defendant needs to do to win one. In other words, no matter what you say, there is always another question.

After the professor has grilled you for a while, other students may raise their hands to talk. The professor may or may not acknowledge the volunteers. At some point, the professor will try to coax from you the legal principle involved in the case: "What do you think we ought to get out of this case?" And you might respond that intent is a state of mind where knowledge that consequences are substantially, not absolutely, but substantially certain to follow, and anything short of this must be negligence. "Whose mind?" Excuse me? "Whose mind do we look at to determine knowledge—the defendant's?" Well, the case says a reasonable person. "So you're telling me that it's not what the defendant actually knew but what some abstract, fictitious 'reasonable' person knew that counts?"

Here, the discussion might dwell briefly on the difference between a subjective standard, looking at the defendant's own state of mind, and an objective reasonable person standard. "*Garratt* didn't mention anything about reasonableness did it?" The last case, you think to yourself. He's asking about the last case. "You do remember the last case don't you?" Yes, of course, you reply, having used the instant to flip back to your *Garratt* brief. The Restatement doesn't mention reasonableness. "Did the judge here just make this stuff up, or what?" The one thing you don't want to say is, I don't know, but you don't, so you do. Smiling that gotcha smile, the professor suggests, "You might want to check that out after class."

The professor might have asked you why the defendant was arguing that his conduct was intentional. You were ready for that one. The statute of limitations had passed, so if defendant's conduct was an assault and battery, the plaintiff could not recover. It was pretty slick of the plaintiff's lawyer, you note, to transform this case into a negligence action.

4. Note Taking

Another skill critical to success in the classroom is effective note taking. You have to find a note taking system that works for you. Here is one formula: brief your cases in a separate notebook for each class. If you use a laptop, you can take notes in the same document that contains your case brief. It may also prove helpful to use different colors for professors' comments, classmates' thoughts, and your own notes. Thus, you can segregate the professor's ideas for later study purposes. Student comments may or may not prove valuable. Your own notes represent a synthesis of what you have heard and what you have read. Remember, also, that you tend to stop listening when you write. Some students find it more productive to just listen in class, then take notes immediately afterwards. Most people don't have enough confidence in themselves as listeners to be able to do this. However, if you manage to cut down your writing time and increase listening time, you will learn more in class, particularly if after class is over you immediately reread your notes and fill in the gaps.

Another helpful hint is that the professor's questions are as important as the answers. Ask yourself what question the professor is posing, particularly when the professor raises questions that are never answered or leaves you with a question at the end of class. Also, listen carefully for phrases and statements by the professor that recur with enough regularity to be considered themes. Try to think about common threads that tie large blocks of material together. Look beyond the individual cases, and try to get a feel for what the course is all about, especially as seen through the eyes of the professor.

Develop a set of shorthand symbols that you use consistently in all classes to save writing time in briefs and notes. A list of commonly used symbols is found on page 65. You will undoubtedly make your own additions to this list as time passes.

Modern technology offers additional help with note taking. Cassette recorders permit you to make tapes of classes that you can replay later. Some students listen to their tapes in the car while commuting; others use the recordings to go back and clarify their recollections and fill in gaps in their written notes. Beware: some professors object to the use of tape recorders in class, so find out in advance if the practice is permitted.

An increasing number of students are bringing laptop personal computers to class. Not only can these students type their notes directly to a disk, but they can access their briefs electronically as well. Unfortunately, some old-fashioned professors may fail to see the benefit of classroom computing, just as some oppose tape recording. The times are changing, however, and the computer illiterate eventually will give way to the technologically savvy. The computer and the tape

Note-Taking Symbols

P or π	Plaintiff
D or △	Defendant
TP or ⊖	Third Party
CA	Cause of Action
Q or ?	Question
H	Holding
BP	Burden of Proof
K	Contract
T	Tort
IT	Intentional Tort
N	Negligence
SL	Strict Liability
Df	Defense
CN	Contributory Negligence
AR	Assumption of Risk
4C	Foresee
PF	Prima facie
DM	Damages
BR	Breach
Du	Duty
BFP	Bona fide purchaser
PUN	Punitive
STD	Standard
RIL	Res ipsa loquitur
NPS	Negligence per se
ORPP	Ordinary Reasonably Prudent Person
L	Lawyer
W/	With
W/O	Without
&	And
v.	Versus
Aff	Affirmed
Rem	Remanded
Rev	Reversed
Ct	Court
J	Judge
Jmt	Judgment
RS	Restatement
Ø	Not

Note-Taking Symbols (continued)

∴	Therefore
b/c	Because
EX	Except/Exception
EV	Evidence
INF	Infer/Inference
Prof	Professor says
s/be	Should be
=	Same as, equal to
≠	Not the same as, equal to
SoL	Statute of Limitations
§	Section
¶	Paragraph
Art.	Article
Hypo	Hypothetical
s/w	Spoke with
@	At
PH	Procedural History
B/w	Between
gov't	Government

recorder are just two tools for the use of law students and lawyers. If you possess the technology, you should use it. See page 78 for additional thoughts on the application of technology in the law school setting.

B. After Class

1. After Class Review

For many students, when class is over, it is on to the next assignment. They may discuss what transpired in class with a few other students, but for the most part the rule of the day is: never look back.

If you assume that learning takes place in the classroom setting, and that you may lose 50 percent or more of what you learned within 24 hours after leaving class, you might conclude that it would be worthwhile to take steps to retain as much as possible of what you have learned while it is still fresh on your mind.

A simple technique requiring 15 minutes or less per class will allow you to maximize your retention. As soon as possible after class, go to a quiet place such as the library and read through your notes. Fill in any blanks you find. Two months from now you will not remember what any of your half-completed sentences or chicken scratchings mean. Highlight questions and comments that you consider particularly important. Add your own personal ideas, particularly answers to the professor's questions. Reformulate your statements of the issues and holdings in the cases if classroom discussion suggested that changes are in order. Highlight case holdings, either your original or revised version. By doing this simple daily review, you should be amazed how much simpler your later study efforts become.

2. Talking to Professors

Many professors talk informally to their students after class is over. Frequently, they will provide insights into the material that were not clear in class. Even if you do not have any questions to pose, it may be fruitful to go down and listen.

If you have specific questions, or if you are unusually confused, your professors will be available to talk with you. Some students are reluctant to interrupt their professor or to appear to their classmates to be currying favor. These fears are generally groundless. Your professors, however, are not likely to respond favorably if they feel you are using them simply as a substitute for doing your own thinking. Professors who are unwilling to spoon-feed you the answer (if there is such a thing) during class will be unwilling to spoon-feed you after class also. If you go to see a professor about a question, you should have taken the time to think about it, formulate your own statement of the problem, and consider possible answers. You should have reviewed any cases on the subject. The question, "Excuse me, professor, but what did you say the holding in *Spivey v. Battaglia* was?" will probably be met with icy silence. On the other hand, the following approach is likely to produce a more favorable response: "I was troubled by our discussion in class on the *Spivey* case. Don't you think that women should have a legal remedy against unwanted advances? The court basically ignores the real issue here by talking about intent." "When was this case decided, Ms. Jones? 1971? Were courts back then—in Florida—likely to be responsive to sexual harassment claims?" "Yes, but we have to start somewhere." "Maybe we did. What happened in this case that was unusual?" "Well, for one thing the plaintiff's lawyer gets around the statute of limitations problem by arguing negligence." "Right. So by letting Spivey go forward on the negligence theory, the judge is giving her a remedy, or at least a shot at it. Was the defendant's conduct intentional? Probably, by the Restatement definition. When he put out his arms to hug her, he knew with substantial certainty that offensive if not harmful contact would result. Is the court wrong in *Spivey?*" "Maybe, but I'm glad she can argue negligence, even though she ought to sue the bastard for sexual harassment." "And today, Ms. Jones, she would."

In short, when you see a professor privately, you can expect the same kind of exchange that you would get in class, although it may seem that the professor is much more willing to provide answers (or at least opinions) than during class. As in class, however, you have to meet the professor halfway for the dialogue to work. Most students who take the time to talk to their professors outside of class are surprised by the professors' openness and candor.

Many professors are accessible by e-mail. If you have questions, you simply go online and ask. The professor can respond, and the exchange may continue through several messages. Online discussion groups also provide opportunities for outside class exploration of the issues with your professor.

3. Outside Reading

Professors will often cite cases, articles, web links, and hornbooks not included in the casebook. These references should be checked out. I remember Professor Loisieux in Contracts, who used to say periodically at the end of class, "See what the UCC has to say about that." Now we didn't open the UCC all year long. We studied common law contracts. But, guess what? The final exam was all UCC.

In college, everything you needed to know in American History was contained in your American History book, or the professor's lectures. In law school, your casebook and classroom discussions are but two tools to help you understand the subject matter. There are many others. One resource is hornbooks, such as Prosser and Keeton on Torts (see Appendix B, pages 170–178). Hornbooks are annotated discussions of the law in a particular subject area. Another resource can be found in the restatements, such as the Restatement (Second) of Torts (see Appendix B, pages 178–179). Restatements are summaries of the law in a field synthesized by leading authorities on the subject. Other aids include nutshells (see Appendix B, pages 180–184), short (150 pages) overviews of the law in a given area, and commercial outlines (see Appendix B, pages 185–192). Additionally, an increasing number of products are available in electronic form. You will note that the resources referred to in Appendix B all address the same issue of intent raised in *Garratt*, *McGuire*, and *Spivey*. The resources all offer additional insights to help you understand the concept.

Although all your professors may have told you to avoid commercial outlines, almost all students buy and use them. These comments are offered on the assumption that you will not be deterred from your reliance on these products. First, you do not need to buy every commercial outline on the market. The leading outlines are Gilbert's, Legalines, Emanuel's, West's Black Letter Law Series, and multistate bar review outlines (produced by several vendors). At some schools, you can purchase outlines specific to courses and instructors at that school. Find a series that is easy for you to follow. The professor, when pressed, may even begrudgingly acknowledge her personal favorite for her subject area.

The commercial outline can only be used effectively as a supplement to your own outline and study materials. As will be suggested later in this chapter (see page 71), the process of outlining itself is integral to the learning process. If you are merely taking someone else's work product, whether it is that of another student or the professor who did the job for Gilbert's, you will not force yourself to organize and conceptualize the principles in your own mind. You will be memorizing a bunch of rules.

A second important caveat if you use commercial outlines is to study the course you actually took, not the course as seen through the eyes of the outline's author. Different professors organize the material differently, view the cases differently, and emphasize different areas to a greater or lesser degree. So, unless your professor is actually the author of that commercial outline, remember that the author will not be grading your exam. With these warnings in the back of your mind, you may find these outlines extremely helpful to clarify your own thoughts, provide concrete examples, and give you some reasonable basis for reviewing your own work product.

Because there is so much review material, it is important to know when to stop. When you practice law for a living, you can always find another case or law review article to read. But because your client is paying the bill, you must decide at some point that your research is sufficient. In law school, it is impossible to leave "no" stone unturned; you simply have to turn over enough stones to get the job done. The skills of knowing when to say enough and learning not to follow time-consuming dead-end trails are critical. Many students actually hurt their performance by engaging in academic overkill.

4. Synthesizing

The process of synthesizing is overlooked by a great number of students. Synthesis is an ongoing process, which, in the context of legal education, means pulling together disparate concepts into a comprehensible body of information. The process of synthesizing may be undertaken through a series of discrete steps. A few comments will help you to approach this process sensibly.

The time to engage in synthesizing is at the end of each chapter in your book. This probably will be every one, two, or three weeks. Chapters in the casebook were created to place conceptually related topics together in the text. By taking one or two hours at these natural break points in the course, you can take advantage of logical divisions in the subject matter.

It is important to transform your study material from a case-oriented document to a concept-oriented one. The briefs and class notes as recorded in your notebooks or computer reflect an artificial organization of the material, based on the chronology of the discussion and study. You need to create an outline that presents the ideas in a logical order that you can understand.

The first step in this process of synthesis is to reread your notes, particularly the highlighted portions of your briefs (as depicted in your postclass review). Then, extract from your earlier notes the rules, ideas, and principles you have identified. One convenient way to do this, which will support your subsequent outlining, is to organize these statements in a spreadsheet. You do not need to write out case names or other citations, just the concepts. Record the day or days (because you may find that some ideas are discussed in more than one class) when the idea was discussed.

In the cases on intent in this chapter, you have already seen a number of concepts that you will need to understand:

- intent as a motive to cause harm
- intent to bring about consequences
- knowledge
- substantial certainty
- reasonable belief
- intent exercised by children
- intent exercised by insane persons

Reviewing your notes you may find other concepts. Whether you use a spreadsheet, note cards, make lists, or work from class notes, you should not overlook this step. Some students will utilize their computers during the synthesizing process, while others will do the job manually. In any event, the product should be a mass of information ready to be outlined.

Assuming your law school classes average about three cases per day, the discussion of *Garratt, McGuire,* and *Spivey* represents approximately one day's worth of law school work in one course. A typical class such as Torts will meet 28 to 30 times during the semester, and you will probably take five classes. This means that you now have covered about 1/150 of the information you will need to assimilate in the first semester alone.

5. Outlines

The bridge between classroom participation and studying for exams is outlining. Many students misunderstand the purpose of outlining, and therefore fail to benefit from the process. Others get too far behind in class preparation to properly utilize outlining techniques. Their last-ditch efforts before exams are too little, too late.

The course outline has two basic purposes: first, it is a continuation of the synthesis process. It represents a reduction of the vast amount of material into a manageable, organized format. Second, the outline allows you to transform the case-oriented classroom discussion into the topic-oriented summary of what you have learned.

You may outline material at the end of each chapter in the casebook after your synthesis. Because the authors have grouped the material by chapters in a logical way, you will find it easier to grapple with ideas at these times. When you go back to study at the end of the course, you may find that some of your earlier impressions and statements were offbase. You may find it easier to revise your earlier synthesis and outline than to start from scratch.

Many students wait until later in the semester to do their outlines in order to give them the benefit of cumulative learning. Many find that their ideas early in the course have been modified by subsequent readings and discussions. The downside risk in waiting to do your outlines is that you may not have enough time at the end of the semester to do an adequate job. If you have been religious about reviewing and synthesizing the earlier material, however, preparing an outline should be a manageable process.

Different people use different outlining structures. Generally, a topic outline will be adequate, but you may need to use sentences as well to state rules of law with specificity. You probably will feel most comfortable with an approach to outlining that you already know. As long as you can organize major topics and subtopics in a systematic way, the particular format is not important.

If you are using a personal computer, you probably already have access to an outline feature in your word processing program. The outline feature in Word can be turned on and off easily. Such programs provide a greater degree of flexibility and efficiency than handwritten outlines. In addition, word processing outlines can be revised easily, since they typically renumber automatically if you make changes.

It is critical to remember to create a topic-oriented substantive outline, rather than one based on the cases. You may place a case name at the end of a statement in your outline if it helps you to remember the context in which you studied the idea. You may be able to collect bonus points if you can connect a concept with a case name, although just throwing out case names without saying what they stand for will not get you anything. Because professors are more interested in your knowledge of substantive legal principles than they are in hearing you recite case names, this approach makes more sense in exam preparation.

How do you put these general outlining principles to work? The form on page 73 presents a detailed organizational plan for a law school outline. As you can see, it focuses on concepts rather than cases, although cases are included along with class hypotheticals. The segment called "keys" is optional, but it may be useful to include in one place insights or hints to help you grasp the concept. Usually, the

Law School Outline Organization

OUTLINE

I. Topic

  A. General principle

    1. Rule of law (majority)
      a. Elements, test, etc.
      b. Terms/definitions
      c. Examples
      d. Cases

    2. Exceptions
      a. Examples
      b. Cases

    3. Minority view
      a. Examples
      b. Cases

    4. Comments
      a. Professor
      b. You
      c. Others

    5. Mnemonic devices, etc.

rule followed in the majority of jurisdictions is covered first, but frequently, one or more minority positions will need to be included as well. Minority rules may be discussed in the court's opinion, a dissenting opinion, note cases, or classroom discussion.

Using the information you have gathered on the three cases covered in this chapter, try your hand at producing an outline on intent. Although there is obviously more to the topic than you have had a chance to learn here, assume for purposes of this exercise, that the universe of law on the subject of intent is contained in these three cases. After you have prepared your outline, look at page 75 to view a sample outline on the same subject. If your outline is substantially similar to the model, you are on the right track. If your outline is very different, you may want to reconsider your work product. In Chapter 5, on taking exams, you will have another opportunity to practice outlining, if you need it. Outlining is something most people have done since elementary school, so law students may overlook the fact that GOOD outlining is a skill essential to success in law school, because the outline is the vehicle through which you make all the information you have assimilated manageable.

The end product of your effort will be a document that reflects what you learned in the course you actually took. Even though you may need to do some research at the end of the semester to fill in gaps in your notes, if you have worked steadily throughout the semester you should have virtually everything you need to do your outline right in front of you when you need it. If you haven't prepared efficiently throughout the semester, the burden will be insurmountable. You will probably either cut corners on your outline, finish your outline with no time to study it, or resort to reading a commercial outline or one produced by a classmate.

Sometimes study groups prepare outlines by dividing subject matter among themselves. These individual efforts are collated, photocopied, and distributed to members of the group. If you accept the assumption that the importance of outlining is the process rather than the work product, you should agree that this approach is not sound. Group outlining will leave you highly informed about the areas you have outlined personally, and unclear about others you have not. It is a better practice for each person in the study group to prepare an outline individually, but work as a group to compare notes, discuss inconsistencies, pose hypotheticals, and look at thorny issues.

Sample Outline

TORTS

I Intentional Torts
  a. Intent
    1. Substantial certainty that
       consequences will follow (scc)
       a. Reasonable knowledge
       b. D's state of mind
       c. Children (Garratt)
       d. Insane (McGuire)
    2. To cause harm (either/or)
       a. Motive
       b. May be more "wrong"
    3. Contrast
       a. v. knowledge of risk (neg.)
       b. Gun
          (1) Desire to kill v.
          (2) Pulling trigger in crowd (scc)
    4. Essential element in intentional torts
  B. Battery
    1. Elements
       a Harmful or offensive
       b. Intentional
       c. Contact with another
       d. Unconsented

As you study, you may develop an outline of the outline, reducing the longer document into a shorter one as you master the material. And that outline may be distilled further, until three or four major points trigger all of the knowledge derived from the original outline. Some students even tape their outlines and play them on the car radio while commuting.

Whereas outlining is an integral part of learning, it is possible to become so obsessed with the process of preparing the outline that the objective of learning is overlooked. Never forget that the outline is a tool. Just as your briefs can be too long, your outline can say too much.

6. Checklists

Another useful device is the checklist. A checklist includes key words comprising a body of knowledge you need to know. This checklist may be broad, such as the main headings of your outline, or specific, such as in the elements of a tort. A checklist can help you avoid leaving out important points in your discussion. You can use mnemonic devices. Mnemonic devices use a series of letters representing concepts you want to remember in a word or phrase. If you ever took music, you learned that the lines on the treble clef were E, G, B, D, F because "Every good boy does fine," and that the spaces were F, A, C, E. In law you can use similar tools to help remember the large number of rules and principles you must know. You may want to remember that intent requires "substantial certainty that consequences will follow." A shorthand form of this formula, SCCF, might be easily recalled by the phrase "Sharon could climb forever."

C. Other Concerns

1. Memorization Versus the Big Picture

A common question posed by many first year law students is, "How much of my time should I devote to memorizing the law?" The simplistic answer is that you should focus more on the big picture than on memorization of case holdings. Getting the big picture means coming to grips with how the principles involved in the course fit together. It suggests an overall understanding of the material. And it is almost impossible to do well in law school without such an understanding. Thus, your professors all will admonish you not to simply memorize the black letter law.

On the other hand, it is difficult to get the big picture if you don't understand the underlying rules. And no matter how well you understand the rationale of proximate cause as discussed by the leading luminaries in the field of torts, if you can't remember the elements in a negligence suit, you might as well turn in your Gilbert's. In truth, there is a great deal of memorization in law school, but it is memorization within a larger context. It is different from cramming for a history exam in undergraduate school; in those days you could forget the facts you memorized as soon as you walked out of the exam. In law, you will be using many of these rules for the next 30 to 40 years. Your goal should be to internalize these concepts by learning how everything fits together.

2. Study Groups

Another question students ask is, "Should I study alone or with a group?" Part of the answer is that it depends on you. Some people study best alone, and find that the group merely slows them down. If the group's orientation is more social than study, the group will detract from the learning process. If one or more members of the group fail to do their share of the work, everyone is hurt. If the group serves simply to cut corners in studying, you might as well invest in a set of canned briefs and commercial outlines.

If the study group is properly utilized to supplement the individual efforts of its members, and if the group dynamics are good, study groups can have a positive effect on law school success. Learning the law frequently entails spirited discussion of the issues. You engage in such discussion in class, and informally when class is over. Study groups can provide another forum for dialogue on the issues.

There are two keys: All participants should be roughly equally prepared. Second, you must stick to the subject; if the discussion evolves into an anecdotal bull session, it ceases to be productive. Remember that your group doesn't have to be the same in each class nor does it have to be large. One or two good study partners may work better than a group of seven or eight duds.

3. Computers

The final question, which an increasing number of students ask, is, "Can I use my personal computer to help me study?" By all means, do it. In addition to the obvious application of typing memos and briefs, your computer can be used for outlining, taking notes (if you have a laptop), organizing your schedule, managing your budget, and conducting your job search. See Chapter 6 for more information on using computers in law school.

D. Using the Library

Your school's law library is a vast resource, which is always available to you. During the next three to four years, you will spend countless hours doing legal research, studying, and reading. Determine at an early stage of your law school career how to exploit the library's collection.

Whether your library has as few as 100,000 volumes or over 500,000, there are a number of common parts. You will find reports containing published decisions of courts in different jurisdictions. You will also find law reviews and other scholarly journals, treatises, legal encyclopedias (e.g., CJS, ALR) and indexes. Not all the books are on the shelves either. The library will have many lesser used volumes on microfiche. It will also have access to electronic databases such as LEXIS and WESTLAW, as well as CD-ROM technology that permits the storage of vast amounts of information on compact disc. Finally, the library has special collections that relate to areas of emphasis in the law school curriculum, multimedia collections such as videotapes, and directories (e.g., *Martindale-Hubbell Legal Directory*). Furthermore, if your law library does not have a volume you need, it may be able to obtain the book through interlibrary loan from your university, public, or neighboring law library.

A library is more than books; it is people. The professional librarians are trained to help you with your scholarly endeavors; some of them may have a law degree in addition to a master's degree in library science. You should get to know the reference librarian and other members of the library staff, because they will be able to help you in ways you might not even anticipate as you begin your legal education.

If the library is books and people, it is also a place. It was designed to give you somewhere to study. Many law schools provide ample study space, private carrels, and discussion rooms. The libraries in other schools may be cramped, and not conducive to studying. Some libraries may be too noisy, too drafty, too dim, or too cramped. Such limitations may affect your use of the facilities. You should explore the physical layout of your law library in order to find a study area that works for you. If you can sign up for a study carrel, do so early before they are all taken. This may not be an option, however, if the school allocates a limited number of carrels to upper division students.

CHAPTER **5**
Taking Exams

This chapter deals with law school exams. Probably no aspect of legal education produces as much stress as first year law school examinations. These tests are physically and intellectually draining. They can make you or break you academically. They are also the subject of considerable myth and misinformation. In order to perform successfully on law school exams, you must master four key elements of exam taking: substantive legal knowledge, analysis, writing, and management of time and stress. Law school examinations require you to do all these things well.

A. The Role of Ongoing Study

The previous chapter suggests that an organized plan of ongoing study throughout the semester is the best way to prepare for law school exams. In undergraduate school and graduate school before, you may have succeeded in blowing off the semester until the night before the exam, and then cramming madly and somehow pulling out a decent grade. The chances of your repeating the feat in law school are highly unlikely. First, the learning process is very different here. You have to do more than just recite facts. During the second and third year, after you have learned to think like a lawyer, many of the steps that took forever during the first year will become second nature to you. For this reason, your study time will be reduced—although ongoing study still will work better than cramming. Second, there is just too much material to cover for short-term cramming to be a feasible approach to law school study. Not only is the volume of material vast, but the level of detail that you must comprehend is great. Third, the competition is too good. Because law schools accept only the best undergraduate students, the middle and bottom of the college curve is gone. And if you fall victim to lazy study habits, you will find yourself holding up the bottom of the class in law school. In fact, even if you study as hard as you can, you may still wind up in the middle of the class, although chances are you will not be at the bottom. The word is this: don't take chances. The stakes are too high. Your best shot at mastering law school exams is to prepare continuously throughout the semester.

B. Review for Exams

1. By the Professor

Many professors provide review sessions prior to exams. In these sessions, they give you some idea of what will be covered on the exam, how to study for their exam, and an overview of the substantive law. They may also discuss particularly difficult parts of the curriculum and answer questions. If your professor offers such a review session, take full advantage of the opportunity. Some professors will allow you to record these sessions. If they do, bring your tape recorder and leave your pencil at home. You can always transcribe the tape, so use the review session to actively listen to what the professor has to say.

Back in the old days, review sessions were unheard of. In fact, my Contracts class pleaded with Professor Loisieux to give us a review session because we were all so confused. After much gnashing of teeth, he relented. On the appointed day, we were all sitting expectantly in the classroom waiting for Professor Loisieux to arrive. When he did, a hush fell over the assembled throng. Now at last the truth. Instead of pulling stone tablets from his briefcase, Professor Loisieux looked around the room and smiled. Then he said, "Well, all year long you people have accused me of hiding the ball. There is no ball." And he walked out. The review didn't help much with the Contracts exam, but it has remained one of the most enduring and accurate lessons of law school. The lesson in its brevity teaches two things: First, there aren't any stone tablets. Second, to learn it, you have to do it yourself.

2. By Yourself

Because the bulk of your study time will be spent working alone, it is important to find a study place that is comfortable, convenient, and free from distractions. Some law students move away from their families, take leaves from their jobs, and curtail regular activities during the exam period. This may not be an option for everyone, but it is important to create an environment where you can devote your full attention to study for substantial periods of time. The law library becomes packed during finals, and may prove to be a less hospitable study environment during exams than it was earlier in the semester. Plan out your study schedule from the last week of classes, through the reading period and exams. Try to block out periods of time to study, and designate what you plan to do at each stage. Allocate time according to the relative credits required in each course. Stick to your schedule.

Eat well and get plenty of sleep. Part of being mentally ready for exams is being physically prepared. If you are tired or weak, you will not perform as well. Law school exams tend to be emotionally and physically draining, so a good meal and good sleep will help to put you back on track.

If you become sick during exams, do not try to take them. Call the dean in charge if you can't get out of bed, and supply medical documentation if necessary. Most deans do not look favorably upon butterflies in the stomach as sufficient grounds for postponing exams, but they will be understanding about legitimate illness. If you eat well and sleep well during this period, the chances of becoming ill are less.

After exams start, it is important to put the exams you have completed behind you, and move on to the ones ahead. There will be plenty of time for celebration after the last exam. If you had a particularly bad exam, do not worry about it now. You will be able to survive one bad grade, but if you let it affect your performance on other tests, you could be in trouble. Remember, too, that just because you thought you did poorly does not mean you did. Your reaction may arise from the fact that you saw clearly the complexity and difficulty of the issues addressed in the examination.

3. With Your Study Group

If you have a study group, schedule study group sessions as a balance to your individual work. As with your personal schedule, the study group schedule should be clearly spelled out, and adhered to. There may be a tendency to want to dissect completed exams rather than study for upcoming ones. Make every effort to avoid giving in to this temptation.

4. Practice Exams

Most law school libraries keep on file past exams by your professors. At the very least, you should read through these exams in order to get a feel for what the professor is likely to ask this time around. You might spend some of your study group time discussing the old questions. The best use of old exams is to sit down and take them. Don't just answer the questions, but take the entire exam, adhering to the time limitations provided in the instructions. This will give you the opportunity not only to deal with the substantive questions, but also to get a feel for the professor's approach to the exam process itself. You will be able to ascertain, to a degree, whether you answer questions too quickly or too slowly. In some cases, the professor's exam will not be on file, or the professor will be new. If so, you may just have to look at exams prepared by other professors. However, you should be able to do practice exams for at least some of your classes.

C. What Kind of Exam?

There are several different kinds of law school exams. Not surprisingly, you will approach different exam formats differently. Furthermore, generalizations about exam taking do not apply equally to all types of exams. Thus, before you begin to study for an exam, you should attempt to ascertain its organization and structure.

1. Essay Exams

The most common first year examination is the traditional essay exam. Tests are normally scheduled for two, three, or four hours, depending on the credit hours for the course. Essays may be 45 minutes, 1 hour, or more in length. The number of questions on a given test will depend on the length of the test and the individual questions. Longer questions, as you might expect, tend to cover more issues and utilize more complex fact patterns. The issues are also usually multilayered, so that most students will see the basic problem, and fewer students will catch more subtle questions. This may account for the phenomenon many law students experience: doing well on exams they are sure they flunked and performing poorly on exams they thought were easy. An exam may seem easy for someone who misses a number of significant issues and difficult for someone who recognized those issues.

Take a look at the sample essay question below, which was used in an actual first year Torts exam. You can see that the question involves a series of events, and you need not have gone to law school to recognize a number of injuries and potential lawsuits. The question asks, "Who is liable to whom?" (perhaps the broadest possible question "call"). It also calls for a discussion of theories, damages, and defenses, suggesting that specific points will be awarded for addressing these matters. Because of the complexity of long essays, your organizational skills are critical. It may help to label issues and subissues, as well as to underline key words and phrases.

Because you have not taken the entire Torts course, this question is probably beyond your ken at this point in time. Right now, you should read it to get a sense of the length and complexity of extended law school essay questions. You may want to return to it late in your first semester of law school as you begin to prepare for exams. Additional long essay questions may be found in Appendix D, pages 204–216.

Sample Essay Exam Question

Construction was progressing on the new wing of the Camelot Law School. Although the project was far from complete, the faculty wing had been occupied prior to the beginning of the fall 1985 semester. A hallway connected the faculty offices with the rest of the law school; rooms along the hallway were still under construction.

The general contractor, Marvin Mercenary, had requested that his site supervisor, Joe D. Furious, protect the property by placing warnings in the hall to keep out everybody but faculty members, and to warn faculty using the hallway of potential dangers on the constructtion site. Furious put up two signs: one said "No students;" the other, "Be careful."

Furious also told his workers, Larry Comical, Klaus vonKurtson and Marjorie Schoolgirl, to keep the hallway clear and to avoid using sloppy methods in their work. Despite these admonitions, Comical left an open bucket of white paint in the hallway near the top of the stairs leading to the faculty offices. Schoolgirl and vonKurtson were carrying several sheets of plywood down the hall when vonKurtson stepped into the open paint bucket, causing him to lose his balance and drop his end of the load. Schoolgirl, being small of stature, could not hold on to her end of the plywood sheets, and she tumbled down the stairs.

At the very moment this happened, M. B. McManymen, Dave Fish, and Phyllis Bookends, faculty members at the law school, were returning to their offices from a faculty meeting in the law school. As they ascended the stairs, Schoolgirl and the plywood were descending at a great rate of speed due to the law of gravity. The faculty members did not notice the oncoming objects because they were involved in an intense discussion about the gravity of law.

At any rate, Schoolgirl's fall was broken when she fortunately landed on McManymen; McManymen's leg was broken when she unfortunately fell back down the stairwell. More unfortunately, the injury did not heal, and two years later cancer developed at the point of the break and her leg had to be amputated.

Meanwhile, the plywood struck Bookends, causing her to lose her balance. She instinctively reached out to grab something to maintain her footing. What she grabbed was an electrical cord hanging from the ceiling. Although there was no obvious exposed wire, Bookends was shocked as she held the cord. Fish, attempting to be civil, reached out to help her up, causing the current to proceed through his body as well. Bookends survived the incident, but she was in the second month of pregnancy and the child she was carrying did not. Nor did Fish, whose pre-existing heart condition was aggravated by the electric shock. The next day he collapsed and died of a heart attack.

The bucket of paint rolled down the stairs, coming to rest on the Torts notes of first year law student Gilbert Outline, who was studying at the foot of the stairs some 50 feet from the place Comical initially had left the bucket. Outline's notes were ruined; he failed the Torts exam and was dismissed from school for academic deficiency.

In addition, there was a statute in the state of Camelot, which provided that, "any building contractor who leaves an open container of paint in any enclosed area on a construction site shall be guilty of a misdemeanor." The legislative history indicated that fumes from open paint cans in enclosed areas had resulted in several explosions in recent years in the state of Camelot.

What tort liability issues are presented by this fact situation? Who is liable to whom? What damages are recoverable if the injured parties prevail? What theories of law are most likely to be used by potential plaintiffs in subsequent lawsuits? What defenses may be presented by potential defendants?

2. Short Answer Exams

A second type of exam is the short answer or short essay exam. In this format, the questions are usually 10, 15, 20, or 30 minutes and address a limited number of issues. A short answer test will have many more questions and may limit the amount of space allocated for writing your answers.

Short answer questions are problematic in that they are narrowly drawn to cover a limited number of issues; if you miss the issue here, you are out of luck. Sometimes short answer questions contain enough issues that they could be long essays except for the fact that you have only a limited amount of time to discuss them. The key to answering short answers is to get right to the point, stating the issue(s) immediately, and answering the question concisely and clearly. There is less need to organize your answer than on a longer essay, but logical thinking is still important.

The sample question below is an example of a fairly long short answer question; we will return to it later in this chapter. Appendix E, page 217, contains additional examples of short answer questions. Some of them relate to topics addressed in this book; others deal with problems you will not cover until later. Again, these sample questions may prove valuable to you when you practice for exams later in the first year in law school.

Sample Short Answer Question

Sally Westchester decided to go shopping one day in Manhattan. She took Metro North to Grand Central where she disembarked, and started up Fifth Avenue, store by store. Eventually, she turned down one of the cross streets as she worked her way toward Madison Avenue and Bloomies. As she was passing a construction site, she had to walk through a temporary covered walkway separated from the street and the construction by metal bars. The bars would permit a person to pass through only with difficulty, especially a person such as Sally laden with packages. On the construction side of the passage was a chain link fence; in the street there was a considerable amount of traffic.

About halfway through the passage, Sally looked up to see a scruffy looking man standing directly in her path. She clutched her purse tightly, but the man did not move. He stared at her for what seemed like an eternity, and then spoke, "Hey lady, you got a quarter for a cup of coffee?" Sally said nothing, but weighed the situation. Out of the corner of her eye she could see another man standing at the end of the passage from whence she had come, but she could not tell if he had any connection to the man who had spoken.

"Lady, you wouldn't want a poor homeless man to starve would you?" the man continued. Sally still said nothing, and the man, growing agitated, shouted, "You think you're too good to speak to me. You're lucky I don't break you like a stick, or smear that pretty makeup all over that pretty face." At this moment, Sally noticed that the second man had entered the walkway and was approaching her from behind. Summoning all her strength, Sally pushed the scruffy man in front of her as she ran to get out of the passage. He fell backwards between the metal bars and into the street, where he was struck and killed by a car carefully driven by Tom Tourist. Discuss the possible torts and defenses in this scenario.

3. Multiple-Choice Exams

A third exam format utilizes multiple-choice questions. Taking multiple-choice tests involves a specific skill that everyone has learned through standardized testing beginning in grade school. Some students are clearly better multiple-choice test takers than others. Since the advent of the multistate bar examination in the mid-1970s, multiple-choice exams have proliferated at many schools.

On the next pages are three multiple-choice questions from a first year Torts exam. Although the fact patterns for many law school multiple-choice questions may be longer than these, they represent a standard format with four choices. Often you will be able to eliminate two of the options immediately, leaving two plausible answers. Multiple-choice questions tend to test your ability to make distinctions about fine points in the rules of law. Multiple-choice tests place much greater emphasis on the "black letter law" and less on the "big picture" than essay tests. Multiple-choice tests reward skill in taking standardized-type tests, while essay tests reward written communication skills.

Just as a poor writer will have difficulty on an essay exam, a person who struggled through the SAT, GRE, and LSAT will struggle through law school multiple-choice exams. If your skill in taking multiple-choice exams is weak and you know that you will be getting multiple-choice exams, try to get some practice, or assistance; otherwise multiple-choice tests will continue to be your Achilles heel. A guide that deals with multiple-choice test-taking skills generally, such as *Barron's Guide to the LSAT*, may prove helpful. Another possibility is to gain access to materials produced for bar review courses dealing with preparation for the Multistate Bar Exam, a multiple-choice test. Find out from your professors early in the semester if they plan to use multiple-choice questions (some may give a test that is part multiple-choice and part essay). You can expect between twelve and thirty multiple-choice questions per hour, depending on their length (the ones below are the two-minute variety).

Sample Multiple-Choice Exam Questions

15. Smoke and soot from D's factory blew over P's property causing eye irritation and damage to his property. D showed that his factory could not be operated with a lower smoke and ash emission and that the neighborhood was mixed residential and industrial. P alleges that the factory is a nuisance and seeks an injunction and damages.

    a. P has shown that the interference with his property and health is substantial, and he is entitled to a directed verdict.

    b. It is for the jury to determine whether D's conduct is substantial under all the circumstances.

    c. The interference need not be substantial so long as it is unreasonable.

    d. The interference must be substantial and unreasonable. Both are questions of fact.

16. D built a high brick "spite fence" on his property line within six inches of P's building and thereby cut out light, air, and view of the residents. It was alleged that this was done maliciously and for the sole purpose of injuring P.

  a. There was no actionable wrong as P has no right to use D's property.

  b. D may not use his property to the injury of P when his only motive is spite and malice.

  c. The owner of land has a right to make any reasonable use of his property without liability.

  d. A lawful act is not actionable even though it proceeds from a malicious motive.

17. P, a coal mine operator, built an earthen dam to hold waste water from its operation so that "tailings" could settle to the bottom before the water flowed into a stream. The dam was located above a narrow valley containing many small homes. P was aware that other such dams had broken in the past under pressure of flood water. Ds, residents of the valley, dynamited the dam in such a way as to permit the water to escape without flooding. P sues for trespass and resulting damages to the dam.

  a. Ds are not liable. Under the circumstances, they were entitled to use self-help to abate the nuisance.

  b. Ds are liable. They should have first notified the owner and demanded removal of the nuisance.

  c. Ds are liable. They used unnecessary force in abating the nuisance.

  d. P is entitled to no recovery as he is clearly the wrongdoer.

4. Combined Formats

In reality, many of your exams will employ a combination of long essays, short essays, and multiple-choice questions. Because each type of question measures different aptitudes, a multi-format exam is likely to provide a better measure of all students than a single-format one, which may benefit some students and disadvantage others.

Since different formats require different study techniques, the multi-format exam may also present more challenges in preparation. Professors generally tell their students what kind of test to expect, but if your professor does not say anything, be sure to ask. Additionally, many schools keep old exams on file, so you can actually see what kinds of questions your professor might ask.

5. Other Testing Options

Although most law school exams fall under the descriptions above, several other testing options deserve mention, because you may see them on occasion. These include:

- Take home exams—An increasing number of law school exams fall into the category of "take home." The professor typically lets you pick up or download the exam within a window of time and complete it within a prescribed period. For instance, you may be able to download the exam at any time during the school's final exam period, but once downloaded you will have 24 hours to complete the exam. Take home exams are not usually given in first year courses, but appear with greater frequency in upper level electives. Having access to unlimited resources may be deceptively appealing, until you realize that having access to more information raises the bar as to what you are expected to know. Most students like take home exams, because of the scheduling flexibility afforded to students.
- Open book exams—A majority of law school exams are "closed book," meaning that you cannot bring any notes, outlines, or written materials with you into the exam. Some professors, however, do allow students to bring, not only notes and outlines, but casebooks and other materials. In courses that use statutory or regulatory materials (such as Civil Procedure, Tax, and Professional Responsibility, there may be a supplement to your casebook containing relevant rules and procedures. In some cases, the professor will reprint statutory or other material in the exam itself. And occasionally the professor might permit Web access for exam takers.
- Quizzes—Traditionally, law school courses had one exam at the end of the semester, and that exam was the basis for students' grades in the course. Some professors today may give quizzes during the course of the semester, in addition to the final exam, although this testing approach remains fairly rare.

- Problems, papers, documents, and research memos—Some classes, particularly clinical and skills courses, may call upon you to draft a variety of products reflecting your work in the class. These might include answers to hypothetical problems (answered individually or in a group), research papers (either optional or mandatory), legal documents associated with the subject matter of the class, and memoranda of law requiring substantive research.
- Self-reflection instruments—You may be asked to keep a journal, time records, or other record of your experiences or insights. You may be asked to offer a self-critique of your work—both oral and written. Or you may be asked to use some other self-assessment tool. Like problems and papers, you are more likely to see this approach used in clinical and skills courses rather than traditional law school subjects.
- Oral exams—Although fairly uncommon, a few professors may give oral exams. Anonymous grading generally discourages this approach, and logistics makes it impractical for large classes. An oral exam might be feasible in a small, high-level elective class.

As you can see, law schools are not limited to the traditional model for law school exams. Many professors are experimenting with new teaching methods, including evaluating student performance. Although you will not see all of these testing methods all the time, you will undoubtedly encounter some of them before you graduate.

D. The Examination

Whatever generalizations may be made about law school exams as a whole, every exam is an effort by an individual professor to test your knowledge of a legal subject. Professors vary in their approach to the law, testing methods, and grading criteria. Long before you sit down to take an exam, you should attempt to get some feel for the professor's mind-set. What has the professor said about this exam? What points has the professor emphasized and de-emphasized in class? What concepts recur periodically throughout the course? What are the professor's old examinations like (because many law schools keep old exams on file on the law school web site or in the library, you can frequently obtain these documents)? What do former students of the professor say about their experiences in his or her examination?

If you look at these questions, you may be able to anticipate the exam. Certainly, the professor may fool you, but generally professors are somewhat predictable.

1. Beforehand

You can help yourself out immensely if you tend to a number of logistical matters before the exam even starts. These include:

- Find out in advance what materials you can have with you in the exam room. Although most first year exams are not open book, some courses that rely heavily on statutory material (e.g., Civil Procedure) may permit those materials to be used in the exam.
- Make sure you know whether you will need pencils, pen, paper, or other supplies.
- Law schools usually provide blue books and answer sheets, but may or may not supply you with scratch paper on which to take notes.
- If you will be using your laptop, make sure advance procedures, like loading exam software, have been completed. Get a spare battery if you are not sure you will be able to connect with a power source.
- Check your computer's functionality before the exam.
- Make sure you know the room number where you will take the exam.
- Have a watch or clock with you. And, of course, because law school exams are graded anonymously, don't forget your anonymous number.
- Get plenty of sleep the night before the exam.
- Eat a good meal before you take the exam.
- Make sure to arrive in plenty of time.
- Go to the bathroom before the exam begins. Despite the fact that you can leave during the exam if nature calls, you can ill afford the time during the test.

These logistical suggestions are as important to effective test taking as drafting a good answer. When you sit down in the exam room, get comfortable and relax.

2. Instructions

When you get the exam, read the instructions and allocate your time among the questions. As a professor, it is astounding to see the number of students who misread or fail to read the instructions on their exams. And if the majority of students got the instructions right and you got them wrong, it is more likely your fault than the professor's. If an exam instruction seems unclear to you, ask a proctor for clarification.

Look at the time allocation for all questions. Remember to stay on schedule. If you get behind, you are dead. Poor use of time is probably the most common cause of otherwise well-prepared students performing below their expectations. It is probably best to answer the questions seriatim rather than to spend time trying to decide which question to answer first.

3. Read the Question

When you start on the first question, read it once through, underlining key words and making notes. Try to get a picture of the problem. Who are the parties? What is the history of the case? What are the basic facts? And, most importantly, what question or questions does the professor ask at the end? Your mission is to answer the question the professor asked rather than the question you would have preferred. The question itself gives you information about how to write the answer. For instance, the question may say,

"You represent the plaintiff in this case. Against whom would you proceed? What actions would you bring? What arguments would you make? What arguments and defenses do you anticipate from the other side?"

Or, it might say,

"As law clerk for the judge in this case, draft an opinion based upon the issues presented in these facts, explaining how the court should decide and why."

Or my favorite,

"Discuss."

Each of these requests by the professor leads you to answer the question in a different way. If only law students would read the question carefully, they would obtain insights into their answer.

4. Organize

Read the exam question again, outlining your answer as you go. Note unusual or salient facts, problems, or issues. Unlike on those Poli Sci exams in college, you can't just start writing and hope to say something memorable. On the other hand, you can't spend so much time organizing that you don't have time to write your answer. A well-organized essay will inevitably account for several points on your final grade. What do you want to say? How do you want to say it? What logical arguments can you make? What counterarguments can you make?

Don't spend so much time on the outline that you don't have time for your real answer, leaving all your good points on the scratch pad. Some students devote as much as one third to one half of the allocated time to reading and organizing their thoughts. Some people write or type faster than others; if your writing is more deliberate, you may not have the luxury of spending much time organizing your answer. If nature has afflicted you with a slow hand, you have to compensate by reading faster and organizing mentally in order to stay even.

One way to think of this organization step is to picture your professor as someone who is intelligent, but ignorant of the law. Your job is to take him or her by the hand and walk through the problem, explaining as you proceed. It is wise to discuss the most important issues first, followed by subissues and secondary issues. If you run short on time, you can give a quick sketch to minor issues having already addressed the major ones fully.

Before proceeding to discuss the specifics of exam taking, it is necessary to read one more case, *Katko v. Briney*. *Katko* involves the privilege of defense of property, a variation of self-defense. A valid privilege will excuse an otherwise actionable tort. A person is privileged to exercise force to defend himself or others, even deadly force in response to deadly force. Other nuances of self-defense can wait for Torts class. The question raised by *Katko* is whether one may use deadly force to protect property. Before proceeding, you should read and brief this case.

4. DEFENSE OF PROPERTY
KATKO v. BRINEY
Supreme Court of Iowa, 1971.
183 N.W.2d 657.

MOORE, C. J. The primary issue presented here is whether an owner may protect personal property in an unoccupied boarded-up farm house against trespassers and thieves by a spring gun capable of inflicting death or serious injury.

We are not here concerned with a man's right to protect his home and members of his family. Defendants' home was several miles from the scene of the incident to which we refer infra.

Plaintiff's action is for damages resulting from serious injury caused by a shot from a 20-gauge spring shotgun set by defendants in a bedroom of an old farm house which has been uninhabited for several years. Plaintiff and his companion * * * had broken and entered the house to find and steal old bottles and dated fruit jars which they considered antiques. * * *

The jury returned a verdict for plaintiff and against defendants for $20,000 actual and $10,000 punitive damages.

After careful consideration of defendants' motions for judgment notwithstanding the verdict and for new trial, the experienced and capable trial judge overruled them and entered judgment on the verdict. Thus we have this appeal by defendants. * * *

[The house was inherited from Mrs. Briney's grandparents and had been unoccupied for some time. There had been a series of intrusions.] Defendants through the years boarded up the windows and doors in an attempt to stop the intrusions. They had posted "no trespass" signs on the land several years before 1967. The nearest one was 35 feet from the house. On June 11, 1967 defendants set "a shotgun trap" in the north bedroom. After Mr. Briney cleaned and oiled his 20-gauge shotgun, the power of which he was well aware, defendants took it to the old house where they secured it to an iron bed with the barrel pointed at the bedroom door. It was rigged with wire from the doorknob to the gun's trigger so it would fire when the door was opened. Briney first pointed the gun so an intruder would be hit in the stomach but at Mrs. Briney's suggestion it was lowered to hit the legs. He admitted he did so "because I was mad and tired of being tormented" but "he did not intend to injure anyone." He gave no explanation of why he used a loaded shell and set it to hit a person already in the house. Tin was nailed over the bedroom window. The spring gun could not be seen from the outside. No warning of its presence was posted. * * *

[Plaintiff] entered the old house by removing a board from a porch window which was without glass * * * As he started to open the north bedroom door the shotgun went off striking him in the right leg above the ankle bone. Much of his leg, including part of the tibia, was blown away. Only by * * * assistance was plaintiff able to get out of the house and after crawling some distance was put in his vehicle and rushed to a doctor and then to a hospital. He remained in the hospital 40 days. * * *

There was undenied medical testimony plaintiff had a permanent deformity, a loss of tissue, and a shortening of the leg. * * *

The main thrust of defendants' defense in the trial court and on this appeal is that "the law permits use of a spring gun in a dwelling or warehouse for the purpose of preventing the unlawful entry of a burglar or thief." * * *

Instruction 6 stated: "An owner of premises is prohibited from willfully or intentionally injuring a trespasser by means of force that either takes life or inflicts great bodily injury; and therefore a person owning a premise is prohibited from setting out 'spring guns' and like dangerous devices which will likely take life or inflict great bodily injury, for the purpose of harming trespassers. The fact that the trespasser may be acting in violation of the law does not change the rule. The only time when such conduct of setting a 'spring gun' or a like dangerous device is justified would be when the trespasser was committing a felony of violence or a felony punishable by death, or where the trespasser was endangering human life by his act." * * *

The overwhelming weight of authority, both textbook and case law, supports the trial court's statement of the applicable principles of law. * * *

Restatement of Torts, section 85, page 180, states: "The value of human life and limb, not only to the individual concerned but also to society, so outweighs the interest of a possessor of land in excluding from it those whom he is not willing to admit thereto that a possessor of land has, as is stated in § 79, no privilege to use force intended or likely to cause death or serious harm against another whom the possessor sees about to enter his premises or meddle with his chattel, unless the intrusion threatens death or serious bodily harm to the occupiers or users of the premises. * * * A possessor of land cannot do indirectly and by a mechanical device that which, were he present, he could not do immediately and in person. Therefore, he cannot gain a privilege to install, for the purpose of protecting his land from intrusions harmless to the lives and limbs of the occupiers or users of it, a mechanical device whose only purpose is to inflict death or serious harm upon such as may intrude, by giving notice of his intention to inflict, by mechanical means and indirectly, harm which he could not, even after request, inflict directly were he present." * * *

The facts in Allison v. Fiscus, 156 Ohio St. 120, 100 N.E.2d 237, decided in 1951, are very similar to the case at bar. There plaintiff's right to damages was recognized for injuries received when he feloniously broke a door latch and started to enter defendant's warehouse with intent to steal. As he entered a trap of two sticks of dynamite buried under the doorway by defendant owner was set off and plaintiff seriously injured. The court held the question whether a particular trap was justified as a use of reasonable and necessary force against a trespasser engaged in the commission of a felony should have been submitted to the jury. The Ohio Supreme Court recognized plaintiff's right to recover punitive or exemplary damages in addition to compensatory damages. * * *

In addition to civil liability many jurisdictions hold a landowner criminally liable for serious injuries or homicide caused by spring guns or other set devices. [Citations] * * *

[The court declined to rule on whether punitive damages were allowable in this type of case because defendant's attorney had not raised that issue in the trial court.]

Study and careful consideration of defendant's contentions on appeal reveal no reversible error.

Affirmed.

LARSON, J., dissented, noting that the trial judge's instructions "failed to tell the jury it could find the installation was not made with the intent or purpose of striking or injuring the plaintiff," and that the principle espoused by the court had never been applied to a burglar, but only "in the case of a mere trespasser in a vineyard."

---

1. The Brineys had to sell 80 acres of their 120-acre farm in order to pay the judgment in this case. Their appeal to equity to block enforcement of the judgment failed. See Briney v. Katko (1971) 197 N.W.2d 351. Further background about the case can be found in Palmer, Katko v. Briney: A Study in American Gothic (1971) 56 Iowa L.Rev. 1219.

2. A strange development later arose between the parties. When the 80 acres were put up for judgment sale and there were no bids above the minimum price of $10,000, three neighbors purchased the land for a dollar more, expecting to hold it for Briney until he won his appeal. When he did not win, they leased the land back to him for enough to pay taxes and their interest costs on the money they had borrowed. Some years later the neighbors decided to sell. One of them bought the property for $16,000 and sold it to his son for $16,500. Briney and Katko then got together and jointly sued the neighbors to establish a constructive trust on their profit. Just before the case came to trial, it was settled for a sum large enough to pay the remainder of Briney's judgment to Katko.

3. The United Press International reported the results of the trial court decision in this case stating in part that Katko was "shot and seriously injured in the *home* of Mr. and Mrs. Edward Briney." (Emphasis added.) A public outcry about the decision resulted in the introduction of "Briney Bills" in several state legislatures. The Nebraska Legislature enacted a self-defense act that provided in part that "no person * * * shall be placed in * * * jeopardy * * * for protecting, by any means necessary, himself, his family, or his real or personal property * * *." The statute was held to be unconstitutional by the Supreme Court of Nebraska on the unusual ground of improper delegation of sentencing authority. See State v. Goodseal (1971) 186 Neb. 359, 183 N.W.2d 258, certiorari denied 404 U.S. 845.

4. As in the case of self-defense, the privilege to defend property is limited to the use of force reasonably necessary to the situation as it appears to the defendant. Here again a reasonable mistake as to the necessity will protect him. Smith v. Delery (1959) 238 La. 180, 114 So.2d 857; Bunten v. Davis (1926) 82 N.H. 304, 133 A. 16. But a reasonable mistake as to the existence of the privilege will not, as when the invader is on the land as a matter of right.

5. What constitutes reasonable force is normally a question for the jury, but there are several recognized limitations. When the invasion is peaceful and occurs in the presence of the possessor, the use of any force at all will be unreasonable unless a request has been made to depart. Chapell v. Schmidt (1894) 104 Cal. 511, 38 P. 892 (defendant caned elderly person who was picking flowers); Emmons v. Quade (1903) 176 Mo. 22, 75 S.W. 103. A request does not have to be made, however, when the conduct of the intruder would indicate to a reasonable person that it would be useless or that it could not safely be made in time. See Higgins v. Minaghan (1891) 78 Wis. 602, 47 N.W. 941; State v. Cessna (1915) 170 Iowa 726, 153 N.W. 194.

6. When the invasion occurs in the presence of the possessor he may repel him by use of physical force short of infliction of serious bodily injury. See Palmer v. Smith (1911) 147 Wis. 70, 132 N.W. 614; Ulmer v. Seelman (1909) 159 Mich. 253, 123 N.W. 1124; McIlvoy v. Cockran (1820) 9 Ky. (2 A. K. Marsh.) 271.

7. *Use of Force Calculated to Cause Death or Serious Injury.* The principal case caused a good deal of re-thinking about when, if ever, force calculated to cause death or serious injury may be utilized to defend possession. It is one of the few cases in which a burglar or a thief was able to recover civil damages from his intended victim.

A. When the privilege of self-defense enters the picture in that the invader threatens the personal safety of the defendant or his family, the defendant may use deadly force if it is necessary in the circumstances. This is likely to occur when the invader attempts to enter the homestead at night. See Tipsword v. Potter (1918) 31 Idaho 509, 174 P. 133; Coleman v. New York & N. H. R. Co. (1870) 106 Mass. 160.

B. Still another privilege may also apply. There is a privilege to use reasonable force to prevent the commission of a crime. With a serious felony like burglary the amount of permissible force is greater, and some courts permit a deadly force. See Scheuerman v. Scharfenberg (1909) 163 Ala. 337, 50 So. 335; Gray v. Combs (1832) 30 Ky. 478.

   C. In Ilott v. Wilkes [1820] 3 B. & Ald. 304, 106 Eng.Rep. 674, it was held that a landowner who placed spring guns on his land to keep off poachers was not liable to a trespasser who was shot. The result of this decision was a storm of public disapproval, which led to an act of Parliament making the setting of such devices a crime. In Bird v. Holbrook [1824] 4 Bing. 628, 130 Eng.Rep. 911, a case which arose before the statute was passed, but was decided afterward, the court overruled the Ilott case and a defendant who set a spring gun was held liable to a trespasser.

   D. Most American courts such as the main case and the Restatement (Second) of Torts § 85, have followed Bird v. Holbrook. Many jurisdictions have placed the restrictions on the use of deadly force in their state statutory codes. See statutes collected in Posner, Killing or Wounding to Protect a Property Interest (1971) 14 J. L. & Econ. 201, 228–232. Some statutes and some cases appear to allow the use of deadly force against serious invasions of property, such as burglary, that may be costly to the possessor. There is also some authority that the right of peaceful habitation may be protected by the use of deadly force. See Model Penal Code § 3.06(d)(i) (1962). Compare Bramble v. Thompson (1972) 264 Md. 518, 287 A.2d 265 (german shepherd).

   E. The general rule prohibiting deadly force is modified in some states by permitting it if defendant gives the plaintiff clear notice of the danger. See Starkey v. Dameron (1933) 92 Colo. 420, 21 P.2d 1112 (dictum); State v. Marfaudille (1907) 48 Wash. 117, 92 P. 939. This is especially likely to occur when defendant's use of force involved a vicious dog. See Hood v. Waldrum (1968) 58 Tenn.App. 512, 434 S.W.2d 94; Sappington v. Sutton (Okl.1972) 501 P.2d 814. Compare Loomis v. Terry (1837) 17 Wend. (N.Y.) 496, 31 Am.Dec. 306 (no warning, defendant liable). Barbed wire may give notice in and of itself. See Quigley v. Clough (1899) 173 Mass. 429, 53 N.E. 884. What privilege is operating in these cases? See also Hart v. Geysel and notes.

In some jurisdictions even posted warnings will not protect the landholder if he would not be privileged to use this amount of force were he there in person. See State v. Plumlee (1933) 177 La. 687, 149 So. 425; State v. Childers (1938) 133 Ohio St. 508, 14 N.E.2d 767.

F. Another line of defense that may work for the landholder is the argument that he intended only to frighten and not to injure the intruder. See Allison v. Fiscus (1951) 156 Ohio St. 120, 100 N.E.2d 237, discussed in the principal case.

8. The limitations on the possessor's privilege may also restrict his power to eject the plaintiff from his property into a position of unreasonable physical danger. Thus a tramp stealing a ride on a railroad train cannot be thrown off at forty miles an hour. Chesapeake & Ohio R. Co. v. Ryan (1919) 183 Ky. 428, 209 S.W. 538; Kobbe v. Chicago & N. W. R. Co. (1928) 173 Minn. 79, 216 N.W. 543.

In Depue v. Flatau (1907) 100 Minn. 299, 111 N.W. 1 this was extended even further. Plaintiff, a travelling cattle buyer, called at defendant's farmhouse on a cold winter evening, and was asked to stay for dinner. During dinner plaintiff was overcome by a "fainting spell," and became very weak and seriously ill. He asked permission to stay over night, which was refused. Defendant led him out to his sleigh, put him into it, adjusted the robes around him, and threw the reins, which he was too weak to hold, over his shoulders. Defendant then started the horses on the road to town. Plaintiff was found the following morning by the side of the road about three-quarters of a mile away, badly frost-bitten, and nearly frozen to death. Defendant was held liable. Suppose the landowner places a drunken guest in his car to go home?

9. On the other hand, if the plaintiff's presence endangers the personal safety of those on the premises, the privilege of self-defense, or that of defense of third persons, may justify the ejection. In Tucker v. Burt (1908) 152 Mich. 68, 115 N.W. 722, plaintiff, a member of the family of the janitor of an apartment house, fell ill with a highly contagious and infectious disease. Defendant, the owner of the building, ejected her. She was able to get to a hospital in a taxi. It was held that defendant was not liable.

10. See Bohlen and Burns, The Privilege to Protect Property by Dangerous Barriers and Mechanical Devices (1926) 35 Yale L.J. 535; Hart, Injuries to Trespassers (1931) 47 Law Q.Rev. 92, 101–105. Note, (1972) 24 S.C.L.Rev. 133; Annot. (1973) 47 A.L.R.3d 646.

Don't open your answer with a rambling preamble or restatement of the facts. Don't use any unnecessary introductory or transition language. You don't have to say, "There are three issues in this problem. I will now discuss these issues in order." Nor do you have to say, "The first issue is whether…." It is enough to say, "Was Farmer Jones justified in setting a spring gun in his home to protect it against burglars while he and his family were on vacation?" There is no magic in the order of presentation of issues in a multi-issue exam question. You may discuss the issues chronologically, by type of action, by plaintiff, by defendant, or in the relative order of importance as you see it. Sometimes you have to discuss a preliminary or "threshold" issue before addressing a major issue, or you have to talk about a major issue before tackling one or more subissues. However, there should be some structure to your approach. A random approach generally will not work because the professor reading the question will not have any idea where your answer is going and may conclude that you do not understand the problem. A stream of consciousness style like that of James Joyce is unlikely to produce satisfactory results in law school.

5. IRAC

Some commentators have suggested a system called IRAC for answering law school essay exam questions (I = issue, R = rule, A = analysis, C = conclusion). This approach bears a startling resemblance to the case brief discussed previously. As an approach to questions generally, IRAC can be quite useful. However, students can become bogged down in the methodology of IRAC, particularly on complex, multi-issue questions. They sometimes forget what questions the professor has asked, and their analysis may deal with discrete subissues while neglecting to analyze the relationship among the various issues. Such an answer may fail to perceive, for instance, that the issue in the question is how to characterize the issue itself. It is sufficient to say that all essay exams present legal issues, that they require explication of the law, that they anticipate some rational analysis, and that the conclusions should be supported by the reasoning.

As for spotting issues, your facility will depend upon how well you know the material generally, and how adept you have become at spotting issues. Much of the classroom experience during the first year reinforces the learning of issue spotting. Professors frame the issues through hypotheticals, through the Socratic questioning of students, and through comments. You can practice spotting issues with classmates, or try to predict the salient issues as you study. When you sit down with the exam, you either see the issue or you don't. If you don't, there is absolutely nothing you can do about it, because your discussion is neither right nor wrong, only missing. When in doubt, err on the side of inclusion. Remember, however, that to call something an issue that is not can be damaging too. Some professors include "red herrings" in exam questions; these are facts that lead you to think that a particular problem exists, which on closer analysis proves not to be a problem at all.

I offered this "red herring" on the short answer question involving Sally Westchester and Scruffy Man, included earlier in the chapter on page 87. The question says specifically that Tom Tourist was NOT negligent, but the facts also indicate that Tom's car struck Scruffy Man when Scruffy fell into the street. A number of students could not resist the opportunity to analyze Tom's negligence. On another question from the same test Bob and Otto Palindrome were harmed in various ways by Bob's ex-girlfriend, Allie Stalker. (In case you were wondering, professors do sit up nights thinking of these names.) The question asked what lawsuits Bob could bring against Allie. Again, a number of people got sucked in to a discussion of Allie's liability to Otto. Sometimes the facts will use a buzzword that conjures up memories of a particular case or rule that does not apply to the question at hand at all.

Assuming that you have seen the issue, the next step, as it was in class, is to state the issue succinctly and clearly. The statement should cut to the heart of the problem, and be expressed as narrowly as possible to cover the facts in the case. The wording of the question itself may give you guidance as to how to frame issues on an exam.

After articulating the issue, you should state the applicable law: "In a majority of jurisdictions, a landowner may not use deadly force to protect the property against damage from intruders. A small minority of states would allow such force to be used." State only the law that is applicable to the issue. For instance, you don't need to add, "The homeowner may use deadly force in his home in defense of himself or his family, although a majority of states require the owner to retreat prior to exercising such deadly force." The facts establish that the defendant's family isn't in the building where the intrusion took place, so the issue of defense of others doesn't arise.

Next, apply the specific facts to the law you have stated: "Here, no one was in the house when the burglar was injured by the spring gun. A spring gun may be considered a deadly force. In fact, it killed the burglar. A number of cases, such as *Katko v. Briney,* have established that the use of a spring gun, even if it does not actually kill an intruder, can be considered a deadly force because it had the potential to kill."

A good answer always anticipates the counterargument. "It may be argued that since Farmer Jones placed the gun so that it was pointed at the door two feet above the ground, he intended to use only nondeadly force. However, this argument is unpersuasive because a gun is highly likely to kill at any height. Jones's weapon would have been pointed chest high at a four-year-old."

Finally, your answer should state a conclusion: "Therefore, Farmer Jones was not justified in using a spring gun to protect his house while he and the family were on vacation." The conclusion itself is less important than the rest of the answer. It is important that the conclusion be supported by your analysis, but the "right" answer will mean little if your statement of the law is inaccurate or your logic flawed. It is possible for different students to reach different conclusions based upon the same set of facts. In fact, exam questions are seldom clear-cut. The answers could go either way.

6. Logic

It is important for you to construct a logical answer. The basic analytical tool used on law school exams is the syllogism. Your statement of the law is the major premise: "People who use spring guns to defend their property and cause injury to another may be held liable." The minor premise refers to the facts in the question: "Farmer Jones used the spring gun to defend his property and killed the burglar." The conclusion follows logically from the two premises: "Therefore, Farmer Jones may be held liable."

You do not have to have studied logic in college to handle this kind of analysis successfully. A few helpful hints may make it easier for you to master the process.

First, remember to use deductive logic. The conclusion must be deduced from the law as applied to the facts. Inductive or inferential logic can get you into trouble on law school exams. For instance, if the burglar was injured by Farmer Jones's spring gun while Farmer Jones was on vacation, it might be inferred that Farmer Jones set up the device. Maybe he did and maybe he didn't. The facts suggest that he did, and if there are enough facts, the inference may be a strong one. But a strong inference will never replace a sound deductive conclusion.

Second, avoid making unwarranted assumptions. Assumptions in the context of the law school exam question are facts not stated in the question that are taken by the reader to be true. We all make certain basic assumptions about the facts: "The case took place in an American jurisdiction." "The burglar was there for unlawful purposes." The problem arises when we assume too much: "Farmer Jones feared for the safety of his property and family because of rampant crime." Some students rewrite exam questions assuming away problems they do not wish to address: "Assuming that Farmer Jones set the spring gun for the purpose of protecting his family and forgot to turn it off when they went on vacation, his defense of them may have been justifiable." On the other hand, if the facts are ambiguous, it may be necessary to analyze the situation using different assumptions: "Assuming Farmer Jones was attempting to protect his family, his conduct may have been justified. However, if he was protecting the property alone, his conduct was probably improper."

Third, be prepared to argue in the alternative. On many law school exams, either the facts will lie somewhere between two rules that produce contrasting results, or the facts will fall between two fact patterns that produce different results under the same rule. This "on the one hand, on the other hand" approach is reminiscent of the character Tevye in *Fiddler on the Roof* trying to grapple with his daughter's impending marriage: "On the one hand...On the other hand..." Or *Hamlet,* who saw both sides of every question: "Whether 'tis nobler in the mind to suffer/The slings and arrows of outrageous fortune/Or take up arms against [them]."

Don't get sucked into a conclusion not supported by the facts: "Birds are animals. The burglar is an animal. Therefore, the burglar is a bird." Beyond your analysis itself, the effectiveness of your answer may depend on a number of other factors. Some of these factors should be apparent; others are more subtle.

E. Writing

1. Grammar and Style

Although the heart of your exam is undoubtedly the quality of your analysis, other factors may contribute enough points to make the difference between a good or mediocre paper. Probably the most important of these factors is writing style. If you can't write clearly, your grades will always fall behind your knowledge. To those who argue that this is law school, not freshman English, the best answer is probably that the fundamental skill of lawyering is communication, which involves both written and oral persuasion. More to the point, if the professor can't understand what you are talking about, you will not get a good grade. Every semester I have students who come in to review their exams, and attempt to point out that they knew what they were talking about. I respond that the very fact that they have to explain what they have written in order to make it comprehensible to me demonstrates the inadequacy of their answer. Since the professor may be reading one hundred or more papers, vague, poorly expressed ideas and convoluted prose can be painfully difficult to follow. If the professor cannot follow your train of thought, your exam grade will be derailed quickly.

The basic principles of effective writing should not be new. Use clear, concise prose. Avoid complex sentences. Place the central thought in each sentence at the beginning of the sentence and the most important sentence in each paragraph at the beginning of the paragraph. Avoid long, flowery transitions and lead-ins. Use the active rather than passive voice. Stay away from legalese. If you aren't sure what a word means, don't use it. Say it one time. In short, be brief.

Another common problem on exams is grammar and spelling. It is likely that your sentence construction will not be as clean under the time constraints of the law school examination process as it would have been in less stressful situations. Your writing may, at times, be awkward. Such lapses are unavoidable under the circumstances, and you should not spend valuable time trying to make a problematic sentence sound like it came from a Pulitzer-prize-winning novel. On the other hand, there is no excuse for abandoning fundamental rules of grammar and construction. The same thing may be said of spelling errors. Although many professors claim that they do not grade grammar and spelling, they may make unconscious assumptions about your ability that may influence their willingness to give you the benefit of the doubt on a questionable response.

One difficulty with these suggestions is that if you don't know good grammar or how to spell, you may not be able to identify your own writing deficiencies. And if you haven't learned these matters in 16 or more years of school, nothing you can do the night before exams or during exams can help you. If you have writing problems, you should seek remedial help before the time of exams. Many law schools or their universities offer programs to assist students at improving their writing skills. Writing may also be a concern of yours if you did not do much writing in undergraduate courses, or if you have always had difficulty writing. You may want to get your writing critiqued by a strong writer or editor, but the best thing to do is practice, practice, practice.

2. Legibility

Another aspect of writing is legibility. Although law school professors do not give awards for penmanship, it is important to produce a blue book that the professor can read. Because law school essay exams are long, they strain the hand, and because time is limited, students often rush to finish. Both of these phenomena can have an adverse effect on handwriting. Of course, some people just write almost illegibly regardless of the pressure.

The profs may tell you that they do not penalize bad handwriting, but the truth is that if they are reading 80 or more essay exams, and they can't read what appears on the page, the writer inevitably loses points. If the page looks like Arabic, Russian, or Sanskrit to the eye, the professor may overlook the brilliance of the answer. Take a look on page 109 at two handwriting samples from a recent law school test, and imagine yourself reading 20 or more pages of each.

Which Exam Would the Professor Want to Read?

DID THE SCRUFFY MAN AND HIS
POSSIBLE ACCOMPLICE JOIN TO FALSELY
IMPRISON SALLY? FALSE IMPRISONMENT
OCCURS WHEN A DEFENDANT CREATES
BOUNDARIES THAT RESTRICT A PLAINTIFF
FROM LEAVING OF HER OWN FREE WILL.
THE PLAINTIFF IS NOT AWARE OF ANY
REASONABLE MEANS OF ESCAPE. THE
PLAINTIFF MUST BE AWARE OF THE
CONFINEMENT OR SUFFER DAMAGES.
FORCE IS NOT NECESSARY TO CONTAIN
THE PLAINTIFF. HERE, THE SCRUFFY

False Imprisonment could be charged against
the two men for their action restricting her
in a confined space - taking no action to
let her go + doing all against her will. Sally
had no reasonable, safe way to exit -
(the bars, the traffic, etc.)
But we'd have to prove the 2 men had the
necessary intent: knew that they were causing

As an exam taker, try to write legibly. Don't crowd your answer; the law school will give you as many blue books as you need. Label different parts of your answer, and highlight important words. Write on one side of the page in case you need to come back later and add to or change your answer. Write on every other line. In other words, unless you are given a limited amount of space, spread out your answer on the page.

If your handwriting is not good, the best solution may be to use your laptop to take exams. Even if your keyboarding skills are limited, the output is still easier to read than an illegible handwritten exam.

F. Time

Perhaps the greatest failing of many law students is an inability to manage time during the exam. You may assume that on law school exams you will run out of time more than you will walk out early. If you were the last one to leave the examination room in previous educational incarnations, prepare yourself now for a formidable struggle against time limits in law school. If this is a problem for you, practice answering law school exam questions, particularly those of your professors that may be on file, prior to the exam. Students who have previously taken the same professor can tell you whether the professor's exams are normally difficult to complete in the time allotted. By doing a little preliminary investigation, you can identify potential problem exams in advance. Forewarned is forearmed!

In the exam itself, you have to get a grip on the time. Never just start answering the first question on the test. Carefully read the instruction sheet, because it usually describes the number and type of questions, as well as the time allocations or point values for each. In some cases the professor may have provided this information in advance; regardless of such information, rely only on the actual instructions in the test book. Look through the test book to see how many pages are included, and how much reading you will have to do. Many law school exam questions are long and convoluted, with complex facts and many issues. As you might expect, it is usually the case that the more time you are given to answer the question, the more complicated the question will be.

Don't panic! Remember that somebody (your diabolical professor) thought this exam could be answered in the time allotted. Even if the professor misjudged the time needed, everybody in the exam room has exactly the same amount. Your grade will not be based on some absolute value.

On your college history exam, there may have been 100 multiple-choice questions that look something like this: "In what year was the Declaration of Independence signed? (A) 1776 (B) 1876 (C) 1678 (D) 1767" The answer, of course, is (A). If you got the other 99 questions right, your score was 100 and you got an A on the test. If you missed 11, you got a B. On a law school exam, the professor might have 200 possible points, with the best paper in the class scoring 125. Even on multiple-choice exams, which are frequently modeled after multistate bar exam questions, it is possible to miss a number of answers and still do well on the test. Thus, the question is not what you could say if you had an unlimited amount of time and resources to produce an answer. The question is what you do say in three hours, or whatever time is provided, compared to what other examinees say in the same amount of time.

Think of yourself as a practicing lawyer, sitting in your office. A client comes in and tells you his problem. He was driving down the street in his brother's car when the brakes gave out and he ran into another car that had just run a red light. The doctor had improperly set his broken wrist and he has had to give up his career as a concert pianist. His brother also refuses to speak to him anymore. You explain to the client that he may be able to sue the driver of the other car on a negligence theory, but that under the state's comparative negligence statute, the brother, the brother's mechanic, or the manufacturer of the car might be partially responsible. You tell him that these potential defendants can be expected to compensate him only for the injuries that flow directly from their conduct. You may or may not be able to convince a jury that the subsequent negligent act of the doctor was foreseeable. The doctor can in no way be held responsible for the damage to your client's brother's car, but he may be sued for the damages caused by his subsequent negligent conduct. You tell your client that the fact that the doctor did not know he was a concert pianist, whose career was ruined by the accident, will not preclude recovery, citing the famous "egg-shell skull" case. The client agrees to have you represent him and leaves the office.

You then go into your law library to begin conducting research to develop your case. The spontaneous legal advice you gave your client was based upon the facts presented to you in the client interview. Your answer does not represent a final statement on the problem, and certainly not the level of knowledge you will have attained by the time the case goes to trial. But you had better at least be in the ballpark recognizing the client's problem and offering him legal advice. The law school exam question is like the client interview in that you are presented a problem you have not seen before, and you must identify the issues, articulate the applicable law, and make the basic arguments.

The point is this: you are not expected to write a brief that would be filed with the United States Supreme Court. You only have to answer the question within the framework of the time provided. You do well on the question if you give a better answer than the average law student within that time period; you will do poorly if your answer is worse.

G. Test Anxiety

Everyone feels nervous before examinations. The physical symptoms may vary from a knot in the stomach, to loss of appetite, to irritability, to loss of sleep, to a host of other reactions. More than a few of us have felt the primal fight-or-flight response when we go into the examination room. And rare is the law student who does not recall reading a question and drawing a complete blank.

These are all ways our body deals with stress, and exams are stressful. But if we did not respond to stress as we do, we would not get that jolt of adrenalin that helps us perform at our most efficient level at such times. As disturbing as it is, we need stress; we use stress; we overcome stress. Stress is normal. See pages 140–145, for a more general discussion of stress in law school.

For a small number of law students, stress levels prior to or during exams can become so heightened that they simply cannot perform. For them, stress is an enemy and not an ally. They may become so sick that they are incapacitated. They may become so agitated that they cannot sleep or study. They may feel so overwhelmed in an exam that they stare at a wall for three hours or run out of the room although the exam is only half over. Take heart: this will probably not be you. You will take a few deep breaths and make the best of things. You will do what you have to do. You will survive, even succeed.

Those students whose test anxiety is so severe that they are incapacitated must do something about the problem or they will not stay in law school for long. If you have a history of test anxiety, experience the severe reactions described above before exams begin, or have recently suffered through other highly stressful events, such as a divorce or job layoff, try to stay tuned in to your own feelings. Talk to someone before an exam crisis occurs. Take measures to reduce stress in your life. One of the best things you can do is be prepared. If you get to the exam and suffer from an anxiety attack, contact the dean or administrator on duty (not the professor because the exams are anonymous). If you wait until later, the response will probably be, "Too bad; that's life." Avoid disaster while you can.

H. Practice Questions

Enough talk. It's time to practice your exam-taking skills. If you prefer, you can continue to Chapter 6, and return to this material later. To do justice to these practice exercises, you should give yourself several hours of uninterrupted time. You may be able to divide the material into as many as three separate sessions if your schedule is tight. Either way, the practice will help you to be a better test taker.

1. Problem 1—Sally Westchester

Recall the question about Sally Westchester and Scruffy Man on pages 87–88. Recall also the four cases you have read in this chapter. Review also the materials on intent and battery that appear in Appendix B, page 169. The only other information you need to know is that there is an issue of false imprisonment in this fact pattern. False imprisonment is the intentional, unconsented confinement of an individual within boundaries set by the defendant without reasonable means for the plaintiff to escape. There's a little more to it than that, but for now, this definition should suffice. After you have reviewed the material, sit down and answer the question in the 30 minutes designated.

* * * * * * * * * * * * *

If you have finished, let's look at your answer.

This problem implicates several intentional torts, including assault and battery, which have been mentioned in the cases, and false imprisonment which is defined in the text above. A good answer would have talked about each of these issues. There are peripheral negligence issues as well, negated as to Tom and lacking facts as to the construction company. A reading of the entire question should alert the examinee that the main thrust of the professor is to test intentional torts. Looking at the specific issues (and understanding that you have not studied these various torts in detail), the professor would look at the following:

Assault—Were Scruffy's words alone enough to bring about apprehension of imminent battery? Probably not. In fact, they may have negated intent. But if they didn't, circumstances (the passageway, the other guy, Scruffy's hostile conduct) may be enough to cause Sally to reasonably anticipate harmful or offensive contact. Scruffy's ability to carry out the battery is not a problem.

False imprisonment—Scruffy cuts Sally off on three sides. The other guy is coming up from the rear. We know she can get through the bars sans packages, but the law doesn't require her to imperil herself or abandon her property. We don't know if the two men are acting in concert, but if they are, this may be a confinement. If not, the danger posed by the second man (as seen through Sally's eyes) may effectively negate that exit as a means of escape (the means of escape must be reasonable). But really, Sally doesn't even ask if she can get by; she just pushes Scruffy aside. It's hard to imagine false imprisonment without more facts. If there is a restraint, however, it doesn't matter how long.

Battery—As to Sally pushing Scruffy, clearly the elements of the tort are met. She intentionally caused harmful touching of Scruffy's person without his consent. Her motive does not have to be to cause harm; she only needs to know with substantial certainty that her act will bring about contact with Scruffy's body (as in *Garratt*) If these elements are present, Sally is liable for the harm to Scruffy, and in intentional torts, if she is liable, she is liable for all physical consequences flowing from her battery (here the death of Scruffy). You might argue that, as in *Spivey*, the result was unforeseeable, and that such consequence could not have been known with substantial certainty. In all likelihood, unless Sally's conduct was privileged, she will be held liable.

Self-defense—If Sally is privileged, the battery is excused. The question turns on whether her belief was reasonable as to the danger and whether the force she used was excessive. Her possible mistake as to the threat posed by the second man is allowed (i.e., she perceived him as a threat even if it turns out he wasn't one). Arguments can be made either way as to the reasonableness of her fear. As to force, she is allowed to use force equal to that threatened. Here, she used non-deadly force against nondeadly force. The fact that Scruffy fell into traffic does not make Sally's force deadly. The requirement to retreat prior to exercising the privilege of self-defense may mean that Sally should have taken steps to avoid confrontation before exercising her privilege, if she could do so without increasing her danger. But could she?

Defense of property—As in *Katko* she has a privilege to protect her property, but unlike *Katko* she is personally in danger along with her property (as when a burglar breaks into your house while you are there, as opposed to breaking into an unoccupied building). But her privilege is no greater as to her property than as to her person.

Negligence of the contractor—Although there are no facts in the problem to suggest possible liability, the property owner is certainly a possible target of an injured person.

Negligence of Tom—The facts said he was driving carefully, so a discussion of this possible action is off base.

In light of these comments let's look at two actual student answers that follow. The first answer was one of the best in a class of eighty. It is clear, direct and easy to understand. The issues and the relevant law are articulated accurately. The analysis is sound. The second answer was one of the poorer papers in the class on this question. The writer just never seems to get going. You will note that even the "good" answer does not hit all the issues addressed in the comments. It just covers more of them, and better. Following the two sample answers is an evaluation checklist. Use it to rate the two answers and then your own answers. If you can be brutally honest with yourself, such self-evaluation can be an effective tool for improving your test-taking skills.

QUESTION 2

WE HAVE 2 ISSUES OF INTENTIONAL TORTS, AND 1 ISSUE OF NEGLIGENCE. THE POSSIBLE INTENTIONAL TORTS THAT MR. SCRUFFY COMMITTED AGAINST SALLY ARE THOSE OF ASSAULT, AND FALSE IMPRISONMENT.

THE FACT PATTERN FAILS TO ESTABLISH A PRIMA FACIE CASE OF FALSE IMPRISONMENT BECAUSE IT IS UNCLEAR WHETHER MR. SCRUFFY WAS IN FACT RESTRICTING SALLY'S MOVEMENT. WE DO NOT KNOW WHETHER THE SECOND MAN WAS INVOLVED OR NOT. IT CAN BE ARGUED THAT SCRUFFY INTENDED TO RESTRICT SALLY'S MOVEMENTS, BUT SINCE NO SPECIFIC REQUESTS WERE MADE BY SALLY TO PASS ALONG HER WAY. WE CANNOT BE CERTAIN. IT IS CERTAIN THAT SALLY FELT RESTRICTED, BUT THIS IS NOT SUFFICIENT TO ESTABLISH A PRIMA FACIE CASE.

THERE IS, HOWEVER, SUFFICIENT EVIDENCE OF ASSAULT. SCRUFFY'S COMMENTS WERE DESIGNED TO PUT SALLY IN FEAR AND APPREHENSION OF A BATTERY, THEREFORE HE HAD INTENT. SALLY CLEARLY FELT THREATENED BY A LIKELIHOOD OF IMMINENT OFFENSIVE CONTACT TO HER. THERE IS A CAUSAL LINK BETWEEN SCRUFFY'S WORDS AND SALLY'S FEAR AND APPREHENSION. IT IS OFTEN HELD, HOWEVER, THAT WORDS ARE NOT SUFFICIENT TO ESTABLISH ASSAULT. IN THIS CASE, HOWEVER, SCRUFFY IS STANDING IN SALLY'S WAY AND SHOUTING AT HER MENACINGLY. HE ALSO SPECIFICALLY MENTIONS PHYSICAL HARM TO HER.

IN ADDITION TO SCRUFFY'S INTENTIONAL TORTS, SALLY COMMITS AN ACT OF BATTERY AGAINST SCRUFFY. ALTHOUGH SHE HAS INFACT COMMITTED A BATTERY (INTENDING TO TOUCH SCRUFFY, OFFENSIVELY TOUCHING SCRUFFY, CAUSING HARM AS A RESULT OF HER ACTIONS), SHE IS ABLE TO CLAIM AN AFFIRMATIVE DEFENSE OF SELF DEFENSE. ALTHOUGH SCRUFFY DIED AS A RESULT OF SALLY'S BATTERY, THIS WAS CLEARLY AN ACCIDENTAL RESULT. THERE IS NOTHING TO INDICATE THAT SALLY USED DEADLY FORCE. IT MAY BE ARGUED, HOWEVER, THAT SHE USED UNREASONABLE FORCE, OR PERHAPS SHOULD NOT HAVE USED ANY FORCE. THE ORDINARY PERSON IS SALLY'S SHOES WOULD PROBABLY HAVE ACTED SIMILARLY.

SCRUFFY'S DEATH IS ACCIDENTAL AND TOM TOURIST IS PROBABLY NOT LIABLE FOR THIS TRAGEDY.

SALLY MAY ALSO FIND NEGLIGENCE IN THAT THE CONSTRUCTION CONTRACTOR HAD A DUTY TO PROVIDE AN ADEQUATE WALKWAY ALLOWING PROPER SPACE AND THAT A BREACH OF THIS DUTY RESULTED IN SOME DAMAGE (LOST PACKAGES, MENTAL DISTRESS (VOMITING) FOR WHICH SHE MAY BE LIABLE

Question 2.

Sally W. was assaulted by scruffy
because he placed her in fear of
imminent battery, Sally Then
used an amount of force that
may have been excessive but because
she was put into fear by scruffy's
threats and his relevant size and
probable ability to harm her she was
justified under the doctrine of
Self defence. Scruffy's death
while arguably tragic was not
caused by a tort on Sallys part
(she was acting as one reasonably so situated would under the circumstances)
but may have been caused by the
Negligence of the Construction Company
for not making the (cite) safe enough
by limiting the width of the side walk

area, but not fencing the side facing
traffic. This may be because they undertook
to control the flow of pedestrian
traffic and didnt follow through or
because they had a duty to the
pedestrians because they were negligent
in leaving the site only partially
protected but obstructed and unsafe.
(Also could be negligence per se if in violation of OSHA statute)
Tom Tourist is not liable
So long as he didn't have a (last) clear
chance to stop. Which if he were
driving carefully would have.
The man following had no duty to
any-one unless he were in on a
joint venture with scruffy to rob   Concert
other pedestrians or whatever
although this is a stretch.

Critique Form

Evaluation

Points

(1) Issues

_____(10)   Did the person state the basic issues?

(2) The law

_____(20)   Did the person correctly state the law?

(3) Analysis

How did the person apply the law to the facts in
_____(40)   the case?

(4) Conclusion

Did the person reach a conclusion on each issue?

_____(5)   What was it?

_____

_____

(5) Other factors

_____(5)   a. Was the answer well organized?

Did it make sense?

_____(5)   b. Was the answer logical?

Did it apply a rational, deductive analysis?

_____(5)   c. Was the answer well written?

Were there grammatical, spelling, or structural
errors?

_____(5)   d. Did the answer deal with the problem on a
superficial issue or address the complexities?

_____(5)   e. Was the answer persuasive?

_____
Total 100

2. Problem 2—Ronnie and Nancy

In this problem, you get to look at another body of law. This problem involves the issue of strict liability for abnormally dangerous activities.

In strict liability cases, the defendant may be held liable for reasons other than fault, such as a particular fact pattern where the activity involves a degree of danger that cannot be made safe through ordinary care, such as blasting, keeping wild animals, or damming up water that can escape and cause flooding.

* * * * * * * * * * *

Practice Question and Answer

Ronnie and Nancy maintained a pond on the ranch that was used to water cattle. The pond was on the land when Ronnie and Nancy bought the land several years earlier. The pond was man-made, having been created by an earthen dam on a small creek. Through no negligence on the part of Ronnie and Nancy, the earthen dam broke after several weeks of unseasonable rain.

Water from the pond produced a flash flood damaging property for several miles downstream before the creek bed emptied into a larger stream. The damage included the Ferraro Bait Shop minnow tanks and worm troughs, three autos at Hart's Used Cars, and some vestments belonging to a Rev. Jacks at the Church of Freedom, PAC. Wally Mondell, who was camping in the dry creekbed, was swept away by the flood while he slept.

The cattle on Ronnie and Nancy's ranch stampeded when the dam broke. They broke through the fence on the ranch and ran onto Jeannie K's truck farm where they trampled several thousand head of cabbage.

Consider the issues raised in this fact pattern and discuss them in terms of strict liability theories of recovery.

Answer

This question deals with two primary issues involving strict liability for damages caused by 1) the breaking of the dam and 2) the stampeding cattle. In each situation the issue is whether liability should attach for certain conduct absent a showing of negligence because of the nature of the instrumentality causing the injury. The concept of strict liability holds liable owners of animals trespassing and persons who engage in abnormally dangerous activities if their animals or activities cause harm, regardless of fault. The rationale behind the strict liability theory is that the defendant is in a better position to bear or insure against the loss than the innocent plaintiff in part because the defendant controls the instrumentality, in part because he benefits from its use. In this question, the application of the general rule is slightly different in each situation.

1) The breaking dam—the traditional rule articulated in *Rylands v. Fletcher* imposes strict liability on the owners of land for the non-natural use of the land causing damage to the property of another. Lord Cairns modified Judge Blackburn's rule in the lower court that one is strictly liable whenever he brings something dangerous on his land, it escapes and causes damage. The Cairns view limited liability to things or activities unduly dangerous and inappropriate to the place maintained in light of the character of that place and its surroundings. Many American Courts rejected *Rylands* by mistakenly using the Blackburn view, although many of those courts later accepted the doctrine under the rubric of "absolute nuisance." An additional issue is whether the unseasonable rain was "an act of God" cutting off liability. If unforeseeable, sudden or destructive, the outside force may act as a superceding, intervening cause; here, it probably does not.

In this fact pattern, Blackburn's view would probably hold Ronnie and Nancy liable to Ferraro's Bait Shop, Hart's Used Cars, and Rev. Jacks, because the water was a dangerous thing brought on the land; it escaped and caused damage. However, under the Cairns view, it is unlikely that a jury would find a cattle pond inappropriate to the place in light of the surroundings, if the ranch is in a rural area where cattle ponds are common. The heirs of Wally Mondell will have greater difficulty because Wally's conduct placed him in the path of the water. Did Wally have full knowledge of the danger? Probably not. Although contributory negligence is not a factor in strict liability, plaintiff's conduct may bar recovery if it is sufficiently reckless. If Ronnie and Nancy are negligent, that is another matter, but absent a showing of inappropriate use strict liability is unlikely to be applied.

2) The stampeding cattle—at common law, owners of livestock have been held strictly liable for damages caused by the livestock trespassing on the land of another. This issue was complicated by the passage of "fencing in," "fencing out," and "free choice" statutes. Under "fencing in" statutes the defendant has the burden of fencing his cattle in; under a "fencing out" statute, the plaintiff has the burden of fencing out the cattle of defendant. A "choice" statute would allow the community to choose either option.

The answer to this question depends upon the statute involved. If there is no statute, Ronnie and Nancy are probably liable to Jeannie K., because under the general rule their cattle escaped and caused the damage. If there is a "fencing in" statute, they are probably liable also because the defendant's duty is to keep the cattle fenced in and he did not, while the plaintiff has no duty to keep the cattle out. If the cattle escape and do damage, the defendant should be liable. If there is a "fencing out" statute, Ronnie and Nancy may be relieved of liability if Jeannie K. has not fenced her property in order to keep the cattle out. If she has met this burden, however, she may recover for damages caused by the cattle, although the facts here do not indicate which is the case.

Look at the evaluation sheet here and on the next page to see how the sample answer might be scored.

Evaluation

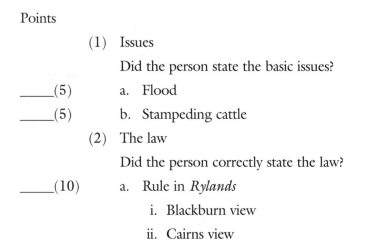

Points

    (1) Issues

        Did the person state the basic issues?

_____(5)   a. Flood

_____(5)   b. Stampeding cattle

    (2) The law

        Did the person correctly state the law?

_____(10)   a. Rule in *Rylands*

            i. Blackburn view

           ii. Cairns view

            iii. American "misinterpretation"

            iv. English view

_____(10)   b. Rule on trespassing cattle

            i. General rule

            ii. Fencing statutes

    (3) Analysis

        How did the person apply the law to the facts in the case?

_____(20)   a. The flood

_____(20)   b. Stampeding cattle

    (4) Conclusion

_____(5)   Did the person reach a conclusion on each issue?

        What was it?

        a. The flood _____

        b. Stampeding cattle _____

    (5) Other factors

_____(5)   a. Was the answer well organized?

        Did it make sense?

_____(5)   b. Was the answer logical?

        Did it apply a rational, deductive analysis?

_____(5)   c. Was the answer well written?

        Were there grammatical, spelling, or structural errors?

_____(5)   d. Did the answer deal with the problem on a superficial level or address the complexities?

_____(5)   e. Was the answer persuasive?

_____

Total 100

3. Problem 3—Sam Student

Our final practice question involves another legal question, whether the violation of a statute can be used to establish a breach of the standard of care for a defendant whose conduct unintentionally causes harm to another. Individuals are normally supposed to take reasonable precautions to avoid injuring others, and if they fail to do so, they can be held liable for the harm they cause. In these questions, the defendant has not only caused the plaintiff's injuries; she has also violated a statute that arguably establishes a standard of conduct.

In those cases where the statute articulates a standard of conduct, courts often adopt the statutory standard as the standard of care for negligence. For instance, if there is a law requiring people to stop their cars at stop signs and someone fails to stop, if that person hits another car, he can be found negligent because the law established a standard of care and he breached it. Courts often say that in order to apply the statutory standard, the legislature must have intended to protect the class of persons of which the plaintiff is a member against the type of harm that occurred. Sometimes the legislative intent itself is not clear, and the court must look for the intent in the language of the statute, the legislative history, and other principles of statutory interpretation. It is also noteworthy that courts in different jurisdictions give different evidentiary weight to statutory violation as a basis of liability.

****

After you have answered the question, look at the model answer, and then critique your answer using the evaluation form that appears on page 120. By now, you should be able to evaluate your progress. If your test-taking skills are wanting, make sure you get more practice before you undertake the real thing. Many universities have test-taking labs. Professors and student mentors are frequently willing to offer advice. Just don't ignore the symptoms. Since most readers of this book either have not yet or just recently begun law school, these exercises are less a measure of your knowledge than your ability to communicate your thoughts on paper. For now, that should be enough of a head start to permit you to begin your legal education with confidence.

Practice Question and Answer

Sam Student decided to fly his kite while at the beach one day. He did this despite knowledge of a local ordinance that prohibited kite flying on the beach and punished offenders with a $25.00 fine. Sam was not holding onto the kite string very tightly and when an unexpected strong gust of wind materialized, it blew the kite out of Sam's hands. The wind carried the kite about 5 miles until it crashed into the windshield of Pete Plumber's truck, which Pete was driving at a speed 10 miles above the legal limit. The kite shattered the glass and forced Pete to cancel all of his afternoon appointments. Discuss Student's liability to Pete.

Model Answer

The first issue is whether Sam may be liable to Pete for damages in tort due to his violation of a statute prohibiting kite flying on the beach. Generally, one may be held civilly liable for statutory violations if the statute provides a standard of conduct. The test is whether the plaintiff was in the class of persons the legislature intended to protect by passing the statute, and whether the harm that resulted was the type the legislature intended to protect against.

Here, there is no information about the legislative intent. However, if the purpose of the legislature had been to provide for the safety of people on the beach (e.g., being run over by people trying to get or keep their kites up), the harm to Pete would probably not be within the scope of the legislative intent; nor would Pete be within the protected class. If the legislature meant to provide some broader protection against errant kites, then Pete may be within the class and the harm exactly what the legislature contemplated. However, the statutory language limiting the prohibition to "on the beach" suggests that such a broad interpretation is not warranted. Even if the legislature, in response to injuries caused by loosed kites on the beach, drafted narrow language limited to kite flying on the beach, it is unclear whether an injury occurring 5 miles away caused by an unexpected gust of wind was contemplated. The answer may turn upon how common such strong gusts of wind were on this beach; in other words, was the propulsion of Sam's kite this distance a foreseeable event, which the legislature contemplated in drafting the statute.

It is likely that Sam will not be held liable in this case because the statute was not intended to protect the class of persons of which Pete is a member or against the harm that occurred.

If the statute applies, however, an additional question arises, whether Pete is contributorily negligent for exceeding the speed limit. Using the same test for civil liability in case of statutory violation, exceeding the speed limit is not likely to provide a basis for contributory negligence. Pete could have hit the kite at any speed, so violation of the statute was not a cause of the injury. Thus Pete cannot be found contributorily negligent in this case.

Go back to the evaluation form on page 123 and, based on your reading of the answer, evaluate the answer.

These practice exams questions are designed to give you a taste of what to expect in law school. Real law school exam questions may be longer, more complex, and more comprehensive. However, if you possess the skill to write short answers, you can develop the skill to write longer ones. Right now, you have not learned enough law to address more than basic questions. The day you face real exam questions will arrive soon enough.

I. Conclusion

In the end, it's just you and the exam book. For the most part, in law school there are no homework assignments, no pop quizzes, no bonus projects to factor in with the final exam, to produce your final grade. Everything comes down to this three-hour intellectual duel. Assuming that you have prepared throughout the semester and studied effectively in the days preceding the exam, you now have an opportunity to demonstrate how much you know. Taking law school exams requires a special set of skills. Some students who are very good in classroom discussions perform poorly on tests. Every year, many students fail to establish on paper what they know in their heads. On the other hand, there are some students who get better grades, not because they know more but because they know more about taking tests. One final recommendation you should heed is to review all your exams, whether you did well or not. Most schools provide for exam review, and if you did poorly, you need to know what you did wrong. Conversely, if you did well, you will want to know how to replicate the feat.

CHAPTER 6
Managing Technology in Law School

Law school is more than briefing cases and reciting in class. Computer and other technologies pervade legal education just as they do other parts of the university. If you graduated from college within the past few years, you probably already have utilized these technologies in a variety of ways. You may wonder whether or not law school will require the same technology skills on a regular basis. The answer is yes. If you have been out of school for a decade or more, you may be surprised at how the educational process has changed, although chances are you have already experienced the technology revolution in the work place or at home.

A. Electronic Learning

Law schools today provide a network, or intranet, for members of the law school community. The network is anchored with an Internet site and e-mail system. Even before you enter law school, you can visit law schools' web sites for information. Most law schools allow students to apply for admission online. Many law school courses utilize e-mail to post reading assignments and other messages. Some schools provide class bulletin boards for the posting of syllabi, sample exam questions, supplement readings, and other materials. Even some law school casebooks are available electronically. Many classes include an online discussion group, or a listserv. Some professors ask for written assignments to be submitted electronically. Distance learning, participating in a course which is offered electronically at a remote location, is becoming more prevalent. And a variety of electronic tools are regularly used by law students these days.

The fact that a number of activities associated with legal education take place in cyberspace broadens the arena in which legal issues are discussed and learning takes place. Professors and classmates are instantly accessible through e-mail. If you have a question about something that came up in class, you do not have to find a time to meet the professor in his office outside of class. You can just send an e-mail message. If you cannot attend class because you are ill, you can inform the professor through e-mail. If you want a professor to review a draft of something you are writing, you can attach the document to a message. If you participate in a study group or student organization, you can arrange meetings or discuss issues electronically.

The law school may rely on e-mail to convey important announcements and to post administrative policies and other information. Offices such as the registrar, financial aid, and career services may communicate with students or directly provide services online. For instance, the registration process, financial aid application process, or interview scheduling process may be computer-based. Reliance on technology varies from law school to law school, so check with the administrative offices in your school to find out which functions operate online.

B. Legal Research

One area that will require some new learning on your part is legal research. The majority of legal work requires research into cases, statutes, and other sources of legal information. Traditionally, information was kept in books, was stored in law libraries, and researchers learned to find the information they needed by going to the library and digging through the books. A significant part of your first year in law school will involve learning to conduct legal research. Electronic research today is rapidly replacing book research in the legal field.

Most of the information available in law libraries, including virtually all reported cases from American jurisdictions, is available electronically on a number of searchable databases. Your law library will have a research librarian, whose role is to help users access online databases and information. The Internet gives legal researchers access to a vast amount of information that was difficult to locate or obscure in the past. Legal research is a skill that you will use not only in law school but also in practice once you graduate. For this reason, it is well worth the investment of time and energy to become a skilled researcher. Learning to conduct proficient legal research early in your law school career will pay big dividends throughout your legal career.

Many law school classes will be taught in a traditional Socratic way, but an increasing number hold in-class Internet sessions. More and more professors are experimenting with new and exciting teaching methods, teaching classes in real time to students in one or more distant locations.

C. Computers

Law schools permit (and some require) the use of laptops in the classroom, and have classrooms wired for the Internet. In addition to writing your papers using a word processing program, you may be able to submit your work for review by professors electronically. Most schools permit students to take their exams on a computer using special exam software.

Clinical education and practice skills courses designed to train students for the practice of law are likely to incorporate technology used by actual practitioners, such as calendaring, timekeeping, case management, and document assembly systems, in addition to electronic research. Students with strong technology skills will find it fairly easy to learn these new applications and to hone their skills before graduation.

Technology can help you to be a more efficient student. If you know how to use the tools that are available to you, you can find and manipulate information quickly and accurately. You can manage aspects of both law school and your personal life. You will want to have a calendar program, contact list, word processing, spread sheet, and financial management programs at your disposal.

A significant number of law students use laptop computers. Law schools typically provide either wired or wireless Internet access within the law school building, and many provide remote access as well. You should plan to have a personal computer of some kind during law school, and a laptop gives you the greatest flexibility for working in a variety of locations, such as home, the law library, in class, at friends' apartments, or wherever else you need to do work.

If you purchased a computer when you went to college four years ago, you should consider replacing your machine with one that is more state of the art. You will need a system with Internet access, a reliable printer, a large screen (17" for a desktop, 12+" for a laptop), and one or more flash drives. Consider purchasing a PDA (Personal Digital Assistant), which can be linked to a desktop calendar and contact program. Active law students may also want to keep a digital wireless or cellular telephone with voice mail. Although some schools and many professors disapprove of students leaving cell phones on during classes, many students enjoy the portability of these devices.

Another emerging technology that may help law students, particularly those who are very slow at keyboard entry, is voice recognition software (VRS), which allows the user to dictate into a microphone connected to a computer. The VRS converts the audio into digital text files that can be read by your word processing software for editing. The cost of this technology can be substantial, but may be less than many people think. Considering the benefits that may be derived from effective use of technology, the investment is probably a sound one.

CHAPTER 7

Avoiding the Pitfalls
of Law School

The road through law school, like the road to hell, is paved with good intentions. Victory here is never absolute. There always is one more case you could have read. Another source you could have checked. An additional hour you could have studied. There probably is not a lawyer alive who would not have done something or other differently in law school to improve his or her performance.

In law practice, you develop your skills as a lawyer through experience. If you are a trial lawyer, you argue cases in court. If you are an estate planning lawyer, you draft increasingly complex instruments. As a new lawyer, your mistakes will be corrected by senior lawyers, judges, and your own desire to improve. Competence is a constantly receding goal.

In law school you only get one chance. Whereas you certainly can improve your performance after a disastrous first year, you do not have the luxury of years to hone the skills needed for success. This chapter addresses some common pitfalls for the unwary law student, and offers suggestions on how to avoid them. It deals with time management, money management, stress management, alcohol and substance abuse, and other problems.

A. Time Management

Time management is the most pervasive problem you will encounter in law school. Not only is the work voluminous, but also the need to make choices is inevitable. Your ability to get a grip on your schedule and discipline yourself to establish a flexible but workable routine will have a major impact on your success in law school.

1. Common Difficulties

Law students procrastinate. They are overwhelmed by choices they have to make. They are overcommitted. All these difficulties are related. We often procrastinate when we have many things to do; we simply don't do the most onerous tasks. We make too many commitments because we can't make decisions, and so just say yes to everyone. In the most basic sense, time management is learning to make decisions in a timely way about matters important to us, and acting upon those matters when it is most advantageous to do so. Law school imposes an entire set of inevitable demands that can only be controlled, not eliminated. Although it may be easy to recognize the objectives of time management, it may be more difficult to become an effective manager of time.

2. A Time Management Model

If you are a full-time law student, you will have approximately 33 months separating first year orientation and graduation. If you had a full-time, 40-hour-per-week job, you could expect to spend 5,500 hours on the job during this 33-month period. Many lawyers work considerably more hours than this. On the other hand, a law school will prescribe roughly 1,200 hours of classroom work. If you spend 3 hours outside class for each hour in the classroom (a suggestion that many professors offer but few students accept), you would still spend less than the time demanded by your full-time job on legal studies. To be sure, because of semester breaks, summer jobs, and vacations, the actual work load during school is greater. (If you are carrying 15 classroom hours per week, and spending 3 hours outside class, your work load is actually about 60 hours per week.) The point, however, is that there are plenty of hours to go to law school and lead some semblance of a normal life. If there are 24,000 hours during the 33 months of your legal education, and you spend 12,000 of them eating, sleeping, and grooming, you still have 12,000 hours left for school, work, play, and commuting.

The evening law student may not have such a good situation. Even carrying a reduced load of 10 or 11 classroom hours, applying the 3:1 study to classroom ratio, the evening student is frequently carrying two full-time jobs during periods when school is in session and only one during breaks. Such a schedule requires significant sacrifices, careful planning, and dogged perseverance. Pursuit of a part-time legal education is not for those who are marginally committed or perennially disorganized.

What you must do is *hire yourself* as a law student. Get out of the student mentality and think of your job as attaining a legal education. Make the commitment to yourself that you will spend a minimum of some specified number of hours per week over the next 33 months (45 months if you are an evening student). Give yourself two weeks vacation per year and appropriate holidays, but otherwise go to work every day as a law student. And pay yourself. Once a month, reward yourself with some treat as compensation for doing your job. Your pay might be something esoteric, like dinner and a movie; physical, like a new article of clothing; edifying, such as a (nonlegal) book to read; or psychological, like vegging out in front of the TV. This is not the only relaxation you can have during law school; it is one form of R&R that acknowledges your ongoing work.

Your friends, family, and loved ones must understand your commitment to law school. Just as they should know the demands of any job you take, they need to know the demands of this job, so they will not make competing demands (too often). It will help to set aside a certain time each week for family activities. If you use your time well, there will be time for relationships. Whether you "work overtime" or bring your work home with you is a separate question.

Some readers may question the need for a device such as the one just described. Some readers may possess the discipline to do their work without creating the fiction to assist them. Unfortunately, many do not. This exercise forces those students to make commitments to set aside the large blocks of time required for law school, while maintaining a big picture of how law school fits into their broader existence.

3. Establish a Schedule

A second technique for managing your time is to establish a weekly schedule. There are many commercial products, such as the "Weekly Planner" that you can buy. If you have a personal computer, a number of programs, such as Microsoft Outlook, have scheduling features. You may have developed your own system over the years in school or business. Whatever system you use, set up and follow a weekly schedule. Make sure the schedule is workable. If you don't allow yourself enough time to get from home to school each day, you will always be late. If you stop to get coffee each morning in the student lounge, put it in the schedule. Set aside blocks of time to study.

You walk a fine line, when you schedule your time, between inflexibility and anarchy. No schedule can be inelastic; things come up that you can't anticipate. On the other hand, if the schedule is honored more in its breaking than in its observance, it is useless. As a rule of thumb, the schedule should represent accurately your actual utilization of time. If more than 10 percent of your time is spent on unplanned activities, you need to get better control of your schedule.

4. The Daily List

A third simple device for time management is the daily list. While your schedule may govern the allocation of major blocks of time during the day, you still must find a way to deal with the urgencies of the day. Every morning, when you get up, make a list of the nonroutine things you have to do that day. Routine things (e.g., reading the paper, getting the mail) should already have a place in the schedule. Nonroutine matters, such as class assignments and personal obligations, should be included on your list. Then, rank the items in their order of importance, with the things that absolutely must be done today at the top and matters that you hope to finish today at the bottom. Within the times allocated for the appropriate activities, take care of the things at the top of the list first and handle the less important matters if you can. If some item stays at the bottom of your list for a period of weeks, drop it from the list, because you will never do it.

5. A Tickler System

In law practice, you may utilize a device called a tickler system. A tickler is a perpetual calendar that reminds you of critical dates. You can set up a tickler file now using a personal information manager like Microsoft Outlook. A tickler can help you make appointments, remember birthdays, organize a study schedule, and meet deadlines for papers, registration, and so on. You can also use a commercial software program; you do not have to be a computer whiz to apply this easy study aide.

B. Money Management

Several years of service on a law school academic standards committee have produced these observations. Next to personal and family problems, money problems are most commonly cited by students in academic difficulty as a major cause of their plights. And personal/family problems often have money issues at their root. Financial worries overwhelmed their consciousness and eliminated any possibility for effective study. These comments are intended for every law student who cannot sit down and write a check for $60,000 without grimacing.

In 2008, law school tuition ranged from less than $10,000 to more than $40,000 per year. In addition, the cost of living for housing, food, transportation, entertainment, and other expenses will run $10,000–$15,000, or more, depending upon your location, lifestyle, marital status, and pre-existing obligations. Before you begin law school, you should budget carefully, considering your needs, law school expenses, and sources of income.

1. Financial Planning

Many students enter law school without a clear financial plan. They literally live from hand to mouth day by day. They are forced to take jobs in restaurants to pay expenses, constantly fight with family to obtain financial help, and frequently ignore school work because they are struggling with financial matters. If you prepare a realistic budget and the numbers just don't add up, it is probably better to postpone law school for a year or two or, after having started, take a leave of absence than to continue your legal education with inadequate resources. If you are committed to the idea of attending law school, make arrangements to set aside a portion of your earnings in a money market or other savings plan until you have saved enough to enter law school with some degree of financial security.

2. Financial Aid

There are alternatives to deferring law school enrollment that you should consider also. Talk to the financial aid officer at the law school(s) where you are admitted to determine whether the school can put together a package with which you can live. You will have to complete a Free Application for Federal Student Aid (FAFSA) form (available at *http://www.fafsa.ed.gov*) in a timely manner. You may also have to fill out special applications for specific scholarship or loan programs. The Financial Aid Office may be able to combine scholarships, work-study, and student loans in such a way that you will be able to survive. Most law students are not supported by their parents and therefore qualify for higher loan limits than younger students living at home. Convincing the Financial Aid Office that you are not in the same boat as an undergraduate student may prove problematic at some schools. One caveat concerning student loans deserves mention: the more you borrow, the more you have to pay back. A heavy debt load at graduation may force you into career choices you would not otherwise make. Because loan repayment commences with graduation from law school, there is great pressure to obtain the highest paying job possible immediately after graduation in order to pay the bills. For instance, many students do not pursue prestigious federal/judicial clerkships because the pay may be less than half what they could make in large law firms. For a more thorough discussion of student financial aid, see *Barron's Guide to Law Schools*, published biannually.

3. State Versus Private Schools

If you wish to avoid going into hock up to your eyeballs, you may consider attending your state law school instead of the expensive private school you always dreamed about. Most state law schools have sound programs and excellent resources. The best state law schools compare favorably with the leading private institutions. At many state schools, tuition pays for only a portion of the cost of running the law school, so tuition is only a fraction of that of a private school, which must cover its operating expenses with tuition revenue.

4. Working

Consider working full-time and going to school at night. Many law schools have evening division programs for students who choose not to go to school full-time. Whereas a part-time education takes four years and terrific discipline, the educational experience is substantially the same as that of a full-time program. Some schools permit you to change from one division to the other depending on your needs. Remember, however, that full-time students take 14–16 semester hours, while part-time students take 10–11. Thus, as a part-time student, you take only 1–2 fewer courses per semester than your full-time counterparts. The main advantages of enrolling in a part-time program are that you can carry a full-time job, and that the tuition is only about three-fourths of that for a full-time student.

American Bar Association standards limit full-time law students to 20 hours of outside employment per week. Many law students· clerk in law firms during their second or third year of law school (see Chapter 9). The same ABA standards discourage first year students from working at all. By the second year, you should know whether you will be able to handle outside employment and still keep up with your law school work. Furthermore, after the first year you can adjust your course load to accommodate your work schedule by bunching your classes on certain days, taking a lighter load in some semesters, or attending summer school.

During the first year, your schedule is inflexible, and you really don't know how much time it will take you personally to do the work necessary to succeed at this enterprise. It makes more sense to hold off working until after the first year is over if at all possible. If you must work, try to find a job with flexible hours so that you can take time off to study for exams, prepare for moot court, and meet other law school obligations. Some students have successfully located positions that allow them to study while they work (e.g., night security guard, police dispatcher in a rural police department). Try to find a job that is close enough to the law school that transportation is not a problem. Avoid work that is physically or emotionally taxing. Some students engage in entrepreneurial activity, running their own businesses (e.g., computer consultant, writer, private investigator), so that they can control their schedules better. In short, don't work unless you have to, but if you do, try to pick something that you control or that doesn't impinge on your law school work.

Many students use summer earnings to finance law school. If you can find a summer job that pays well, in a law firm or elsewhere, it can alleviate money pressures during the school year.

5. Scholarships

A final comment on financing your legal education involves scholarships. If you are resourceful, you may be able to identify scholarship money that is not available through the university, law school, or Financial Aid Office. Many private organizations offer scholarships to individuals who meet special criteria. These include private foundations, religious organizations, ethnic and cultural support groups, states and municipalities, the military, and other institutions. If you can identify such independent funding for your legal education, you may be able to avoid many of the pitfalls described above. Every year in the United States, countless scholarships go unclaimed because no one applied for them. For more information on student financial aid, see *Barron's Guide to Law Schools.*

6. Budgeting

Once you are in school, money management involves keeping track of your finances. The time management section of this chapter suggests hiring yourself as a law student. To carry this analogy further, the business entity hiring you as a law student is "your future." As in any business, this one must be properly capitalized, as the preceding section indicates. The enterprise also needs to be run in a businesslike fashion. This means that you operate as efficiently as possible within a budget and keep accurate financial records. In other words, you are your own CFO (Chief Financial Officer).

If you have a personal computer, there are a number of excellent and inexpensive personal financial management software packages (e.g., "Quicken") on the market that allow you to keep track of your finances. These systems are usually easy to use and require no formal accounting training to operate. Manual systems depend largely on your business/financial/accounting acumen. As with any business, "your future" depends on adequate cash flow. You have to have enough money in the bank at times when bills are due in order to pay them. Even students who have addressed the problem of financing their legal education may face short-term difficulties if they cannot get to their resources when the rent is due, the tuition bill arrives, and other expenses arise.

On the whole, you will find the law school experience much less painful and probably more meaningful if you get a grip on your finances from the start. If you have financial problems, don't wait until disaster is impending to seek help. After all, law school gives you enough to worry about without having to struggle with money matters on an ongoing basis.

C. Stress Management

The point has already been made that law school is a high stress environment. Everything seems designed to produce anxiety, particularly during the first year. You will often hear the argument that learning to survive the pressures of law school will prepare you to cope with the pressures of practice.

Understanding that law school is stressful is one thing; doing something about it is quite another. Different people cope with this stress with varying degrees of success. Because stress can effect your performance, it is important to develop effective stress management skills.

One misconception is that all stress is bad. On the contrary, stress is a motivator. It helps us to deal with the problems and conflicts that life throws at us. The only truly stress-free state is death.

You need to make stress work for you. If the pressure isn't great enough, you have no motivation to act. If it is too great, you may be immobilized and unable to act. The following suggestions are designed to help you manage stress. Some of the ideas presented have been discussed already in this book in conjunction with other issues; others are introduced for the first time as techniques to deal with stress generally.

1. Responsibility

Take responsibility for what happens to you. Victims are almost always more stressed out than those who accept responsibility for their own decisions, because victims don't have any control over what happens to them. For instance, the victim would say, "That #!)/[* > Munneke gave us too much to read in Torts again," instead of "I didn't read my Torts last night." When you decide that you are in control of your own destiny, you will feel better equipped to deal with whatever obstacles law school throws at you.

2. Commitment

Believe in something. Dr. Ted Edwards, who runs The Hills Medical Sports Complex in Austin, Texas, and who has spoken to lawyers all over the United States on stress management, has stated repeatedly that individuals who are committed to something are less likely to have strokes, heart attacks, and other stress-related illnesses than those who are not. For some people, this may be a belief in God or some secular value system. For others it may be commitment to a cause or to family or loved ones. As much as drifters make popular movie heros, they may not fare as well on the streets of life as they do on the silver screen. In law school, the translation of this principle is fairly simple. Those who have a strong sense of purpose find it easier to endure the pressure than those who don't.

3. Little Aggravations

Don't sweat the small stuff. One of the difficulties with stress is that it doesn't always come out in response to what is really bothering you. The week before your brief is due, you yell at your spouse for being 15 minutes late getting home from work. You threaten to sue the grocery checker for neglecting to give you credit on your Peter Pan peanut butter coupon. You make obscene gestures at drivers who impede your progress in traffic with seeming maleficent purpose. You may do all sorts of uncharacteristic things in response to what is going on at school.

It is important to remember that stress is cumulative. All the pressures add up. Studies have shown that individuals who experience a large number of stressful events in their lives within a year often fall victim to physical illness shortly thereafter. If you let the little things get you down, it will be harder to deal with the one big stress you can't escape: law school.

When you feel like blowing up at someone or something, count to ten. Yes, just like your mother told you when you were a little kid. Wait a few seconds, take a deep breath, and think about whether it's worth it to waste your valuable anger on something like this. If it is, by all means, give them hell. Sometimes you just need to get a load off your mind. Those who do not know how to express their anger, frustration, or unhappiness, or who refuse to recognize their stress, have as much of a problem as those who express their anger too easily.

4. Signs of Stress

Learn to recognize the signs of stress. Although we all react to stress somewhat differently, there are a number of common symptoms that can signal us that the stress level is high: tightness or tension across the shoulders and the neck region, bulging blood vessels in our temples and neck, clenched teeth, clenched fists, sweaty palms, a knot in the stomach, heart palpitations, feelings of rage or panic, or compulsive behavior such as craving for cigarettes, food, drugs, or alcohol. If you know how to recognize these stress reactions in your own body, you can frequently cope with the anxiety even if you are not aware of the stress cognitively. A lawyer I know found that she was digging her fingernails into her palms at times she didn't even know she was under stress. However, she learned that when she did this, there usually was something bothering her.

5. Stoicism

A little stoicism goes a long way. Learn to accept the things you cannot change. Every indignity is not your personal war. Pick your battles and save your anger. We all feel a little like David Banner (a.k.a. "The Incredible Hulk") who responds to the bad guy twisting his arm, "Please don't do that. You really wouldn't want to see me when I'm angry."

6. Causes

Recognize what causes your stress. In law school, this means recognizing the times when you face the most stress: when you get behind, when you take exams, when major assignments like briefs are due, when you have to speak in class or do an oral argument, and when you have trouble understanding something. Although you can do something about some of these stressors (like getting too far behind), many of them are just part of law school. To the extent that you know what they are and when to expect them, you will find it easier to cope.

7. Coping

Learn some simple coping mechanisms. Deep breathing can lower your heart rate and blood pressure and actually reduce stress. When you recognize signs of stress, take several deep cleansing breaths, breathing in slowly through the mouth with the diaphragm and breathing out through the nose. If you can, sit down. If you can't, drop your shoulders and open your palms. Close your eyes and fantasize about something wonderful. Massage the spots where you feel the stress (e.g., temple, jaws, shoulders). A formal program of yoga or pilates can help you to engage in stress-reducing coping activities as well.

8. Exercise

Get some exercise. One of the best ways to get rid of stress is to work it out through exercise. The opportunities for physical exercise are virtually unlimited: tennis, basketball, running, jogging, walking, aerobic dancing, sex. Many law schools have intramural programs, tennis and golf matches, kickboxing, and exercise classes. There always are health clubs, exercise centers, weight rooms, and leagues sponsored by your local parks, Y.M.C.A., or other organizations. Whatever you decide to do, whether it is an individual or group activity, just try to get out regularly during law school. You will find it much easier to survive.

9. Diet

Eat well. There is a difference between eating much and eating well. Many law students experience eating disorders; some of them balloon, whereas others waste away. Many students subsist on junk food, particularly those who work all day, go to school at night, and grab a "Big Mac" in between. A well-balanced, high protein, low fat, low cholesterol diet can actually contribute to stress reduction. Switch to decaf coffee. Caffeine is probably the most widely used drug in America. It is addictive (if you don't believe it, try going cold turkey from your coffee). It can produce anxiety (haven't you ever found yourself literally walking the walls after too many cups?). Try brewed decaf; it's just as good.

10. R & R

Make sure you get rest and relaxation. Get plenty of sleep. You really don't function all that well with long periods of two to three hours per night. And get away from studying every once in a while. Go to a party. Read something unrelated to law. Watch T.V. Spend time with your family. Just don't get carried away with it.

11. Meditate

Clear out the cobwebs in your mind on a regular basis. The process of clearing your mind is called meditation. You don't need a mystic guru, incense, or a mantra in order to meditate. All you need is a little bit of quiet time alone each day. Get away from noise, interruption, and distractions. Some people find a peaceful or relaxing setting like a park, a garden, a church, or a quiet comfortable room. Sit down, and begin to breathe slowly and deeply. Shut your eyes, and try to clear out all the mental noise that keeps trying to intrude. "Oh, my God. I have 30 pages of Torts to read for tomorrow." "Will I ever get a job?" "Wow! Did Mr./Ms. X really look good in class today." To help you clear your mind, think of something far away and peaceful, like standing on a tropical beach under the full moon, watching the waves roll in one after another. Or coasting down a lazy river on a comfy raft. Or going out of your body to float among the clouds, removed from the conflicts of life below. If reading these suggestions makes you uncomfortable, you are probably already over-stressed and could benefit from these suggestions.

When you have blocked out the intrusive thoughts begin to think about different parts of your body one at a time: your fingers, your arms, your toes, your legs, your stomach, your back. You will find that you can tune in, very acutely, to how each part feels. Then, think to yourself that each part is very relaxed. Let your hands feel heavy. Let the tension in each fade away. When you have been through your entire body, return to your deep breathing, open your eyes, and sit quietly for a few moments returning again to face the world. The whole exercise takes no more than five or ten minutes and can do wonders for your mental well-being.

12. Help

Don't let your problems get too big. This is what the late T. J. Gibson, for many years associate dean at the University of Texas School of Law, used to say to each entering class. Too often, people let problems build up until they cannot deal with them. Frequently, law students fail to confront serious problems until it is too late to do something about them. Sometimes students fail to acknowledge the symptoms of stress until their bodies or minds simply revolt. Almost any law school administrator who has been in the business for any length of time can recount one or more suicides among the ranks of former students. So, Dean Gibson's message was, "Talk to someone." You will find people in the law school who are willing to listen and help when you are troubled. They may or may not have formal training as counselors. Some of the most formidable law professors may be the most sympathetic and concerned human beings when one of their students is facing a legitimate crisis. Many universities and some law schools have a formal counseling center equipped to deal with personal problems of law students. Many law students have access to a minister, priest, or rabbi with whom they can share their concerns. There is nothing wrong with getting help. It is better to take a semester off from law school to get your life together than to stay in and flunk out.

None of this is intended to frighten or intimidate you. It is rather an attempt to present some of the negative realities of law school in a way and at a time when you can do something about them. This could be a very stressful time, but you have the potential to not just survive, but to thrive and grow, which is something you must do in order to succeed in law school.

D. Sex, Drugs, and Rock-and-Roll

1. Life in the Fast Lane

Every law school has its share of party animals. As mentioned previously, all work and no play is not the best approach to law school. Conversely, all play and no work is an invitation for academic disaster. Life in the fast lane has a certain allure to a fair proportion of law students. These students enjoy living life on the edge. They play hard. They may even work hard. They have been described as "Type A" personalities. The legal profession seems to attract a large number of such individuals. They seem to love the thrill of being overwhelmed, not knowing whether they will complete their brief by the 5 o'clock deadline, make it to a hearing on time, or survive their unmanageable caseload.

Certain parallels between these hard-living law students and their lawyer counterparts are inevitable. Moreover, practicing lawyers who have problems related to substance abuse frequently developed an identifiable pattern during law school or earlier. Thus, even if life in the fast lane doesn't get you now, eventually it will catch up with you.

2. Prognosis for Type A's

What is the prognosis for "Type A" personalities in the practice of law? Even without alcohol or drug problems, the likelihood of career upheavals resulting from an inability to work with more stable partners and associates is constant. At home, the prognosis for divorce and personal crises is greater. Moreover, the chances of making a critical error, missing an important deadline, or forgetting about a crucial hearing are greater for those who live on the edge. The possibility of exposure to legal malpractice or professional discipline is increased.

Studies have shown that there is a correlation between abuse of alcohol and/or drugs and the incidence of malpractice among lawyers. Many bar associations have developed crisis intervention programs that attempt to place problem lawyers into treatment centers before they can make mistakes that can result in malpractice or disbarment. If the problem were simply one of what you could do to yourself, we might say that if you want to die sooner, it is your choice. However, when your conduct has an impact on clients, it becomes a concern of other lawyers and the courts.

3. A Nonreligious Argument for Slowing Down

This section is not meant to sound like a sermon. It is not a moral argument against drugs, alcohol, or wild living. It is simply a statement that many lawyers are prone to chemical abuse and dependancy. For many of them, the results will be professionally self-destructive.

For them, being successful in law school requires eschewing a lifestyle that is likely to lead to diminished performance. If you see a pattern of abuse in yourself, you should seek treatment now. If you are aware of problems among classmates, you may be able to help them. Slow down. You will live longer, remain happier, and achieve greater success as a law student and lawyer if you do.

E. The Job Market

Almost anyone who has looked for a job in law will tell you that it is a challenge to find the right position. Practicing lawyers will tell you that there are "too many lawyers," but they do not want the competition. Reporters will tell you that if you didn't graduate from Harvard or Yale that you might as well drive a truck, but for them it's just another story. Your classmates will tell you stories of their unsuccessful attempts to find jobs, but they are as nervous about the future as you are. Even the professors will tell you that they are glad they have jobs. Only the career services director will remind you that the vast majority of last year's class found employment.

This scenario could describe the job market in 2008, or 1978, or 1958, or 1928. It will probably be the same in 2028 and beyond. The job market is always lousy. There are always too many lawyers and not enough jobs. And always, somehow, people with law degrees find jobs. Maybe we are just a more aggressive, adaptable, and employable lot than most. Maybe legal problems (at least in many areas) are not tied to the economic cycle. Maybe it's easier to talk about our problems than our successes. Who knows?

The fact is, if *you* do not have a job, 100 percent of the people who count are unemployed, and as long as you are looking for a job, there is 100 percent unemployment. And when you finally persuade someone to hire you, there will be 100 percent employment (at least in your job market). The fact is, looking for a job is arduous, tedious, terminally fruitless work. Putting yourself on the line and getting shot down repeatedly is not great for the ego. The fact is, during law school you will spend what seems like an inordinate amount of time looking for a job and an excessive amount of psychic energy thinking about what to do with your life after law school. There may be exceptions, but for most of you, this is true.

If you will necessarily spend a great deal of time dealing with career issues during law school, you need to do things right. First, do not let the job market or job search get you down, and do not become so obsessed with getting a job that your academic career falters (such a result is truly unproductive). Other parts of this book deal with time management, attitude, and organizational skills, and that advice certainly applies to job hunting.

Second, start to deal with career issues early in law school (now is not too early). Many students think that they have made their final career choice when they decided to attend law school, though, actually, that is just the first of many career decisions. Talk to your law school career counselor about your career plans. Read about the career planning process. *The Legal Career Guide: From Law Student to Lawyer*, by Gary A. Munneke and Ellen Wayne, and *Nonlegal Careers for Lawyers*, by Gary A. Munneke, William D. Henslee, and Ellen Wayne, both published by the American Bar Association, as well as *Careers in Law*, also by Gary A. Munneke, published by VGM Professional Career Series, offer a range of information on legal careers and specific advice on the career planning and job search processes.

Finally, get involved with lawyers and the legal profession. Join student sections of bar associations. Attend programs for lawyers and law students at school and off campus. Look for legally related work during law school, including clerking for law firms, agencies, and courts, researching for professors, and volunteering for community service activities with legal overtones. Begin now to develop a network of contacts and to become an integral part of the legal profession. Your network might be drawn from some or all of the following groups: family, friends, high school and college classmates, associates in religious/political/social organizations, colleagues from work, professional advisors, and people you meet through hobbies and personal interests. It is always easier to find work as an insider than as a newcomer in any line of work; law is no exception. And no amount of reading or counseling can substitute for firsthand knowledge gained through personal experience.

Unless you are one of those rare individuals who never plan to work as a lawyer, or intend to use a law degree in some other field, the job market is something you just have to confront. Make the best of your opportunities, and be ready for whatever comes along. Be patient, and wait for the right choice to come your way. Remember that your career is a path and not a destination. In short, the job market can be a major pitfall in law school, but only if you let it.

CHAPTER **8**
Diverse Students

The bulk of this book has dealt with problems of "typical" law students. In reality, no law student is typical. Law school student bodies are far from homogenous. They are a mix of ethnic backgrounds, sexes, socioeconomic statuses, and ages. Many of these students have unique concerns that can hinder their chances for success in law school.

A. Women

Since the early 1960s, when only a handful of women attended law schools, the number of women students has grown to almost half of the American law school population. At many schools, the percentage exceeds 50 percent. Women have entered a profession that traditionally was male-dominated and seemingly determined to stay so. Although the attitudes towards women and opportunities for employment in the profession have changed drastically in the past 30 years, many women students still find vestiges of the old patterns of behavior. Today, large numbers of women are confronted with the dilemma of having to choose between career advancement and family. Many complain that male students, professors, and professional colleagues place more attention on stereotypical factors, such as their looks and dress, than they do for their male counterparts.

A large percentage of law school women have children and primary child care responsibilities. Although there are exceptions, many husbands give little more than lip service to support their wives in this regard. Nor do most law schools help in terms of providing day care, flexible scheduling, or other accommodations. Women have tended to seek out other classmates in similar situations to find both empathy and assistance.

One of the major causes of stress for law student moms (and in some cases dads) is child care. Although it might make some sense to wait until the kids are themselves in school to begin a legal education, many young parents do not choose to wait. Even older children impose their own demands. With older children, particularly teenagers, it is important to get them on board to support your educational goals. Unsupportive children can be as much of a headache as an unsupportive spouse. For young children, the problem is likely to be reliable babysitters. Get someone you can depend on, or you will end up in a perpetual state of crisis.

Women often bear a heavy burden when it comes to other family members as well: aging parents, disabled adults, profligate relatives. It is important to either restructure family relationships to deal with these situations or to seek outside help. Women who try to do it all often find themselves in a perpetual pressure cooker.

B. Racial and Ethnic Minorities

African Americans, Latinos, Asian Americans, Native Americans, and other ethnic groups have not always had the same representation in legal education as Anglo students. Without going into the historical reasons, it is enough to say that despite the fact that law schools have opened their doors to minority students, there is a perception among non-majority students that the atmosphere in many law schools is still less than favorable. Although faculty and administrators try to be responsive to the needs of diverse groups, channels of communication are not always as good as they could be.

Many students have special issues that affect their law school academic progress. Some attended weak inner-city schools as children and still are trying to catch up. For some English is a second language. Others are economically disadvantaged and must work just to stay in school. Obviously, some nondiverse students have these problems too. And some diverse students come from wealthy families and the best schools. However, more ethnic minority students face difficulties such as these in law school. And like women, they will graduate into a profession in which their group is at best, benignly underrepresented and, at worst, is actively excluded. If you have special problems, go to faculty members for help before exams. Take advantage of university and/or law school programs. Talk to administrators such as the financial aid officer and placement officer regularly about your needs and concerns; seek out other students in similar situations for support.

C. Second Career Students

A growing contingent in law school comprises students returning to school after another career. In recent years, the median age of law students has increased. There are more post-thirty students today than ever before. These students often have special concerns about their careers. They go to school in an environment populated by twenty-five-year-olds. Many of them have been out of the educational world for years (even decades), and discover that the transition back into academia is not a smooth one. They may have greater financial needs than young, single postcollege students. Although most schools have few programs to assist them, many older students are imbued by experience with the ability to take care of themselves. They find it easier to discuss problems with faculty members and administrators who are their chronological contemporaries. If you are a second career student, use your maturity to the best advantage. Get remedial help to ease your return to school. Reading this book is a good start.

D. Physically Challenged Students

A small number of law students have sight or hearing impairment, chronic illness, wheelchair confinement, and even learning disorders such as dyslexia. At one time many of these individuals could not dream of going to law school; or perhaps it would be better to say that at one time most law schools would not dream of educating these students. This is no longer the case. Although impediments often remain, law schools today are attempting to create opportunities for physically challenged students. In addition to a variety of state laws providing benefits to physically challenged individuals, the Americans with Disabilities Act (ADA) now mandates that institutions make reasonable efforts to accommodate people protected under the act. You should discuss with relevant government agencies the type and level of support you will be able to receive while you attend law school. Sometimes the school must construct special programs and facilities to aid physically challenged students. If you have a condition, consult with the Admissions Office to work out a plan to tackle law school successfully.

CHAPTER 9

After the First Year

Ultimately, success in law school is predicated on more than one year's performance. To suggest that this race will be won on the basis of first year achievement is as misleading as assuming the mile race will be won by the runner leading the race at the end of the first lap. To be sure, first year grades are important. Many law school awards and honors are determined on the basis of first year grades. Many law firms make permanent employment decisions during the fall semester following the first year, with only those grades to review. Psychologically, success in the first year gives many students an edge that they exploit throughout law school.

On the other hand, it is possible to recover from even a disastrous first year. It is sometimes easier to find a job if your grades have improved steadily throughout law school than if they tapered off each semester. If your first year record was impressive, you will want to keep it that way; if less than memorable, you will want to find ways to improve.

A. Academics

1. Class Rank

Many law schools publish class rankings after the first year. These rankings establish your place in class either as a number (e.g., 15 out of 150) or as a percentile (e.g., top 10 percent). These class rankings are often used in the hiring process by legal employers who have difficulty evaluating differences in the meaning of grades from school to school. Not only do different schools use different grading systems, but the same grade may not mean the same thing at different schools with externally similar systems. In this sense, your employability is defined at least in part by comparing you to your classmates. On a different level, employers also compare law schools. They may consider candidates from the top 50 percent of one law school, well known to them, and only the top 5 percent from another.

Some schools that consider themselves "prestigious" have eliminated class rankings or devised grading systems that make it more difficult for employers to rank their students. These schools operate on the theory that all their graduates are good and rankings would create artificial distinctions among the students. In practice, however, only a handful of institutions can impose such policies.

It is possible to be so obsessed with class rank that you forget about education. Some students take only courses they consider easy in order to maintain or improve their grade point average, usually to their long-term detriment.

2. Classroom

The classroom experience is usually quite different in the second, third, and fourth years. Fear of the professors is replaced by guarded respect. Students in class are more likely to challenge the professor if they believe she is wrong or disagree with her point of view. The level of participation in many classes will wane, as many students withdraw from what they view as intellectual game playing. Classes are frequently smaller and, because the students have chosen to be there, there probably will be a core of students in every class who are both highly motivated and possess special skills and experience in that area. Professors in upper level courses are more likely to tell you the law as they see it rather than hide the ball. You may be exposed to other kinds of teaching methods, such as clinical instruction, simulation, research, drafting, and oral presentation. It is perhaps an overly broad generalization to say that the first year of law school is spent learning to think like a lawyer, the second year learning the substantive law, and the third year preparing for the practice of law by applying the knowledge gained during the first two years in practical settings. If you are a night student, you can add another year of learning the law in the middle.

During fall semesters, classroom participation may drop off in proportion to the level of student participation in on-campus interviews with law firms. Absenteeism often increases as students pursue part-time jobs, student activities, and other interests. It is important to remember that the classroom experience remains integral to the learning process. Ideally, outside activities should supplement rather than supplant classroom learning.

3. Course Selections

Students at many schools have a wide range of choices of courses to take after the first year. Most schools have a limited number of upper division required courses. Thus, students have considerable freedom in course selection. Course selection definitely plays a part in law school success. There is no one right way to select courses. Individual choices may be influenced by the school's lottery registration system, advisors, friends, work schedules, or other extra variables. However, there are a number of general approaches.

You can choose courses on the basis of substantive interest. If you have strong interests in a particular area of law (e.g., tax), you may want to take as many courses as possible in that area. If you are uncertain about your career plans, you may want to try to take a variety of survey courses to help you make career decisions.

Some schools offer concentration or certificate programs at the J.D. level in selected substantive areas. If you were thinking about starting a solo practice or going into a job where you will have immediate responsibility for your own caseload, you may want to choose courses that have a practical orientation. This approach presupposes that you can actually get a feel for what kind of law you will like to practice from a law school course, which may or may not be the case.

A variation of the substantive course selection theme is the bar review approach. If you know what courses the bar examiners in your state test, you can try to take courses in those subjects. Although a steady diet of esoteric courses (e.g., "post-Marxist Bosnian Civil Rights Law") may have a certain appeal, a curriculum that totally ignores core legal subjects is often unsatisfying in the end. On the other hand, students who choose their classes solely because the subject will be tested on the bar exam may miss unusual academic opportunities.

Some students make course selections for pragmatic considerations. They may hear that the grades in a particular course are high. They may take classes that give them a favorable final examination schedule. They may choose courses so that they only have to come to campus two or three days per week. Or they may take courses that require a take-home exam or paper or no examination at all.

Perhaps the best way to choose courses is to take them from professors you enjoy and from whom you will learn. If you find a particular professor boring, you are unlikely to learn much in that course. If you harbor some antagonism for the professor, you may find it difficult to learn. Chances are good that you will do better in courses you enjoy. And taking courses that are stimulating and challenging is the best defense against upper division ennui. If you miss one or two courses that are tested on the bar exam, you will still have an opportunity to pick up the information during a bar review course after graduation.

B. Student Activities

Remember those tables set up at first year orientation? By the second year of law school, you will have a better idea of organizations that interest you and how much time you can afford to devote to student activities. Many law school activities have an educational component, an intrinsic pedagogical value.

1. Law Review

The quintessential law school activity is law review. The tradition of student-edited journals in law is unique in American education. Law review membership looks good on your resumé. Traditionally, law review members were selected on the basis of grades from the first year class. Today, at most schools, grades represent only a portion of the selection criteria. Students are required also to participate in a writing competition or other form of review. Aside from the aura that often attaches to law school participation, law review experience is generally a valuable educational one. Legal research and writing skills learned during the first year are enhanced by editorial training unparalleled anywhere in the law school. In addition, law review members learn discipline and attention to detail. Editors hone their organization and leadership abilities. Many schools have not only *the* law review, but one or more specialized law reviews as well. And there usually is some pecking order of prestige among these journals.

Doing law review well requires a significant commitment of time, but the rewards far outweigh the cost of investment. Legal employers typically recognize the importance of law review experience as a qualification for new lawyers.

2. Moot Court

The second traditional cocurricular activity in law school is moot court. Most law schools require every law student to participate in some form of moot court experience during the first year. For many students that is quite enough oral argument to satisfy them. Other students, however, thrive on these competitions. It is possible to participate in a variety of different moot court, mock trial, client counseling, negotiation, and other competitions after the first year of law school. Some of these are school sponsored for their own students; others are interscholastic, bringing teams from law schools all over the country to compete against each other. These events may be very prestigious, attracting prominent jurists as judges. At many schools, a moot court board analogous to the law review editorial board is responsible for coordinating these various competitions, and its membership is often comprised largely of the student representatives on the various interschool teams.

3. Student Government

The law school has its own student government, called the Student Bar Association, or SBA. The function of the SBA may vary from school to school. At some schools it may sponsor social events, speakers, and other activities. At many schools the SBA is responsible for student appointments to faculty committees. At some schools the SBA is responsible for allocating budgetary funds to all student organizations. One indication that the sun is in its heaven and all is right with the world will be the fact that the same girl who was always running for student council in your fifth grade class will be running for SBA rep in law school, and 20 years from now for U.S. senator. A separate avenue of experience for students interested in exercising professional leadership is to serve as a liaison to the American Bar Association Law Student Division, to a state or local bar association, or to some other professional group. There are a number of such opportunities at every law school.

4. Special Interest Groups

Because law schools themselves are insulated from much of the undergraduate university student life, law school activities have evolved independently of their undergraduate counterparts. In addition to student government, many law schools have their own newspapers, yearbooks, intramural programs, and other organizations. You will find legal fraternities, honorary organizations, and special interest groups. Some of these include organizations devoted to a particular substantive area of law (e.g., real estate, health law, international law, environmental law), outside interests (e.g., film forums, wine tasting, literature study groups), and activities that advocate various political, economic, and social points of view. At most law schools, there exist organizations of women students, minority students, gay and lesbian students, older students, and others. You can probably find some group of students that has your same background, interests, and concerns. During the first year, your friendships with other students were linked to your class schedule, particularly the smaller sections such as legal research and writing. In the second year and beyond, many students find a "home" in a student organization where they feel compatible with the other members. Those who do not connect with some student group often feel alienated from the law school experience generally, and this can affect their performance.

C. Other Learning Experiences

Post-first year legal education offers a wide variety of other learning experiences for students. The boon as well as the bane of the curriculum at many law schools is its flexibility. In addition, many of the cocurricular and extra-curricular activities contribute to your development as a lawyer. It is a little like visiting a cafeteria without your parents when you were a kid. You can get all desserts if you want to or you can select a well-balanced meal. The wise student will take advantage of this flexibility to make selections of courses and activities consistent with his or her career objectives. One important opportunity you should not pass up is the chance to develop your legal research and writing skills.

1. Scholarly Writing

Although some law schools require an upper division writing experience, many do not. On the other hand, even if you were not selected to write for your school's journal, there are plenty of alternatives. You can enroll in one or more upper division seminars that require a paper in lieu of a final examination. Seminars are usually limited to a small enrollment because of the demands on faculty members to work individually with each student. It may also be possible to arrange for independent study with a professor in a subject area that interests you. Many schools give academic credit for papers produced in such a one-on-one setting. Independent study usually works best if you go to the professor with a specific idea for a paper. If you look around your school, you will notice posters advertising various legal essay contests, some offering fairly substantial monetary prizes. You may be able to conduct your scholarly research in one of these areas.

2. Research Assistants

A different approach to scholarly research is to get a job as a research assistant for one of your professors. Law schools usually have funds to cover student research assistants for professors. In such a position, you will do background research, drafting, and cite-checking for your professor's article or book. Instead of producing a finished product of your own, your satisfaction will derive from a small monthly paycheck and a footnote acknowledging your assistance in the professor's final work. Research assistants also benefit from their service by gaining a legitimate legal experience and a strong reference for their résumés. And beyond the actual experience, they get to know their professor on a personal basis—a relationship that will continue long after law school.

3. Nonlaw Courses

In some instances, you may find that the law school curriculum does not offer courses in a field of interest to you. At many law schools, it is possible to take graduate level courses at the affiliated university. It usually is necessary to obtain permission to take such courses, but you may find the experience a welcome respite from the Socratic dialogue.

4. Clinical Education

Every law school today has some form of clinical legal education program. In a clinic, students work with actual clients and real problems under the supervision of a faculty member who directs the clinic. The substantive areas covered will vary from school to school and program to program. However, the lawyering skills one can develop have wide applications after graduation. Unfortunately, most schools do not have enough seats in their clinical program to allow all students to participate. Be sure to investigate the clinical offerings at your school to determine how and when to enroll.

5. Skills Training

Law schools also offer skills training courses in such areas as trial advocacy, client interviewing and counseling, negotiation, instrument drafting, and law practice management. These courses often use simulated situations, "learning by doing" problems, and computer modeling, as learning devices. For instance, in a trial advocacy course you may be required to make motions and present arguments to the court concerning a hypothetical fact situation. In client interviewing and counseling, you may be asked to interview someone role-playing a client coming to you with a problem.

A 1992 American Bar Association report, *The Report of the Task Force on Law Schools and the Profession: Narrowing the Gap*, declared what many critics of legal education have said for a long time: law schools do not prepare students to practice law. The report urges schools to offer more skills and clinical courses, and many schools are rethinking their entire curriculum in light of this suggestion. While you should not expect to see wholesale abandonment of traditional legal education any time soon, you can anticipate that at most schools there will be more opportunities than in the past to develop the practice skills you will use as a lawyer.

6. Summer School

Whether or not your law school offers a summer session, many law schools do. Summer school offers law students scheduling options sometimes not apparent immediately. The most obvious rationale for going to summer school is to accelerate graduation, or to lighten the course load the following year. Some students use summer school to take courses either at their law school or another law school that would not be available during the academic year. Summer school abroad, offered by numerous law schools, may be of special interest to many students. The summer session may be an opportunity to enroll in a difficult course, work on a paper, or enroll in a clinic.

7. Foreign Study

Many law schools offer programs of legal study in a foreign country. Most of these are held during the summer, but some are given during the regular school year. Generally, the program will be associated with a foreign law school or university, although the classes will be taught in English, usually by American professors. Foreign law study presents an alternative to the routine of law school at home. Since you will receive credit for your coursework abroad, you should not delay your graduation by attending one of these programs, although before enrolling you should make sure that your law school approves the specific courses you take. In addition to course offerings, many schools provide international internships for their students in a variety of settings.

8. Specialized Curricula

Some law schools offer special programs of course concentration in areas like tax, environmental law, trial practice, and others. A few grant certification in these programs. Many schools sponsor joint degree programs (e.g., J.D./M.B.A.). You may want to investigate these specialized offerings if you have a particular career interest. For a more complete listing of specialty and graduate law programs, you should consult *Barron's Guide to Law Schools*.

9. Work Experience

After you finish the first year, most of you will consider obtaining legal work experience. A full discussion of placement opportunities is beyond the scope of this book. Take some time to visit your career services office to discuss career plans before the end of your first year. See also the section on "The Job Market" in Chapter 7, page 146.

Law students work in a wide variety of part-time and summer jobs for law firms, corporations, government agencies, and other organizations. Except in the largest firms and corporations, the pay may not be great. But the experience will help you to learn about the practical side of law. Unfortunately, the quality of clerkships varies widely; there are good and bad lawyers as well as ethical and unethical ones. Generally, however, the experiences of law students are positive ones, supplementing their classroom education and helping them to make sound career decisions based on personal experience. If you do work after the first year, don't forget about your education. It is possible for the practical and the theoretical to go hand in hand.

Some students work in areas outside the law because they can make more money, or they enjoy returning to the job they had before law school, or they welcome a break from the rigors of the law. Before pursuing a nonlegal job, you should weigh the benefits of the nonlaw position with the benefits of gaining valuable legal work experience.

D. Problems

After the first year, law school will seem much easier. You will know more about what you need to do to succeed. You will have solved many of the problems that plagued your first year. But, two new upper division problems will confront you.

1. Waning Interest

The first of these derives from waning interest in law school itself. As you move into your final semesters, this problem may become acute. If you decide that you have learned all you can (or want to) from your professors, that work or student organizations are more important than school, or that the result is not worth the effort in terms of grades, you will miss out on an important part of legal education.

After the first year, learning can be fun if you throw yourself into it. Seek out professors and classes that intrigue you. Fight the temptation to coast into graduation. Once you leave law school, it is unlikely that you will have the opportunity to pursue legal issues that interest you at your own pace. You will have your clients' problems and their deadlines. You will face partners' demands and judges' orders. The day will come when you will look back longingly on the leisurely days of law school. Enjoy it now. You only go around once.

2. Self-fulfilling Prophecy

The second problem involves the tendency of many students to perform at the level of their first year grades. If you did well, this may be fine. If your grades were not as high as you would have liked, you may have to struggle to avoid letting your first year record become a self-fulfilling prophecy. For one thing, you will have to go back and reassess your whole approach to study and exams. Schedule appointments with your professors to discuss your exams, focusing on what you could do differently. Look honestly at your study habits to see if they could be improved. Take steps to remedy weaknesses such as issue spotting, writing, and analysis. You are not destined to mediocrity, but you may need to do more work than other students to get ahead. Reevaluate your schedule to make enough room to study. Some students will become lazy after the first year, so there is always room to move up.

3. Jobs

As you proceed through law school, you will be confronted with the prospect of finding a job. Unless you are independently wealthy, the time will come when you will have to earn a living as a lawyer and begin to repay student loans. In the first two years, you may be thinking more of summer and part-time employment, but eventually the short-term question will be transformed into an existential inquiry: "What am I going to do with my life?" In this quest, you should get to know the career counselor at your career services office. You should talk to professors and other lawyers you know. You should read, for example, *The Legal Career Guide: From Law Student to Lawyer*, by Gary A. Munneke and Ellen Wayne. You should test the marketplace for legal services personally. Too many students fail to do these things and sacrifice career opportunities unnecessarily.

CHAPTER 10
Conclusions—
What Is Success?

This book started with the question, "What is success?" That is a good place to end. Much of the text has offered specific suggestions to help you make the best of your law school career. Underlying these recommendations is an assumption that you will maximize your opportunities if you maximize your potential. Stated another way, doing the best you can is the surest guarantee to the most career options possible. And doing your best does not mean just trying hard. You can work very hard in law school and get very little to show for it. You need to work hard *and* work smart. This book has provided some hints on how to work smart. The rest is up to you.

In a larger sense, success cannot be measured over the short term. You may win a battle here or there but still lose the war. The long-term view is ultimately what counts. Furthermore, the only one whose opinion matters is you. The world may declare you a winner, but if you perceive yourself to be a loser, a loser you will be. And vice versa. Law school is just one step in building a successful career.

When you cut away all the complexities and trappings, success is happiness. It is satisfaction with who you are and the choices you have made. It is realizing that enjoyment is not found at some destination, it is encountered in the ride. To be sure, we all have our ups and downs, but if we can make the most out of every day, we will be happy and successful.

What makes us happy? Professionally, we are happy doing what we do well. Ideally, there should be a convergence of work and play in our lives. We should get paid to play. Maybe professional athletes approach this ideal. But they frequently have to pay with pain, and most of them can't do it until they die. So if you really love what you do as a lawyer you really can get paid to have fun.

Unfortunately, many lawyers are not happy. For whatever reasons, work is not play. Despite earning substantial incomes they are not satisfied with their lives. These lawyers often do not feel successful, and surveys suggest that many actually leave the legal profession each year to pursue other interests.

There is a definite link between career satisfaction and commitment. In his book *Working*, author Studs Terkel paints a bleak picture of workers in all walks of life who just put in their time. He also describes a minority who enjoy what they do. The one thing that seems to differentiate the satisfied from the rest is commitment to their work.

I remember visiting France some years ago and observing that the waiters in restaurants seemed genuinely proud of their work. Unlike many waiters in this country, who seem to be passing time in their present occupations until something better comes along, their French counterparts were proud of their work, and it usually showed.

Maybe the American dream sets us up for failure. Maybe we can never succeed because there is always something else to achieve. Maybe we have lost sight of the importance of the simple notion of commitment to doing our jobs well. Maybe it is too easy in our affluent world to slide down the slippery slope of least resistance.

What steps can someone entering law school take to assure success? For starters, if you don't like law, get out now. If you decide to stay, give it all you have. There is an incredible burden of work in law school. The preceding pages describe it in detail; they also give you a formula for managing the load. Nowhere has it been suggested that there exists a shortcut to hard work and commitment to the task ahead.

You can also help yourself by making timely, informed decisions. Throughout law school and beyond, you will make innumerable choices about your career. Every day, you will have opportunities to choose between excellence and mediocrity. If you have a direction in life, it will be easier to identify the courses of action best for you.

The following story, told by Robert Bruce White, a partner in Lucas, Bishop, Bowker and White, Edmonton, Alberta, at a meeting of the American Bar Association Law Practice Management Section, illustrates the point.

A visitor to the Ile de la Cité in Paris came upon a marble quarry. In the quarry he found a man with a chisel chipping marble. The visitor asked the man what he was doing. The answer was, "I'm hacking marble. Isn't that obvious?" The visitor went on, and soon came upon another man, also chipping marble. "What are you doing?" asked the visitor. This man answered with a smile, "I'm earning one franc per week." The visitor walked on until he encountered a third man chiseling marble. When asked what it was he was doing, this man responded with tears in his eyes, "I'm building the cathedral of Notre Dame."

Law is a profession that offers many rewards for those willing to make the commitment. And success in law school as well as practice is not hard to achieve when viewed in this light.

APPENDIX A

Suggested Reading

On Law School

Barron's Guide to Law Schools. New York: Barron's, 2008 (biannual).

Calamari, John D. and Joseph M. Perillo. *How to Thrive in Law School.* Pelham Manor, NY: Hook Mountain Press, 1984.

Carter, Lief H. *Reason in Law.* 3rd ed. Boston: Little, Brown and Co., 1987.

Ehrlich, Thomas C. and Geoffrey Hayard. *Going to Law School: Readings on Legal Career.* Boston: Little, Brown and Co., 1975.

Law School Admission Council. *Financing Your Law School Education.* Newton, PA: Law School Admission Services, 1986.

Llewellyn, Karl. *The Bramble Bush.* New York: Oceana Press, 1960.

Munneke, Gary A., *Careers in Law.* Chicago: VGM Professional Career Series, 2001.

Munneke, Gary A. and Ellen Wayne. *The Legal Career Guide: From Law Student to Lawyer.* Chicago: American Bar Association, 2008.

Munneke, Gary A. *Opportunity in Law Careers.* Chicago: VGM Career Horizons, 2002.

Osborne, John Jay. *The Paper Chase.* New York: Warner Books, 1983.

Research Associates. *Write the "A" Law Exam Answer.* Swampscott, MA: Research Associates, 1980.

Schaffer, Thomas L. and Robert S. Redmont. *Lawyers, Law Students and People.* Colorado Springs: Shepards, Inc., 1977.

Turow, Scott. *One L.* New York: Penguin Books, 1977.

Ward, Kevin P. *Not the Official Lawyers' Handbook.* New York: New American Library, 1984.

Wydik, Richard C. *Plain English for Lawyers.* Durham, NC: Carolina Academic Press, 1979.

On Lawyering

Auchincloss, Louis. *The Partners.* New York: Warner Books, 1975.

Carlin, Jerome. *Lawyers on Their Own.* New Brunswick, NJ: Rutgers University Press, 1962.

Dickens, Charles. *Bleak House.*

Epstein, Cynthia Fuchs. *Women in Law.* New York: Anchor Books, 1983.

Freud, James C. *Lawyering: A Realistic Approach to Private Practice.* New York: Law Journal Seminars Press, 1979.

Johnston, Quintin and Dan Hopson, Jr. *Lawyers and Their Work*. Indianapolis: Bobbs-Merrill, 1967.

Kanter, Arnold. *The Secret Files of Stanley J. Fairweather*. Chicago: Swallow Press, 1980.

Lewis, Anthony. *Gideon's Trumpet*. New York: Random House, 1964.

Mayer, Martin. *The Lawyers*. New York: Harper & Row, 1966.

Munneke, Gary A. and Ellen Wayne. *The Legal Career Guide: From Law Student to Lawyer*. Chicago: American Bar Association, 2008.

Munneke, Gary A., William D. Henslee, and Ellen Wayne. *Non-Legal Careers for Lawyers*. Chicago: American Bar Association, 2007.

Osborne, John Jay. *The Associates*. Boston: Houghton Mifflin, 1979.

Woodward, Bob and Scott Armstrong. *The Brethren: Inside the Supreme Court*. New York: Simon & Schuster, 1979.

APPENDIX B

Resource Materials
on Intent and Battery

Prosser & Keeton on Torts

Prosser & Keeton

INTENTIONAL INTERFERENCE WITH THE PERSON

Table of Sections
Sec.
8. Meaning of Intent.
9. Battery.
10. Assault.
11. False Imprisonment.
12. Infliction of Mental Distress.

§ 8. Meaning of Intent

In a loose and general sense, the meaning of "intent" is easy to grasp. As Holmes observed, even a dog knows the difference between being tripped over and being kicked.[1] This is also the key distinction between two major divisions of legal liability—negligence and intentional torts—and it plays a key role in criminal law,[2] and elsewhere.[3] It is one of the most basic, organizing concepts of legal thinking.

§ 8

1. Of course, a cunning tripper might fool the dog—once, at least.

2. See, e.g., ALI Model Penal Code, 1962, § 2.02(2) (a), (b), defining "purposely" and "knowingly." The contrasting meanings of "recklessly" and "negligently" are defined, id. at (c), (d).

See also Sandstrom v. Montana, 1979, 442 U.S. 510, 99 S.Ct. 2450, 61 L.Ed.2d 39, condemning an instruction to the jury in a criminal case that "the law presumes that a person intends the ordinary consequences of his voluntary acts." Clearly distinguishable, however, is an instruction that "it is ordinarily reasonable (for the factfinder] to infer that a person intends the natural and probable consequences of acts." Hardy v. United States, 1st Cir. 1982, 691 F.2d 39. For further development of this distinction, see infra this section.

3. See infra, §§ 107, 113. See also, e.g., R. Keeton Insurance Law Basic Text, 1971, §§ 5.2–5.4, 7.6, 7.7; ALI Federal Securities Code, 1980, § 202(61)(C).

"Intent" is also one of the most often misunderstood legal concepts, The distinction between intentional and unintentional invasions draws a bright line of separation among shadings of almost infinitely varied human experiences. As might be expected, authoritative definitions that purport to specify exactly where this bright line is to be drawn are not entirely in accord. There is even some conflict between the two major pronouncements on the subject by the American Law Institute—one in the Restatement—now the Second Restatement—of Torts[4] and the other in the Model Penal Code.[5] Still more variations appear in the great mass of statutory and judicial usages, sometimes in explicit definitions and more often among the meanings discovered as implicit when one closely examines the contexts in which statements about intent are made.

The Restatement aims at applying a single, consistent concept of intent throughout. Since the drafters were attempting to "restate" the law of torts, they were aiming for a concept consistent with the most common usage in judicial opinions in tort cases, and it seems a fair assessment that they achieved this aim. Thus, in examining the Restatement concept, we are also examining the most common, though not the only, sense in which courts use "intent" in tort cases.

The three most basic elements of this most common usage of "intent" are that (1) it is a *state of mind* (2) about *consequences* of

---

4. See §§ 8A, 13, 16, 18, 20. For an analysis of the Second Restatement's provisions on intent, with identification of some variations, in form at least, from the first Restatement, see R. Keeton, Computer-Aided and Workbook Exercises in Tort Law, 1976, 1.14–1.23.

5. See § 2.02. Note, for example, that in the usage of the Model Penal Code a person "acts knowingly" with respect to a result of his conduct if "he is aware that it is practically certain that his conduct will cause such a result," § 2.02(2)(b), and that a requirement of knowledge is satisfied "if a person is aware of a high probability of its existence, unless he actually believes that it does not exist." § 2.02(7).

an act (or omission)[6] and not about the act itself, and (3) it extends not only to having in the mind a purpose (or desire) to bring about given consequences but also to having in mind a belief (or knowledge) that given consequences are substantially certain[7] to result from the act. It is also essential that the state of mind of intent exist when the act occurs. Additional elements of the concept concern the extent to which the intent may relate to different persons[8] or different consequences from those at issue.[9]

Much of the confusion surrounding application of the legal requirement of intent arises from lack of a clear understanding of the relationship among act, intent, and motive.[10]

One prerequisite of liability is that the defendant act (or fail to act when there is a legal duty to act). An involuntary muscular movement of a sleeping or otherwise incapacitated person will not

---

6. The Restatement speaks only of an act (not of an omission) in defining intent, in § 8A, and requires an act, as distinguished from inaction, for battery, in § 14 and comment *c* thereto. Also, the Restatement takes the position that purposely failing to act when there is a legal duty to act is negligence. Scope Note preceding § 13, at 24 ("failure to perform [a duty to act for the protection of others against bodily harm] constitutes negligence * * *, irrespective of whether his failure is or is not deliberate and done for the very purpose of causing the other to suffer the bodily harm from which it was the actor's duty to protect him"). This curious usage is confounding, since there is as clear a distinction (1) between purposely failing to act, in order to produce a desired consequence, and failing to act without adverting to that consequence, as (2) between purposely acting to produce a desired consequence and acting without adverting to that consequence. The confusion is aggravated by the assertion that an act is required for false imprisonment (§ 35) and that "refusal" to provide a means of escape when there is a duty to do so is a sufficient "act of confinement" (§ 45).

7. The Model Penal Code uses the phrase "practically certain," § 2.02(2)(b), in contrast with the Restatement's "substantially certain," § 8A. It seems doubtful, however, that any substantive difference was intended by the drafters or by the American Law Institute. See also supra, n. 5, as to differences that are more likely to be substantive.

8. See the discussion of "transferred intent," infra, this section.

9. For example, one who intends only to cause a harmful physical contact but succeeds only in causing apprehension that such a contact is imminent is subject to liability for assault; see infra, § 10.

10. See also supra § 5, concerning motive.

support liability.[11] But an "act," as that term is ordinarily used, is a voluntary contraction of the muscles, and nothing more.[12] An act is to be distinguished from its consequences.

> "Thus, if the actor, having pointed a pistol at another, pulls the trigger, the act is the pulling of the trigger and not the impingement of the bullet upon the other's person."[13]

When "act" is used in this sense, it is tautological to speak of a "voluntary act," and self-contradictory to speak of an "involuntary act," since every act is voluntary. Nevertheless, the phrases "voluntary act" and "involuntary act" do appear in legal prose.[14] Moreover, differences may be deeper than merely a choice of terminology; one who uses the phrase "voluntary act" may be using "act" to mean something different from a mere voluntary contraction of the muscles; sometimes the phrase "voluntary act" is used to mean something closer to the concept of intent (as defined in the Restatement and in common usage), which focuses not upon the mere "act" (in the narrower sense, defined in the Restatement and in common usage) but upon volition in relation to consequences as well as volition in relation to the muscular contraction. The movement of the finger which fires a gun is the same, whether it takes place in a crowded city, or in the solitude of the Mojave Desert, and regardless of the actor's state of mind about the consequences. But the legal outcome will depend on the actor's surroundings and the actor's state of mind. The actor may move the muscles of the finger for the

11. Slattery v. Haley, [1923] 3 Dom.L.Rep. 156, 25 Ont.L.Rep. 95; Stokes v. Carlson, 1951, 362 Mo. 93, 240 S.W.2d 132; Wishone v. Yellow Cab Co., 1936, 20 Tenn. App. 229, 97 S.W.2d 452.

12. Holmes, The Common Law, 1881, 91; Cook, Act, Intention and Motive in the Criminal Law, 1917, 26 Yale L.J. 644; Second Restatement of Torts, § 2.

13. Second Restatement of Torts, § 2, Comment *c*.

14. Even courts citing and following the Restatement definition of "act" have sometimes lapsed, in other passages, into using phrases such as "voluntary act" and "conscious act." See, e.g., Stokes v. Carlson, 1951, 362 Mo. 93, 240 S.W.2d 132.

Moreover, other courts and writers simply do not accept the Restatement of Torts usage. An example is the ALI Model Penal Code, § 2.01, which uses "voluntary act" and defines it in a way that appears to be very nearly if not precisely identical in meaning with "act" as defined in the Restatement of Torts.

purpose of pulling the trigger, for the purpose of causing the bullet to strike another, for the purpose of killing the other, for the purpose of revenge, of defense of country, or of self-protection against attack. "Intent" is the word commonly used to describe the purpose to bring about *stated physical consequences;*[15] the more remote objective which inspires the act and the intent is called "motive."[16] Both intent and motive are steps removed from volition to move the muscles of the finger. Intent is concerned with consequences of that movement; motive, with reasons for desiring certain consequences. Intent is thus less removed from act than is motive. Each has its own importance in the law of torts, and a justifiable motive, such as that of self-defense, may avoid liability for the intent to kill.

Both intent and motive are states of mind. Act is a combination of muscular movement and the state of mind of volition to make that movement.

As already noted, however, intent is broader than a desire or purpose to bring about physical results. It extends not only to those consequences which are desired, but also to those which the actor believes are substantially certain to follow from what the actor does. The actor who fires a bullet into a dense crowd may fervently pray that the bullet will hit no one, but if the actor knows that it is unavoidable that the bullet will hit someone, the actor intends that consequence.

15. See Second Restatement of Torts, § 8A, comment *a*. For a more detailed explanation of this concept, and for discussion of the failure to apply it correctly as a source of error in application of the concept of intent, see R. Keeton, Computer-Aided and Workbook Exercises in Tort Law, 1976, 1.1–1.23. One common source of confusion is failure to focus precisely on *what consequence* must be intended to meet the requirements of the legal theory at issue. In Garratt v. Dailey, 1955, 46 Wn.2d 197, 279 P.2d 1091, second appeal, 1956, 49 Wn.2d 499, 304 P.2d 681, a boy who pulled away a chair just as plaintiff was about to sit down was held liable for battery because he knew that she was substantially certain "to sit in the place where the chair had been," which, without satisfactory explanation, the court treated as the equivalent of knowing that she was substantially certain to suffer a harmful or offensive bodily contact with the ground. Might the boy not believe that she would not be hurt and that she would think it was all good fun?

16. Cook, Act, Intention and Motive in the Criminal Law, 1917, 26 Yale L.J. 644; Walton, Motive as an Element in Torts in the Common and in the Civil Law, 1909, 22 Harv.L.Rev. 501.

Another source of great confusion is failure to distinguish between (1) the factual elements essential to a finding of intent and (2) the elements of proof and argument that advocates and factfinders may bring to bear in addressing the question whether those factual elements are present in a given case. The factfinder need not credit the actor's assertion that the actor did not intend the result in question. One of the common lines of argument against crediting the actor's assertion is (1) that, given the circumstances disclosed in the evidence, a reasonable person in the actor's position would have known that the consequence in question was substantially certain to follow the act, (2) that the evidence shows that the actor was even brighter and shrewder than most others, and (3) that the inference is therefore compelling that the actor knew even though testifying otherwise. If the factfinder credits inference (1) but not inferences (2) and (3), the finding is negligence. But if the factfinder credits all three inferences, the finding is intent to produce the consequence in question. Expressed another way the point is this: Since intent is a state of mind, it is plainly incorrect for a court to instruct a jury that an actor is presumed to intend the natural and probable consequences of the actor's conduct; but it is correct to tell the jury that, relying on circumstantial evidence, they may infer that the actor's state of mind was the same as a reasonable person's state of mind would have been.[17] Thus, when the driver who whips up horses with a loud yell while passing a neighbor's team denies intent to cause a runaway, the factfinder may discredit the driver's testimony;[18] and the defendant on a bicycle who rides down a person in full view on a sidewalk where there is ample room to pass may learn that the factfinder (judge or jury) is unwilling to credit the statement, "I didn't mean to do it.")[19]

On the other hand, the mere knowledge and appreciation of a risk—something short of substantial certainty—is not intent. The defendant who acts in the belief or consciousness that the act is

---

17. Sandstrom v. Montana, 1979, 442 U.S. 510, 99 S.Ct. 2450, 61 L.Ed.2d 39; Hardy v. United States, 1st Cir. 1982, 691 F.2d 39.

18. Lambrecht v. Schreyer, 1915, 129 Minn. 271, 152 N.W. 645. See also Land v. Bachman, 1921, 223 Ill. App. 473.

19. Mercer v. Corbin, 1889, 117 Ind. 450, 20 N.E. 132. Cf. Commonwealth v. Raspa, 1939, 138 Pa.Super. 26, 9 A.2d 925.

causing an appreciable risk of harm to another may be negligent, and if the risk is great the conduct may be characterized as reckless or wanton,[20] but it is not an intentional wrong. In such cases the distinction between intent and negligence obviously is a matter of degree. The line has been drawn by the courts at the point where the known danger ceases to be only a foreseeable risk which a reasonable person would avoid, and becomes in the mind of the actor a substantial certainty.[21]

The intent with which tort liability is concerned is not necessarily a hostile intent, or a desire to do any harm.[22] Rather it is an intent to bring about a result which will invade the interests of another in a way that the law forbids. The defendant may be liable although intending nothing more than a good-natured practical joke,[23] or honestly believing that the act would not injure the plaintiff,[24] or even though seeking the plaintiff's own good.[25]

---

20. See infra, § 34.

21. Hackenberger v. Travelers Mutual Casualty Co., 1936, 144 Kan. 607, 62 P.2d 545; Cook v. Kinzua Pine Mills Co., 1956, 207 Or. 34, 293 P.2d 717. See Second Restatement of Torts, § 13, Comment *d*; Note, 1962, 34 Rock Mt.L.Rev. 268; De Muth, A Comparison of the Conduct Required in Trespass to Chattels and Negligence, 1961, 33 Rocky Mt.L.Rev. 323.

Compare the following statement, which is somewhat at odds with the Restatement definition of "intent":

"If the manifest probability of harm is very great, and the harm follows, we say that it is done maliciously or intentionally; if not so great, but still considerable, we say that the harm is done negligently; if there is no apparent danger, we call it mischance." Holmes, Privilege, Malice and Intent, 1894, 8 Harv.L. Rev. 1.

22. Baldinger v. Banks, 1960, 26 Misc.2d 1086, 201 N.Y.S.2d 629; Restatement of Torts, § 13, Comment *e*.

23. Reynolds v. Pierson, 1902, 29 Ind.App. 273, 64 N.E. 484; State v. Monroe, 1897, 121 N.C. 677, 28 S.E. 547.

24. Vosburg v. Putney, 1891, 80 Wis. 523, 50 N.W. 403; Craker v. Chicago & Northwestern Railway Co., 1875, 36 Wis. 657.

25. Clayton v. New Dreamland Roller Skating Rink, 1951, 14 N.J.Super. 390, 82 A.2d 458 (plaintiff fell and broke her arm; over her protest defendant proceeded to manipulate the arm in order to set it); Johnson v. McConnel, N.Y.1878, 15 Hun 293 (defendant intervened in a scuffle to protect plaintiff and broke plaintiff's leg); Maxwell v. Maxwell, 1920, 189 Iowa 7, 177 N.W. 541, (arrest of insane person for his own protection).

More Extensive Liability for Intent

There is a definite tendency to impose greater responsibility upon a defendant whose conduct was intended to do harm, or was morally wrong.[26] More liberal rules are applied as to the consequences for which the defendant will be held liable,[27] the certainty of proof required,[28] and the type of damage for which recovery is to be permitted,[29] as well as the measure of compensation.[30] The defendant's interests have been accorded substantially less weight in opposition to the plaintiff's claim to protection when moral iniquity is thrown into the balance. Apparently the courts have more or less unconsciously worked out an irregular and poorly defined sliding scale, by which the defendant's liability is least where the conduct is merely inadvertent, greater for acts in disregard of consequences increasingly likely to follow, greater still for intentionally invading the rights of another under a mistaken belief of committing no

26. Bauer, The Degree of Moral Fault as Affecting Defendant's Liability, 1933, 81 U.Pa.L.Rev. 586; Note, 1962, 14 Stan.L.Rev. 362.

27. "For an intended injury the law is astute to discover even very remote causation. For one which the defendant merely ought to have anticipated it has often stopped at an earlier stage of the investigation of causal connection. And as to those where there was neither knowledge nor duty to foresee, it has usually limited accountability to direct and immediate results. This is not because the defendant's act was a more immediate cause in one case than in the others, but because it has been felt to be just and reasonable that liability should extend to results further removed when certain elements of fault are present." Derosier v. New England Telephone & Telegraph Co., 1925, 81 N.H. 451, 463, 130 A. 145, 152. See infra, § 43.
See Green, Rationale of Proximate Cause, 1925, 170ff.

28. Cases are Collected in Bauer, The Degree of Moral Fault as Affecting Defendant's Liability, 1933, 81 U.Pa.L.Rev. 586, 592–596.

29. Thus damages for mental disturbance, whether or not it results in physical injury, are more readily held to be recoverable where the wrong is intentional. See infra, §§ 12, 54.

30. Cases are collected in Bauer, The Degree of Defendant's Fault as Affecting the Administration of the Law of Excessive Compensatory Damages, 1934, 82 U.Pa.L.Rev. 583. See for example the rules applied to innocent and wilful trespassers who remove timber or minerals from land, as to the value of the property converted "in place" or after removal. McCormick, Damages, 1935, 492–496.

wrong, and greatest of all where the motive is a malevolent desire to do harm.

"Transferred" Intent

One definite area in which there is more extensive liability for intent than for negligence is that covered by the curious surviving fiction of "transferred intent." The defendant who shoots or strikes at A, intending to wound or kill A, and unforeseeably hits B instead, is held liable to B for an intentional tort.[31] The intent to commit a battery upon A is pieced together with the resulting injury to B; it is "transferred" from A to B. "The intention follows the bullet."[32]

This peculiar idea appeared first in criminal cases[33] at a time when tort and crime were still merged in the old trespass form of action. It represents an established rule of the criminal law, in cases in which shooting, striking, throwing a missile or poisoning has resulted in unexpected injury to the wrong person.[34]

Restatement (Second) of Torts

§ 8 A. Intent

The word "intent" is used throughout the Restatement of this Subject to denote that the actor desires to cause consequences of his act, or that he believes that the consequences are substantially certain to result from it.

See Reporter's Notes.

---

31. Prosser, Transferred Intent, 1967, 45 Tex.L. Rev. 650.

32. State v. Batson, 1936, 339 Mo. 298, 305, 96 S.W.2d 384, 389.

33. Regina v. Salisbury, 1553, 1 Plowd. 100, 75 Eng. Rep. 158; Queen v. Saunders and Archer, 1576, 2 Plowd. 473, 75 Eng.Rep. 706.

34. Dunaway v. People, 1884, 110 Ill. 333; State v. Williams, 1904, 122 Iowa 115, 97 N.W. 992; State v. Ochoa, 1956, 61 N.M. 225, 297 P.2d 1053; People v. Aranda, 1938, 12 Cal.2d 307, 83 P.2d 928; Coston v. State, 1939, 139 Fla. 250, 190 So. 520.

Comment:

a. "Intent," as it is used throughout the Restatement of Torts, has reference to the consequences of an act rather than the act itself. When an actor fires a gun in the midst of the Mojave Desert, he intends to pull the trigger; but when the bullet hits a person who is present in the desert without the actor's knowledge, he does not intend that result. "Intent" is limited, wherever it is used, to the consequences of the act.

b. All consequences which the actor desires to bring about are intended, as the word is used in this Restatement. Intent is not, however, limited to consequences which are desired. If the actor knows that the consequences are certain, or substantially certain, to result from his act, and still goes ahead, he is treated by the law as if he had in fact desired to produce the result. As the probability that the consequences will follow decreases, and becomes less than substantial certainty, the actor's conduct loses the character of intent, and becomes mere recklessness, as defined in § 500. As the probability decreases further, and amounts only to a risk that the result will follow, it becomes ordinary negligence, as defined in § 282. All three have their important place in the law of torts, but the liability attached to them will differ.

Illustrations:

1. A throws a bomb into B's office for the purpose of killing B. A knows that C, B's stenographer, is in the office. A has no desire to injure C, but knows that his act is substantially certain to do so. C is injured by the explosion. A is subject to liability to C for an intentional tort.

2. On a curve in a narrow highway A, without any desire to injure B, or belief that he is substantially certain to do so, recklessly drives his automobile in an attempt to pass B's car. As a result of this recklessness, A crashes into B's car, injuring B. A is subject to liability to B for his reckless conduct, but is not liable to B for any intentional tort.

CHAPTER 6

LIABILITY FOR INTENTIONAL MISCONDUCT

§ 6—1. Intent

As we have seen (§ 1—3), the early English law of wrongs was not much concerned with the wrongdoer's intent. If his act was voluntary and the resulting physical harm direct, liability usually followed.

Gradually, the actions of trespass and case evolved such that, so far as physical harm is concerned, the distinction between them was no longer whether the harm was direct or indirect, but rather whether the tort could be classified within the confines of the traditional trespass actions—battery, assault, false imprisonment, trespass to land and chattels—or whether the wrong involved mere negligence, for which case was the usual remedy. At the same time the courts came to require fault as a condition to trespass liability—that is, some sort of wrongful intent. Thus, the trespass actions became what we now call the intentional torts.

Morally, greater blame attaches to intentional misconduct than to lesser degrees of fault, and this is reflected in the law of intentional torts. In general, to establish a prima facie case, plaintiff need only prove that defendant intentionally invaded a protected interest. The burden then shifts to defendant to show some justification or excuse. And, unlike negligence actions, actual damages need not be proved. If plaintiff cannot establish any actual harm (tangible or intangible), nominal damages can be awarded.

Traditionally, the intentional torts are those named and discussed in the sections which follow. However, there has come to be recognized a general principle of intentional tort liability, analogous to the general principle of negligence liability (see § 3—1), sometimes called "prima facie tort," which may be invoked when no particular intentional tort applies. Section 870 of the Restatement (Second) as tentatively approved provides:

One who intentionally causes injury to another is subject to liability to the other for the actual harm incurred, if his conduct is culpable and not justifiable. This liability may be imposed despite the fact that the actor's conduct does not come within one of the traditional categories of tort liability.

For a discussion of the elements and limits of this liability, see the Comments to this section; for authorities supporting it, see the Reporter's Notes. A recent case discussing this doctrine is Nees v. Hocks (Or.1975) (wrongful discharge). Of course, it must not be inferred from this that all unjustified intentional wrongs are actionable. But in a proper case, the courts need not and do not consider themselves bound by the traditional intentional tort pigeon-holes.

An intentional tort is an act committed (or omitted) with a particular state of mind. How is the actor's state of mind to be proved? Direct evidence—the actor's own statement of his actual intent—is rarely available. Indeed, after the fact he may claim to have had the best of intentions. Thus, as in all other cases where one's state of mind must be shown, it is usually proved by circumstantial evidence. His conduct, in the context of his surroundings and what he presumably knew and perceived, is evidence from which his intent may be inferred. The law presumes that one intends the natural and probable consequences of his acts in light of the surrounding circumstances of which he may be assumed to be aware.

Intent, in the sense required here, must be distinguished from motive. *Intent* is usually defined as the desire to cause certain immediate consequences. One who throws a rock with great force against a glass window obviously intends that it will be broken. One who points a loaded gun at another and pulls the trigger surely intends that the bullet will strike and injure him. The actor's *motive* for his conduct—revenge, protest, punishment, theft, self-defense, or even a desire to be of help (e.g. the surgeon who operates without consent)—may, in certain cases, aggravate, mitigate or excuse the wrong. For example, malice may permit assessment of punitive damages; self-defense may be a complete defense to tort liability. But to establish a prima facie case, all that need be shown is the defendant's conduct, the invasion of a legally protected interest of the plaintiff, and the requisite intent.

Since intent is a desire to cause certain immediate consequences, very young children may be held liable for intentional torts though so young as to be incapable of negligence.

Intent is a state of mind, a subjective matter. But the law's definition of intent is objective to this extent: an actor is deemed to intend the consequences of his act which he knows are substantially certain to result, irrespective of his actual intent. R. § 8A. Thus, *A* throws a bomb into a room in which *B* and *C* are present for the purpose of killing *B*. *A* knows that *C* is present, but has no desire to hurt *C*, and in fact fervently hopes that *C* will not be injured. Nevertheless, since he knew that physical harm to *C* was substantially certain, he is held to have intended that harm.

Thus, certainty of the harmful consequences is the basis on which we distinguish intentional torts from negligent or reckless ("wilful and wanton") ones. If the result is intended or substantially certain to occur, the tort is intentional. But if the actor's conduct merely creates a foreseeable *risk* of harm, which may or may not be realized, then the conduct is negligent or reckless depending upon the magnitude of the risk.

Unique to the intentional torts, borrowed from the criminal law, the doctrine of "transferred intent" reflects the greater blame which attaches to intentional misconduct. In effect, it is a broadened rule of proximate cause. Thus, where *A* acts with the intent to injure *B*, but at the same time or instead injures *C*, his intent to injure *B* "transfers" to *C* and *A* is deemed to have committed an intentional tort upon *C*, even though he was completely unaware of *C*'s existence or of any risk of harm to *C*. For example, *A* shoots at *B* and wounds or misses him. The bullet strikes *C* who was hidden from view and not known to be in the vicinity. *A* may be liable to *C* in battery. In addition, the intent transfers among the five progeny of the parent trespass action—battery, assault, false imprisonment, trespass to land and trespass to chattels—so long as the harm is direct and immediate. For example, *A*'s intent to commit only an assault upon *B* such as by shooting in his direction to frighten him may support liability for a battery to *C* who is unexpectedly struck by the bullet.

Often the same act is both a tort and a crime. This is especially true with respect to the intentional torts. But despite their common origins, tort and criminal law rules are now more different than similar, and analogies and comparisons between torts and crimes of the same name or having similar bases in conduct should be made only with the greatest caution.

Both a civil tort action and a criminal prosecution may be brought for the same wrongful conduct. The remedies are concurrent, and either a successful or an unsuccessful result in one is ordinarily not a bar to the other. However, since the most common intentional torts are more often committed by judgment-proof persons, and intentional torts are frequently uninsured and in some cases uninsurable, intentional tort litigation is of relatively minor significance in the day-to-day work of lawyers and courts.

§ 6—2. Battery

Battery is the remedy for an intentional and unpermitted physical contact with plaintiff's person by defendant or (now that the distinction between trespass and case has disappeared) by an agency defendant has set in motion. It reflects the basic right to have one's body left alone by others. Secondarily, it seeks to deter relatively minor but offensive contacts which can precipitate breaches of the peace.

Plaintiff's "person" is held to include his body and those things in contact or closely connected to it and identified with it, such as clothing, an object held in his hand, or an object so associated or identified with plaintiff that, considering the nature of the contact, a normal person would deem it an offense against his person.

The tort is the contact, and thus plaintiff need not have been aware of it at the time.

Two forms of contact are actionable. First and foremost are those which cause some *physical harm,* broadly defined to include any physical impairment of the condition of the body (such as a cut, a bruise, a burn, etc., however slight), even if beneficial; illness; and physical (but not emotional) pain. R. § 15. Second, battery also encompasses contacts which do not cause physical harm but are hostile, offensive, or insulting, such as poking with a finger in anger, angrily knocking off one's hat, dousing one with water, spitting in one's face, cutting hair, and even an unwanted kiss. R. § § 18, 19.

The gist of the action is contact without consent, resulting in harm to plaintiff's person or dignity.

The contact must have been intended (unless the doctrine of transferred intent applies); otherwise the action if any lies in negligence. But defendant need not have intended any harm. It is no defense that defendant intended only a joke or a compliment, or even to render assistance. Thus, where a doctor performs surgery without the patient's consent, a battery has been committed.

If plaintiff consents to the contact, defendant is privileged to make it and there is no tort. This is generally true of all torts. See § 7—2. So far as battery is concerned, consent may sometimes be assumed.

Legalines, Torts adaptable to Prosser casebook

Legalines are published by Harcourt Legal & Professional Publications, Inc. (1-800-787-8717)

II. INTENTIONAL INTERFERENCE WITH PERSON OR PROPERTY

A. INTENT

1. **Introduction.** One of the major classifications of tort liability is liability based on the intent of the defendant. It is the intent to bring about certain consequences that is important, not merely the intent to do an act. Intent includes not only the desire to bring about the physical results, but also the knowledge or belief that certain results are substantially certain to follow from the actor's conduct.

   a. **Need not be malicious.** The intent forming the basis of tort liability need not be immoral, malicious, or hostile; instead, it need only be an intent to affect a legally protected interest in a way that will not be permitted by law.

   b. **Objective standard.** The actor's subjective knowledge or belief that certain results are substantially certain to follow from his conduct is determined on an objective rather than a subjective basis. That is, actual knowledge or belief, or lack thereof, on the part of the defendant is immaterial if a reasonable person in the position of the defendant would have believed that certain results were substantially certain to follow from the conduct of the defendant. Of course, the external, objective standard must have certain subjective inputs based upon the position of the defendant; i.e., age, physical abilities, mental capacity, special skills, etc. It is on the basis of the theoretical reasonable person who possesses these same characteristics of the defendant that knowledge or belief for purposes of tort liability is determined.

c. **Intentional acts by children.** Children are charged with what is expected of them considering age, experience, intelligence, etc. They are liable only for what they are capable of, considering the foregoing factors. If they are capable of knowledge of the consequences of an act, they may be liable for these consequences.

Garratt
v. Dailey

2. **Substantial Certainty—Garratt v. Dailey**, 279 P.2d 1091 (Wash. 1955).

a. **Facts.** Garratt (P) alleged that Dailey (D) had *deliberately* pulled a chair out from under her as she was sitting down, causing her to fall and fracture her hip. D, five years old, claimed that he had moved the chair so that he could sit in it himself, and, upon noticing that P was about to sit down, tried in vain to move the chair back in time. On remand, the court found that when D moved the chair, he knew with substantial certainty that P would attempt to sit down where the chair had been. Appeal from a decision denying P recovery of damages for an alleged assault and battery.

b. **Issue.** In an action for assault and battery, may defendant be held liable if he did not subjectively intend to cause the resultant harm but knew with substantial certainty that his actions would likely cause it?

c. **Held.** Yes. Judgment reversed and remanded for clarification.

1) Battery is the intentional infliction of a harmful or offensive bodily contact upon another.

2) An "act" is deemed to be intentional if it is done either with the subjective purpose of causing the contact or the apprehension thereof, or with the knowledge that such contact or apprehension is **substantially certain to result** therefrom.

3) When a minor has committed a tort with force, he is just as subject to suit as any other person would be.

d. **Remand.** On remand, the court found that D knew with substantial certainty that P would attempt to sit where the chair had been located. Based on this finding that D had the requisite intent to be liable for battery, the court awarded P $11,000. This verdict was upheld on appeal. [Garratt v. Dailey, 304 P.2d 681 (Wash. 1956)]

e. **Comment.** Intentional conduct is an act that a reasonable person in D's position would know is substantially certain to lead to the damage of another's legally protected interests.

Spivey v. Battaglia

3. Distinguishing Intent from Negligence—Spivey v. Battaglia, 258 So. 2d 815 (Fla. 1972).

a. **Facts.** Spivey (P) and Battaglia (D) worked for the Battaglia Fruit Co. During a lunch break, D teased P by putting his arm around her and pulling her head toward him. The movement caused a sharp pain in P's neck and paralyzed her on the left side of her face and mouth. More than two years later, P sued for negligence and assault and battery. The trial court granted D summary judgment on the assault and battery allegation because the two-year statute of limitations for intentional torts had run. The trial court also granted summary judgment on the negligence allegation on the ground that D's conduct constituted assault and battery, which is not negligence. P appeals.

b. **Issue.** If a person intends to do an act that produces harm, but does not intend to cause the harm, may the person be liable for negligence?

c. **Held.** Yes. Judgment reversed.

1) Liability for intentional torts does not necessarily rest on a hostile intent or a desire to do harm. It is sufficient if a reasonable person would believe that a particular result was substantially certain to follow. Knowledge and appreciation of a risk short of substantial certainty, however, is not equivalent to intent.

2) The line between negligence and intent is drawn where the known danger ceases to be only a foreseeable risk which a reasonable person would avoid, and becomes a substantial certainty. In this case, the harm suffered by P was not substantially certain to follow from D's conduct. D did not have the intent to cause P's paralysis, and thus did not act intentionally for purposes of tort liability.

3) D may be liable for the unanticipated injury to P if he was negligent. This depends on whether the consequences of his acts were reasonably foreseeable, even though the exact result was not contemplated. The jury should decide this case after being instructed on the elements of negligence.

d. **Comment.** The court contrasted a case in which the defendant had embraced and kissed the plaintiff. During the plaintiff's struggle to resist, she struck her face on an object and suffered injury. That case was an assault and battery and not negligence, because the injury was substantially certain to follow from the defendant's conduct. In this case, by contrast, the injury was a bizarre result.

4. **Mistake.**

a. **General rule.** Normally, good faith mistake is not a defense to a tort suit. Under certain circumstances, however, it may justify assertion of privilege, as when a defendant acted out of a mistaken but reasonable belief that he was being attacked when he injured the plaintiff in self-defense.

Ranson v.
Kitner

b. Application—Ranson v. Kitner, 31 Ill. App. 241 (1888).

1) Facts. Defendants, while hunting wolves, shot plaintiff's dog, mistaking it for a wolf. Defendants acted in good faith, believing the dog to be a wolf. The jury gave a verdict to plaintiff for damages equal to the value of the dog.

2) Issue. Is a good faith mistake a defense to an intentional tort?

3) Held. No. Judgment affirmed.

Gilbert Law Summaries on Torts by Marc Franklin

Gilbert Law Summaries are published by Harcourt Legal & Professional Publications, Inc. (1-800-787-8717)

A. TORTS TO THE PERSON

1. **Battery:** [§ 1] Prima facie case:

   > *Act by Defendant*
   > *Intent*
   > *Harmful or Offensive Touching*
   > *Causation*
   > (*Lack of Consent*—discussed as a defense, *see infra*, §§80
   > *et seq.*)

   a. **Act by defendant:** [§2] The word "act" as used in intentional torts means an external manifestation of the actor's will; it refers to some *volitional movement* by the actor of some part of his body. Thus, if D intentionally drove his automobile into P, the "act" complained of would not be the driving of the automobile, but rather the movement by D of his *arms and legs* in setting the automobile into motion and directing it at P. [Restatement (Second) of Torts ("Rest. 2d") §2 (1965)]

      (1) **Unconscious acts:** [§3] Because of the requirement of a "volitional" movement, the movements of persons having an epileptic seizure or of persons asleep or under the influence of drugs are not generally sufficient "acts" for the purpose of establishing liability for intentional torts. [Lobert v. Pack, 9 A.2d 365 (Pa. 1939)]

      (2) **Reflex actions:** [§4] On the other hand, a muscular reaction by a person in command of his senses is always an "act" unless it is purely a reflex action in which the mind and will have no share. Thus, the blinking of eyelids in defense against an approaching missile is not an "act" because it is purely reflexive. But if someone, finding himself about to fall, stretches his hand out to save himself, the stretching out of his

hand *is* an "act"; his mind has grasped the situation and dictated a muscular contraction in an effort to prevent the fall.

(3) **Acts by incompetents:** [§5] Persons who are not legally competent are still capable of volitional conduct; *i.e.*, insane persons or minors may be held liable for their acts. (McGuire v. Almy, 8 N.E.2d 760 (Mass. 1937); Goff v. Taylor, 708 S.W.2d 113 (Ky. 1986)]

b. **Intent:** [§6] The defendant must have done the "act" with the intent *to inflict a harmful or offensive touching* on the plaintiff or a third person. [Rest. 2d §13(a)]

(1) **Test—desire or belief in substantial certainty:** [§7] Whether the defendant had the requisite intent is measured by whether he acted with the *desire* to cause the result *or believed that the result was substantially certain* to occur; *i.e.*, the defendant must have desired a harmful or offensive touching *or* believed that such a touching was substantially certain to result from his act. [Garratt v. Dailey, 279 P.2d 1091 (Wash. 1955); Frey v. Kouf, 484 N.W.2d 864 (S.D. 1992)]

(a) **Example:** D shoved P, a young child, to get her out of the area in which some boys were playing. P fell and broke her elbow; D has committed a battery. Even if D did not desire the result, he believed that an offensive (if not harmful) touching was substantially certain to occur. [Baldinger v. Banks, 26 Misc. 2d 1086 (1960)]

(b) **Test is subjective:** [§8] The issues of "desire" and what the defendant "believed" to be substantially certain to occur turn on the subjective consideration of what was in the defendant's mind when he acted. Although juries may make inferences about the defendant's state of mind from objective facts, the basic question is *not* what a reasonable person would have desired or believed, but what the defendant *in fact* desired or believed.

(2) **Motives immaterial:** [§9] The same distinction must be made between "malice" and "intent" in tort law as is drawn in criminal law. (*See* Criminal Law Summary.) "Malice" refers to the defendant's *motives* (*why* defendant acted as he did), and motives are generally immaterial. Tort law is concerned only with whether the defendant had the requisite *intent* under the "desire or belief in substantial certainty" test, above.

    (a) **But note:** If "malice" (intent to injure) exists, the defendant may be held liable for *punitive* damages (*see* below).

(3) **Transferred intent doctrine:** [§10] The old common law form of action called "trespass" gave rise to five modern actions: battery, assault, false imprisonment, trespass to land, and trespass to chattels. Under the doctrine of transferred intent, if the defendant acts intending to cause one of these harms to a person, the defendant will be liable on an intentional tort theory if *any* of the five harms occurs to that person or even to *the plaintiff*—even though plaintiff is unexpected and the harm is unexpected.

    (a) **Example:** D attempted to strike X, who ducked. The blow hit P, who had unexpectedly appeared. *Held:* D committed a battery on P. [Carnes v. Thompson, 48 S.W.2d 903 (Mo. 1932)]

    (b) **Example:** D unlawfully shot at X's dog and hit P. Even though D had no reason to know that anyone might be in the area, D committed a battery on P. [Corn v. Shepard, 229 N.W. 869 (Minn. 1930); Altieri v. Colasso, 362 A.2d 798 (Conn. 1975)— attempted assault on X led to battery on P]

    (c) **Comment:** Although phrased as involving "intent," the better explanation for the doctrine is that the courts are imposing strict liability on D because of his serious misbehavior in directing the initial act against X.

APPENDIX C

More Torts Questions

LANE v. KENT
Supreme Court of Columbia, 1995
41 Colum.2d 476

MUNNEKE, Justice. This case involves the liability for battery involving a novel question in this jurisdiction. The plaintiff Lois Lane complains that she was harmed when the defendant Clark Kent brushed against her as Kent rushed down an aisle after receiving a phone call at his desk in the offices of the *Daily Planet*, a newspaper, in the city of Metropolis, where both are employed as reporters. According to Lane, Kent jumped up and announced, "I've got to take care of something out of the office. I'll be back." In his haste to exit the workplace, Kent's arm came into contact with Lane's shoulder as a result of Lane's leaning toward the aisle to ascertain the source of the commotion. Lane also complains that Kent did not apologize for his conduct, and in fact remained away from his desk for several hours after the incident. In his defense, Kent claims that he did not intend to hurt Lane, and that she did not require any medical treatment for injuries associated with the contact. "I may have bumped her, but I was in a hurry." The record does not indicate what might have motivated Kent to leave his desk with such alacrity. As for her injuries, Lane admits that the bump she received was minor, although she notes, "It did hurt. Sometimes I think Clark just doesn't know his own strength."

The trial court with the judge in a bench trial sitting as fact finder found for the plaintiff and awarded damages in the amount of $10,000. The trial court ruled that Kent's motive in bringing about the contact with Lane was irrelevant, and that if he intended any contact at all, he could be held liable. The judge concluded that since the contact was not inadvertent, Kent must have intended some contact, and that such contact amounted to a battery. As to damages, the judge ruled that in a battery action, the plaintiff need not show actual damages, and that the amount of $10,000 was fair compensation for the invasion of a protected interest, i.e., the sanctity of plaintiff's body. From this judgment, the defendant appeals.

There are two issues in this case: first, whether defendant's conduct amounted to intent under the law, and second, whether the damages awarded without proof of actual harm were excessive.

Learned counsel for defendant argue that the evidence demonstrates that Kent did not intend to harm Lane, that his conduct was inadvertent, that it was at most careless, and that it was insufficient to sustain a finding that Kent intended unlawful contact with Lane. Counsel for defendant also argues that even if Kent is found liable in battery, he should only be responsible for nominal damages.

Intent is a critical element of the tort of battery, which may be defined as "an unconsented intentional harmful or offensive contact with another person." [Citation] There is no question in this case as to whether there was contact or whether Lane consented to that contact. We note that the contact required for battery may be either harmful or offensive, and we assume that in the absence of demonstrated physical harm Lane's claim rests on the "offensive" branch of battery. Lane has a right to expect that she will not be subjected to unwanted physical contact by others. Defendant's argument that a certain amount of inadvertent bumping and jostling in modern society is to be expected misses the point. Although some contact with people on the street and other public situations is inevitable, there are many circumstances such as here, where plaintiff is working in the relative peace of her own office, that she is entitled to expect that she will not be subjected to unwanted contact. Furthermore, if an actor's contact is found to be intentional, then he may be liable for battery, notwithstanding other circumstances. The Restatement of Torts §13, Comment (a), says:

"Character of Actor's Intention. In order that an act may be done with the intention of bringing about harmful or offensive contact or an apprehension thereof to a particular person, either the other or a third person, the act must be done with knowledge on the part of the actor that contact or apprehension is substantially certain to be produced… It is not enough that the act itself is intentionally done and this, even though the actor realizes or should realize that it contains a very grave risk of bringing about the contact or apprehension. Such realization may make the actor's conduct negligent or even reckless, but unless he realizes that to a substantial certainty, the contact or apprehension will result, the actor has not the intention which is necessary to make him liable under the rule stated in this section." [Citation]

In *Garratt v. Dailey*, 46 Wash.2d 197, 279 P.2d 1091 (1955), the plaintiff broke her hip when her nephew Brian Dailey, aged five years, nine months, pulled a chair out from under her at a family gathering. The Court, citing the Restatement provision above favorably, held that Dailey could still be responsible for her injuries if he knew to a substantial certainty that the act of pulling the chair out from under her would produce contact with the ground. The fact that the defendant was less than six years old was not an excuse. The question was whether he was able to form the necessary intent, and if he could whether he had in this case.

The question for us is whether Kent knew to a substantial certainty as he ran down the aisle past Lane's desk that his arm would come in contact with Lane's body. It is not enough that he was careless or even reckless. He must possess the knowledge that contact was substantially certain to flow from his actions. Although Kent's own testimony ("I may have bumped her") suggests that he may have had such awareness, the decision of the lower court does not make clear whether or not it found the requisite intent.

On the question of damages, it is clear that offensive battery may not carry with it any actual physical harm. The plaintiff in such an action need not prove that the contact produced injury, only that it was offensive. The trier of fact is entitled, upon a showing of offensive battery, to award damages consistent with the offense. It may award nominal damages, but it may also set the damages at some higher amount as the circumstances dictate. We do not find that the trial judge in his capacity as trier of fact abused his discretion in awarding damages in the amount of $10,000.

We therefore remand this case to the trial court for clarification as to whether the defendant Kent intended with substantial certainty to bring about contact with plaintiff Lane. It is so ordered.

1. In the principal case would it have made any difference if Kent had testified that he didn't see Lane until it was too late to avoid hitting her? Why should that change the situation? At what point can we say that Kent's appreciation of the situation is clear enough to say that he has attained substantial certainty.

2. If A fires a gun into a crowded room, not intending to shoot any particular individual, can it be said that he knew to a substantial certainty that harmful contact would result? What about apprehension? Is the apprehension of harmful or offensive contact called assault? Is it possible to have a battery without an assault?

3. The *Garratt* case says that a child can entertain intent. At what age would a child be able to form intent as defined in the cases? Three? Two? If a child is found to have committed a tort, who pays the damages?

4. The principal case articulates the general rule that intentional torts do not require proof of actual damages. In common law, actions that grew out of the ancient writ of trespass, such as battery and assault, permitted the jury to presume damages. In such cases, the jurors did not have to hear evidence of actual harm in order to assess a monetary award. The offense to the integrity of the plaintiff's legal right was enough. Sometimes juries awarded nominal damages, e.g., $1, to denote the plaintiff's legal right in the absence of cognizable harm.

5. What is the Restatement of Torts referred to in the principal case? Is it binding on the court in the same way that a decided case would be? If not, what is its relevance to the decision?

6. If the defendant need only know to a substantial certainty that a particular result will follow from his actions, what is the relevance of a motive to bring about harm, sometimes called ill will or malice?

7. Why is the case remanded for clarification, and not a new trial? How do you think the case will be decided on remand?

WAYNE v. NAPIER
Supreme Court of Columbia, 1998
99 Colum.2d 1003

MUNNEKE, Justice. This is a lawsuit by Bruce Wayne, a citizen of the State of Columbia, against Jack Napier, AKA "The Joker," for assault and battery. Napier, who has an extensive criminal record, and subsequent to the institution of this action, has been charged with crimes unrelated to the present case. Wayne lives on a large rural estate from which he directs a variety of business enterprises and philanthropies. Napier, for reasons that are not altogether clear, embarked on a personal mission to harass Wayne, his staff and associates, through the commission of a variety of practical jokes. "The Joker," as he prefers to be called, in addition to committing such acts as letting the air out of Wayne's tires and having pizzas delivered to Wayne's estate late at night, took the actions which led to this lawsuit, to wit: he placed a large plexiglass shield in a wooded area behind Wayne's main house near a cave on the property, which Wayne apparently uses for some kind of private work. The defendant then called Wayne on the phone to give him a message, the content of which is not clear from the record, but which prompted Wayne to run from his house to the cave area mentioned above. Unable to see the plexiglass impediment in the path, Wayne ran into the barricade, striking his head and sustaining the injuries complained of in this action.

In a jury trial the plaintiff was awarded $100,000 for medical expenses, pain and suffering, and emotional distress. The trial judge dismissed the assault count on grounds that the facts did not support a finding that the plaintiff experienced any apprehension of imminent battery. The only issue on appeal is the defendant's mental state. For the reasons articulated below, we affirm the judgment below.

Attorneys for Napier argue that their client is insane, and therefore incapable of entertaining the intent required for the tort of battery. They point to his extensive criminal record as evidence of his inability to function in normal society, and that in the pending criminal action, an insanity defense is being considered. An expert for the defendant testified at trial that Napier is a sociopath who does not know right from wrong and is incapable of conforming his conduct to the rules of society. His proclivity for practical jokes is nothing more than an attempt to channel these anti-social tendencies into behavior that is socially acceptable, if not laudable.

We find the defendant's theory intriguing, but not persuasive. The law in this state is well settled that insane persons are to be responsible for their torts. Following the lead of Massachusetts in *McGuire v. Almy* 297 Mass. 323, 8 N.E.2d 760 (Sup. Ct. Mass. 1937), this court has consistently held that mental illness cannot excuse the mischief visited upon others by insane persons. [Citations] The theory behind this doctrine seems to be that even if insane persons are incapable of entertaining intent strictly speaking, that a rule imposing liability for their torts serves as an incentive for families, caretakers, and guardians responsible for them to take steps to prevent harm to others. It has also been argued that as between the tortfeasor and innocent victim that society favors compensation of the victim.

We recognize that a strict analysis of the concept of intent would seem to negate liability. This court has held that children at a certain age may be incapable of intent, and that mental deficiency—in contrast to mental illness—may prevent an individual from knowing with certainty that his act will produce a particular result. We also recognize that the study of the human mind has progressed considerably since the early cases in this jurisdiction and elsewhere were decided. We are unwilling at this juncture to overturn the substantial body of precedent supporting the present rule of law. Particularly in a state where the policy of mental health officials is to "mainstream" patients with mental illnesses, rather than to institutionalize them, we think that a rule protecting citizens of the state from potential harmful acts makes sense.

In another sense, however, we are not even sure whether defendant Napier would be relieved of liability even if we agreed with counsel to change the law. Defendant's condition, which was characterized as sociopathic by defendant's own expert, does not seem to encompass an inability to know that his acts will produce consequences. He may not know right from wrong, or care whether someone could be harmed by his conduct, but it does not follow that when he placed a plexiglass wall at a spot where he knew plaintiff would go, he did not appreciate to a substantial certainty that contact with the glass would follow.

Affirmed.

SUPERMAN v. LUTHOR

Supreme Court of Columbia, 2001
124 Colum.2d 312

MUNNEKE, Justice. The Plaintiff, Superman, a citizen of Metropolis, whose true identity was protected from public disclosure in an earlier action brought under the Columbia Freedom of Information Act, Chap. II, Sec. 12 Colum Stats. (Rev. 2000), by this Court in *Daily Planet v. John Doe AKA "Superman,"* 111

Colum.2d 1211 (1999), sues for damages caused by the alleged battery inflicted on him by defendant Luthor. The trial court dismissed the action after a jury found that Luthor did not actually come in contact with any part of Superman's body.

The facts are these: Plaintiff Superman features himself to be a crimefighter and public servant, who works closely with law enforcement officials to deter criminal activity and to assist in the capture of dangerous felons. He believes that Luthor is the mastermind behind a vast criminal enterprise, who has evaded capture due to his superior (but evil) intellectual capacity. Luthor claims that Superman is delusional and points to his strange garb, a blue body suit with a red cape, to support his position.

On or about January 1, 2000, Superman was called to police headquarters to investigate the crash of the police computer system. Inside the network server, unknown to anyone, was rock, composed of a substance called kryptonite, which had the effect of producing the serious physical injuries complained of in this suit when Superman entered the room. On the desk was a note that read, "Happy New Year, Superman. Lex."

A battery involves physical contact with the plaintiff by the defendant. In most cases, the defendant actually touches the person of another directly, although the cases do not limit contact to this sort of physical touching. A bullet fired from a gun may produce a battery. See e.g., *Soprano v. Santangelo*, 51 Colum 442 (1996). A battery can be inflicted through a chattel. See e.g., *Estate of Doe v. A Car Called Christine*. 67 Colum. 228 (1997). The examples are almost endless. The defendant need not touch the plaintiff's body with his body if the instrumentality causing the contact is, in effect, an extension of the defendant's body, or if the defendant intentionally places in motion the chain of events that produces the contact.

In the same way, the defendant need not actually touch the plaintiff's skin for a battery to occur. The contact may be with something so closely associated with the plaintiff's person as to be seen as an extension of it, such as his clothes. In *Fisher v. Carrousel Motor Hotel, Inc.*, 424 S.W.2d 627 (Tex. Sup. Ct. 1967), a waiter took a plate out of plaintiff's hand, but did not otherwise touch him. To hold otherwise would limit the scope of battery unnecessarily. Civilized society requires that citizens not be allowed to strike their fellow citizens with impunity, but to limit battery to flesh on flesh contact would create a loophole this Court is unwilling to allow.

In the context of this case, we find that if Luthor did in fact place the kryptonite rock in a place where Superman would be exposed to it, knowing that its properties would bring about physical harm to Superman, he may be found liable for battery. Modern science recognizes that radiation is a force that can cause damage, and the fact that this particular radiation seems to affect only Superman does not make it any less a harmful force. If Luthor set in motion the chain of events which produced the harmful radiation, he has committed a battery as surely as if he were in the room and hit Superman over the head with a baseball bat.

The action of the District Court dismissing this action is reversed, and the case is remanded to the District Court for a new trial, consistent with the rule of law articulated in this case. It is so ordered.

CARDOZO, J., dissenting. I am unconvinced that liability should attach in a case like this. It is one thing to say that defendant threw a knife or fired a gun at the plaintiff. In this case, however, the defendant was not in the same room, or the same building, or it turns out even the same city. How far is the scope of liability to extend? In my opinion, the tort of battery requires that the defendant be in the same vicinity as the plaintiff such that the instrumentality used to inflict the battery may be viewed as an extension of the defendant's person.

Using these cases, the material in Appendix B, and the cases you read earlier, try your hand at another sample question. When you have finished, compare your answer to the sample that follows, and critique your answer using the evaluation form found on page 120.

Exam Question
(30 minutes)

Jonathon Harker, an attorney, was retained by Renfield, as agent for Count Dracula, to handle certain property transfers for the

Count, most notably the purchase of a certain property known as Carfax Abbey, and the transport of an undisclosed number of coffins from the Count's homeland of Transylvania, incident to the Count's relocation from Transylvania to pursue international business interests. According to Harker, when he traveled to Dracula's castle in Transylvania, several unknown women in the castle accosted him physically and sexually. Later, according to Harker, the Count made unwanted advances toward his wife, Mina, visiting the Harker's home and then attempting to kiss or otherwise touch Mina's neck, an act which was only stopped by Harker's return to the house from a meeting at the Abbey with Renfield. Dracula claims that his intentions were honorable, and that in his country greetings were commonly exchanged by a slight touching of lips to the neck. Does either Harker, Jonathon or Mina, have a legal claim here? If so, whom may they sue and for what?

Sample Answer
(Don't look until you complete your own answer)

Jonathon and Mina Harker both have a claim for battery, Jonathon against the women in the castle, and Mina against the Count. A battery is an unconsented intentional harmful or offensive contact with another person. The facts here do not seem to suggest that in either case there was no contact or that the contact was consented to by the Harkers. Nor does it seem to be critical as to whether the contact was harmful or offensive—for battery it may be either. The main issue in this case is whether the Count or the women intended their contact with the Harkers.

Intent is defined in the Restatement of Torts as knowledge to a substantial certainty that the consequences will follow a particular act. It is not enough for the act to be careless or even reckless. The defendant must know that his conduct will bring about the contact with the defendant's person. He does not have to be absolutely certain, just substantially certain. Nor does the plaintiff have to show that the defendant intended to bring about harm. The defendant's motive may be relevant to damages, but ill will is not required for there to be a battery. The injury in battery is the invasion of the plaintiff's protected interest in his or her body.

In this case, Jonathon need only show that when the women attempted to touch his neck—assuming that there was contact, however slight—they knew that their conduct was substantially certain to bring about contact with his neck. Although the facts do not indicate that the women made any affirmative statement of intent, the facts do not show either that the women were careless or that they accidentally fell into Jonathon. It is fair to conclude that when a person bends over another's neck, puckers her lips, and then touches the neck that she knew to a substantial certainty that her actions would produce contact with the neck. Accordingly, it appears that the women did possess the required intent to support a charge of battery.

As for Mina, the same analysis would apply to the Count as described for the women above. Here, we even have a statement by the Count, regarding the greeting custom in his country, which supports the conclusion that he knew to a substantial certainty that his kiss would bring about contact with Mina's neck. Thus, he too appears to have intent. The only question in this scenario is whether the Transylvanian custom would somehow negate the intent. Since motive is not determinative as to whether there is necessary intent for battery, I think the only real question is whether the Count knew that his actions would result in contact with Mina's neck. One other question is whether either Mina consented to the contact by inviting Dracula into the house. I think not. Just because she allowed him to enter the premises doesn't mean she consented to him doing anything he wanted while he was there.

In conclusion, Jonathon may sue the women for battery and Mina may sue the Count for battery by showing that there was intent—knowledge to a substantial certainty—to bring about unconsented contact with their bodies.

APPENDIX D

More Long Essay Questions

Question One

(One Hour)

A, B, and C cut across the property of D on their way home after an evening at Tony's Tavern. The footpath across D's land, "Blackacre," frequently was used by patrons of Tony's as a shortcut from the drinking establishment to town where most of them lived. A, B, and C were feeling the effects of numerous rounds of ale quaffed during the course of the evening.

While on the footpath, they were beset by robbers X, Y, and Z. X announced, "Stand and deliver. Your money or your lives." Y struck A and B with a heavy stick, knocking both of them unconscious. Z relieved them of their valuables: wallets, rings, watches, and money.

As Y approached C, C leaped forward and wrestled the stick from Y's hand. Y turned to run, but C hit him over the head, killing him. X and Z, fearing for their lives, ran away, with C in hot pursuit.

Hearing a commotion, D came out of his house and saw C chasing X and Z with stick in hand. Presuming that C was attacking X and Z, he subdued C by confronting him with a loaded gun. Over C's vocal protests, D locked him in a closet until the sheriff could be summoned.

D did not bother to try to stop X and Z. assuming that in capturing C he had rescued them from danger. In fact, the two thieves took the occasion to continue their flight, cutting through the woods of Blackacre. Unfortunately for them, X ran off a bluff on the property, breaking both legs and an arm in the fall, while Z, taking a different route, fell into a concealed pit set out by D to capture bears and other wild animals that roamed Blackacre. Z received a painful injury to his posterior when he landed on a metal bear trap.

Meanwhile, A and B regained consciousness, and discovered Y's body. Thinking, perhaps, that they might be held responsible for Y's untimely departure from this terrestrial orb, they, too, began to run through the woods of Blackacre. Both fell into D's gravel quarry, which was not apparent to them because it was night

The splashing in the quarry aroused D, who had secured C in the closet by this time. When D got to the quarry, he discovered A and B. Because A was closer to shore, D attempted to rescue A by holding out to him a long branch; this attempt was successful, and D was able to pull A to shore. Then, D told A that because B was his (A's) friend, he (A) could rescue him (B) while he (D) went home to wait for the sheriff. A, who was exhausted, did nothing, and B drowned.

In this whole pitiful affair, who is liable to whom for what in civil tort actions that may be brought?

Question Two
(One Hour)

The Exxoff Oil Corporation sold improperly refined jet fuel to Untied Airlines. Untied stored the fuel at its gates at Lax Airport in El Lei, a city on the West Coast. Several of Untied's pilots complained to company brass that they were having trouble getting enough power for liftoff after refueling at Lax. The fleet of Untied jets was inspected, and all were found to be in good condition. Untied did not test the fuel in its storage tanks.

On the night of August 12, Fritz "Flyboy" Mondo and Delia Rownde went out for a wild night in El Lei. "Flyboy" and Delia were pilot and chief stewardess respectively on Untied Flight 13, departing from Lax for Honolulu at 7:55 a.m. Nursing terrible hangovers but otherwise sated from their night of excess, the two appeared at the airport in time to get Flight 13 underway.

With 295 passengers and a crew of ten (10), all normal preflight procedures and safety checks were undertaken, and the aircraft was cleared for departure. As part of the preparation for takeoff, Flight 13 had been refueled using the adulterated Exxoff jet fuel in Untied's storage tanks.

During the previous night, a heavy fog from the ocean just west of the airport had blanketed the city, combining with the normally prevailing air pollution to reduce visibility to a point just above that which would require closing the airport. Air traffic controllers could have increased the intervals between takeoffs as a safety measure, but they did not.

When cleared for takeoff, Captain "Flyboy" noticed as he increased his speed taxiing down the runway that the aircraft was not able to attain full power. Still, he believed he could get the plane off the ground. He did, but it promptly dropped back down, landing in the ocean about one mile beyond the runway it had so recently departed. "Flyboy's" comments, recorded on the plane's "little black box," cannot be reprinted here.

Delia, rather than direct the passengers to the emergency exits, ran screaming to the cockpit to see if "Flyboy" had survived. He had. The tail of the plane broke off on impact with the seats furthest aft, and sank like a rock along with the 70 passengers and two (2) crew members sitting in the seats. Most of the other passengers were injured on impact, but many of them were able to extricate themselves from their seats and escape from the cabin. One man with a heart condition was struck by a heart attack and died in his seat. Once in the water, some of the survivors were able to board inflatable life rafts; others clung to their buoyant seat backs; others attempted to tread water.

When Flight 13 went down, Fisch and O'Kelly were sailing in Fisch's new catamaran in the vicinity. The impact of the crash produced a huge wave, which overturned the catamaran. Fisch was able to swim, and made his way back to the capsized vessel; O'Kelly regrettably could not, and was lost at sea.

Rescue efforts were hampered by the fog; a rescue helicopter sent out by Lax Airport had to return to the airport after arriving at the scene, because visibility was so poor that the pilot thought it would endanger his crew to participate in the rescue effort. Eventually, some 114 survivors were pulled from the drink, including "Flyboy" and Delia, who had made their way together to one of the life rafts. The death toll was set at 195 (not including O'Kelly) after it was determined that four of those who perished were pregnant women. Three of the deceased were eaten by sharks who happened to be feeding in the area.

While the rescue effort was underway, an explosion rocked the sunken plane. This was explained when a note was found at the gate from which Flight 13 had departed at Lax Airport; the note read: "Death to American swine. I carry a bomb which will destroy Flight 13 at 8:25 a.m. You cannot stop me. I die for Allah, Colonel Khadafy, and the revolution. Abdul Chakakhan." Untied's records indicated that a passenger, A. Chakakhan, had boarded the ill-fated flight.

Discuss the issues raised by the facts, including liability of the potential defendants, theories upon which potential plaintiffs might proceed, and damages recoverable. You may assume that there are wrongful death and survival statutes. You do not need to discuss any defenses (e.g.—contributory negligence, assumption of risk).

Part I
Essay Question
(One Hour)

Wilson Badde was the mayor of Filthytown, a large northeastern city. Living in the city were members of FOAM (Filthytown Organization Against Movement), a radical group whose motto, "Filthy Is Beautiful," was lived out in their daily lives. Repeated efforts by the city to get FOAM to clean up its act were fruitless. FOAM members were cited numerous times for violations of health ordinances prohibiting leaving refuse on the premises, keeping livestock within the city limits, and refusing to permit city building and health inspectors into the house to look for other violations.

The city was able to obtain a court order condemning the FOAM house, but the residents refused to leave; in fact, they barricaded themselves inside with an arsenal of weapons which they used to threaten neighbors and passersby.

In response to this crisis, Mayor Badde called in the Filthytown Police S.W.A.T. team which cordoned the area and took positions facing the FOAM house. Fearing a bloodbath if S.W.A.T. stormed FOAM, Badde ordered a police helicopter to drop an explosive device on the FOAM house to open a hole in the roof through which tear gas could be lobbed. Instead of a low grade concussion explosive, a high explosive incendiary device was used, which ignited the wooden structure of the FOAM house.

The fire quickly spread from house to house; soon, the entire block was engulfed. The Filthytown Fire Department was called by Mayor Badde to fight the conflagration. To prevent the spread of the fire, Mayor Badde ordered three houses at the end of the block to be dynamited before the flames reached them. Because of this, the owners were unable to remove their belongings.

One of the fire trucks severed an electric power line. Tad Cobble, a TV news commentator covering the event, stepped on the power line and was electrocuted. Acne Market, across the street, was without power for 24 hours during which time all the frozen goods, meat, poultry, and fish were ruined. Looters removed many canned goods from the market shelves.

The FOAM members in the house were inevitably consumed by the holocaust. Rex Skewer, a bystander, and Smokey deBarre, a fireman, ran into the house to attempt to rescue survivors; they were able to pull out one small child, although they saw a grown FOAM member trapped under a fallen timber pleading for help. Skewer and deBarre decided it was too risky to go back into the building. "I'm not risking my neck for some radical," remarked deBarre. Skewer collapsed of smoke inhalation and was taken to the hospital.

When the havoc was surveyed, twenty houses including the FOAM home and the three houses dynamited to prevent the spread of the fire were totally destroyed. Ten people died including nine FOAM residents and Cobble who was electrocuted. The Acne Market incurred losses of inventory. A number of firemen plus Skewer were treated for injuries. Little Rennie Quist, the child who was pulled from the FOAM house, continues to have nightmares of the event during which he courted death and witnessed the supreme agony of his mother burned to death by the flames.

What tort actions may be brought against whom in this fact pattern? What theories may be used, and what damages may be recovered? What defenses may the various defendants employ? Assume for purposes of this question that the state in which Filthytown is located has not adopted a comparative negligence statute, and that sovereign immunity has been abolished as to municipalities. Assume also that all city employees were acting within the scope of their employment responsibilities.

Essay Question

Union Halide operated a plant that produced fertilizer near Watsamatta, Indiana, a small town on the outskirts of the Chicago metropolitan area. The plant was built in an area populated primarily by dairy farmers, although over the years encroaching suburbs in the form of residential communities and shopping centers had substantially altered the pastoral setting of Watsamatta and environs. By 1985, the town had expanded to the point that residential areas were directly across the Bopaul River from the plant, which had been built originally about five miles from the town.

In 1965, before the present growth of Watsamatta occurred, a number of the local dairy farmers had filed a nuisance action against Union Halide charging that it was dumping chemical waste into the Bopaul River causing damages to them in the form of harm to dairy cattle and grain as well as diminution in the value of their land. A settlement approved by the court was reached under which the plaintiffs in that action received a lump sum award as compensation for all past and future damages incurred as a result of Union Halide's activities.

Since 1965, a number of the farms have changed hands. The new owners fall into two groups: farmers who purchased their land from the previous owners, and suburbanites who purchased their homes from real estate developers who had bought out the original farmers. It is clear that none of the homeowners was informed of the prior suit or of Union Halide's continuing activities by the developers, although careful investigation on the part of potential buyers would have disclosed such facts. The farmer sellers all had communicated to their immediate purchasers that future suits against Union would not be barred because that is what their attorney in the first suit had said.

Many of the new property owners, upon learning of Union's polluting and their own damages, decided to file suit in the spring of 1985. They had gone to company officials to request that the dumping of chemicals cease or that the plant be closed, without success. They had gone to government officials at all levels who were all unwilling to get involved because of the economic benefit Union Halide provides to the region. The property owners believe that a civil suit is the only course of action left to them at this time.

On April 1, 1985, during the evening shift at the Union Halide plant, a leak in one of the chemical storage tanks resulted in the release of a cloud of toxic chemical gas into the atmosphere. The wind carried the cloud across the Bopaul River and over the farms and residential areas on the other side. The ensuing pestilence wreaked havoc on the countryside by destroying crops, killing livestock, and contaminating water. The toll in human life was 489, although countless individuals who did not die suffered injuries, some temporary, but others permanent. Fortunately, the toxic cloud dissipated before reaching the center of Watsamatta or Chicago beyond.

The accident occurred when a valve, which was supposed to control the release of chemical gasses into a purification chamber before releasing them into the atmosphere, malfunctioned. The valve was produced by the Valvo Corporation for Chemtank, Inc., the manufacturer of the chemical storage tank and purification system. The tank and system were built to specification specifically for the Union Halide Watsamatta plant, although similar systems had been produced and were operating without problem throughout the world. In fact, the Watsamatta plant had had no previous problems with the system.

A worker at the Union plant had not turned off the system when the pressure in the tank began to rise above the normal operating range for the system, but the valve malfunctioned at a level of pressure below that for which it had been tested. The test results had been communicated by Valvo to Chemtank and then to Union.

The day after the disaster, Marvin Bellicose arrived in Watsamatta from California where he practiced law, armed with a team of investigators, a legal secretary, and his press agent. Making representations that he was the greatest tort lawyer in the world, that he had won big verdicts in similar cases before, and that he would represent clients in an Indiana suit against Union Halide, Bellicose began the arduous task of lining up clients.

On April 10, the *Watsamatta Tattler* printed an expose of Bellicose and his practices. The *Tattler* purchased the story from a freelance journalist, Patrick O'Kelly, who had made a career of following Bellicose around the world writing stories about his flamboyant behavior and notorious cases. (Ironically, some time earlier O'Kelly had miraculously survived an airline disaster in which Bellicose had represented him and a number of other plaintiffs; unfortunately, O'Kelly lost the case because he was an unforeseeable plaintiff.

O'Kelly's story contained a number of incorrect statements in it, including the following: that Bellicose shared his room at the Watsamatta Hilton with his secretary, and that his contingent fees were higher than those of local attorneys. The article also intimated that Bellicose was not qualified to practice law in Indiana; in fact, although he was licensed in California, he probably could retain local counsel and/or appear pro hac vice in this case. Because of O'Kelly's reputation as a Bellicose authority, the *Tattler* did not check any of the facts in the story for accuracy, but printed it verbatim.

As a result of the *Tattler* story, Bellicose suffered great public humiliation, particularly since the story was subsequently picked up by the wire services and reported nationally. Even more significantly, a number of the clients he had garnered for the Union Halide suit sought other counsel, and he was able to recruit no new clients for the lawsuit thereafter despite continued efforts. Bellicose believed that the story had affected his ability to attract and retain other clients as well.

You are a local attorney in Watsamatta. You have witnessed all these events, and are frankly interested in some of the action(s). Assess the various tort actions that might be pursued as a result of the injuries that have been incurred by the potential plaintiffs described in this fact pattern. Indicate, if you can, the likelihood of success of these actions; if you can't, indicate the facts you would need to know in order to make such a determination.

Part I
Essays

(45 minutes)

Super Sav is a grocery store in a decaying urban neighborhood. Super Sav owns a lot next door to the building in which the store itself is located on which parking for the cars of customers is provided. In order to assure the safety of its patrons, Super Sav constructed a six-foot chain-link fence around the lot and installed floodlights. A loading dock and trash dumpster are located on the lot.

Because neighbors behind the store had complained about the glare of the lights, the noise of trucks unloading late at night, and the smell of trash, the store's management had taken bulbs out of the lights along the back fence, and moved the Dumpster from the back of the lot to the front. In moving the Dumpster, the trash company had broken the fence so that there was a 3' × 5' opening in the corner. Super Sav had been given a check for $500 to repair the fence and signed a release absolving the trash company from any further liability.

On the night of June 6, Katy Turpentine was shopping at Super Sav after parking her car in the back row of the parking lot. By the time she finished shopping, the lot was nearly empty and no other customers were in the lot; nor were there any security guards in the area. As she reached her car, she experienced the touch of cold steel in the small of her back. What she felt was a small handgun, popularly known as a Saturday Night Special, manufactured by Lethal, Inc., held firmly in the hand of Wlad "The Impaler" Jaundice, a local contract killer who had fallen on hard times since botching his last hit. Because it was Saturday night, Turpentine knew she was in trouble. Wlad grabbed her purse, shot her in the arm, jumped into Turpentine's car and drove off.

As Wlad was making his getaway, he approached a manufacturing plant operated by duPoisont Chemical Co. A fog produced by emissions at the plant obscured Wlad's vision of the highway ahead. Because of the poor visibility, he could not see a van belonging to Dean's Furniture Rentals stopped in the road. Wlad hit the brakes but could not avoid slamming into the rear of Dean's truck, injuring both himself and the truck driver, Hal Kelp. In addition, both Wlad and Kelp developed a severe rash from chemicals in the fog.

A story about the entire incident, which appeared in the *Tattler*, the local newspaper, was noticed by D & B Financial Analysts. D & B reported the following in a newsletter circulated for a subscription fee to approximately 50 commercial lenders in the area:

Super Sav Faces Problems

Super Sav Market on Main Street has been plagued by security problems, such as the one described in the June 7 *Tattler* (copy enclosed), and fearful customers appear to be staying away in droves. If Super Sav is unable to address these problems, the store may be forced to close its doors after 70 years in the business.

In fact, this mugging was the first incident of its kind and Super Sav records indicated that the adverse publicity had not hurt business. However, as a result of the D & B report, Super Sav was unable to obtain credit for funds to complete improvements to the parking lot and the store.

Discuss the possible tort actions presented in this fact pattern.

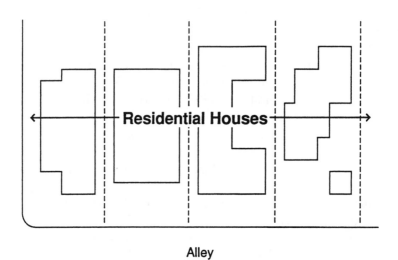

Alley

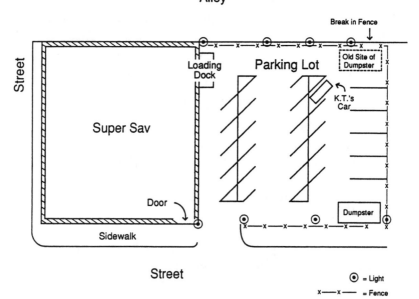

Street

(45 minutes)

Bill Badluck learned that a local gardening club was offering a prize of $200.00 to the community member with the nicest front lawn. Bill decided to enter the competition. He went to the local gardening supply shop ("Guady's"). He told Cal Clerk, an employee of the shop, that he was a novice at lawn care and asked her help in selecting appropriate tools, including an electric hedge trimmer. Cal suggested "Hedgers 100," manufactured by Hedgers, Inc. [For purposes of this exam, the electric hedge trimmer looked and worked exactly like a manual hedge trimmer, except that an electric current flowed into the tool through a long extension cord causing the blades to cross and cut.] There was an ON/OFF switch on one handle that controlled the flow of electricity. The operator needed only to guide the clippers. The clippers came in a box on which it was printed: "These electric hedge trimmers are easy to use and safe for beginning gardeners." Inside the box was a 6-page instruction booklet, which included the following statements:

Page 1   NEVER PUT HANDS OR FINGERS NEAR BLADES unless machine is disengaged.

Page 4   This tool is not a toy. Children should not be permitted to play with it.

Page 6   Guide clippers over hedges slowly, to prevent leaves from catching in the blades and jamming machine.

The "Hedgers 100" model was priced at $50.00. Bill looked at several larger hedge trimmers but rejected them as being too expensive. When Bill arrived home, he took the clippers out of the box and put the instructions away, unread.

Bill's neighbor Norris brought over a bag of fertilizer that he had purchased seven years before from Guady's, but had never used and gave it to Bill. The fertilizer, manufactured by Smelly Stuff, Inc., had the following label affixed to it:

This fertilizer contains chemicals and, thus, like all chemicals, should be treated with care. Always wear gloves when handling fertilizer as it may cause a reaction on skin exposed to it. The liability of Smelly Stuff for any loss due to product's use is limited to a refund of the purchase price.

Bill did not own gloves and decided not to purchase any.

Bill recruited his 13-year-old son Pete to trim the hedges while he spread fertilizer in the garden. All went well for the first ½ hour. However, a piece of shrubbery got stuck between the blades and caused the hedge trimmer to jam when Pete began to go faster. Pete reached in between the blades and dislodged the piece of hedge. The clippers immediately began to move and cut off part of Pete's finger. When Bill saw Pete was bleeding, he covered his face with his hands in anguish. He inadvertently inhaled some of the fertilizer that was on his hands, which caused extensive damage to his respiratory system. Bill developed serious respiratory problems, Pete lost a finger, the hedge trimmer jammed permanently, and Bill lost his opportunity to compete in the competition.

The Badlucks came to see you and asked you to represent them. In the course of pre-trial discovery, you have learned the following facts:

1. On the larger and more expensive models of electric hedge trimmers manufactured by Hedgers, Inc., Hedgers has installed a device that causes the machine to return to the OFF position automatically whenever the blade jammed. Thus, in order to start the hedge clippers operating again, the operator must manually move the switch to the ON position again. Hedgers did not include the device on its "100" size as this model tends to jam quite frequently and this device would have to be replaced after every few uses at a cost of $25.00 per replacement.

2. Smelly Stuff, Inc. has never received any notice that any consumer but Bill suffered a respiratory problem due to exposure to the fertilizer.

Against whom will you advise your clients to seek recovery? On what basis? For what losses will you seek recovery? What defenses do you anticipate the defendant(s) will raise? Evaluate your chances for success.

APPENDIX E

More Short Answer Questions

Sample Short Answer
Exam Questions

Ten-year-old Bobby Scott was driving his daddy's snowmobile over the river and through the woods to pick up grandmother and bring her back for Thanksgiving dinner. He gets to grandmother's, and picks her up, but when he arrives home grandmother is nowhere to be found. The next day grandmother is found frozen in a snowbank. Discuss Bobby's potential tort liability.

* * *

Charles witnessed Diana run over Margaret with a car. Diana's operation of the vehicle appeared to be negligent. Charles ran to help Margaret. While assisting Margaret, Charles was struck by a car negligently driven by Andrew. In the confusion of the accident, a package Charles had set down when he went to the aid of Margaret was lost. May Charles recover from Diana for his injuries? For the loss of his package? From Andrew for either? If Charles recovers a judgment of $10,000 from Diana, and the jury determines that Diana and Andrew were equally responsible for Charles's loss, how much, if anything, may Diana recover from Andrew? If Andrew, at the accident scene, wrote Charles a check for $10,000.00, and Charles signed a note saying, "I, Charles, release Andrew for any future liability for my injuries. I do not release Diana. /s/Charles," will Charles still be able to recover from Diana? Is Diana relieved of liability if an insurance policy owned by Charles pays Charles $10,000.00 for his injuries? What if Charles and Diana are married? What if Charles and Andrew are brothers? What ever happened to Margaret? Explain your answers.

* * *

Mrs. Hapless and daughter Harriet were getting into their car when Roger Reckless drove his auto down the street at a high speed. Reckless avoided hitting Mrs. Hapless only because he turned sharply to the left and into a tree. Mrs. Hapless had her back to Reckless's automobile so she did not realize that he missed striking her by inches. However, she did see him crash into the roadside rotted tree owned by Gary Grumpy. The impact caused the tree to fall in the direction of Harriet. Mr. Hapless, who was still back at the house, heard Mrs. Hapless call out: "Harriet, the tree is going to hit you." Then he heard the sound of the tree contacting the ground. Mr. Hapless suffered a heart attack as a result. Mrs. Hapless fainted. Harriet Hapless escaped all physical injury, because she quickly ran out of the tree's path. However, she began biting her nails after this incident. Discuss the liability of the various parties to each other.

Roger Reckless immediately returned to the scene (see question 4) to give aid. Roger had a certificate stating that he was qualified to administer CPR. The certificate had expired, but Roger began to administer to Mr. Hapless anyway despite a state law that prohibited anyone from administering CPR without a valid certificate. Roger, who had been drinking beer all morning, at first began to administer artificial resuscitation into Mr. Hapless's ear, but soon realized his error and corrected his conduct. Unfortunately, Mr. Hapless died. Bob Bumbling, a doctor, was walking down the street when he saw Mrs. Hapless unconscious on the sidewalk. He ran up to the home of Gary Grumpy and knocked on the door. When Mr. Grumpy answered, Bumbling asked Grumpy to please call an ambulance. Grumpy promised to do so, but as soon as he shut the door, he returned to the football game he was watching. Another neighbor did call an ambulance. Bumbling continued his walk. Discuss the liability of the various parties to each other.

Short Answer Questions

(One Hour)

CAVEAT: DO NOT USE MORE THAN ONE BLUE BOOK PAGE SINGLE-SPACED OR TWO BLUE BOOK PAGES DOUBLE-SPACED PER SHORT ANSWER!!!!

1.   D approaches A, with whom he has argued, and threatens him with a gun, shouting loudly, "I'll kill you, you b———, if it's the last thing I do!" D begins blasting, and A ducks for cover. C, a child walking by, is struck by a bullet from D's gun, and falls to the ground. B, the mother of C, witnesses the event and experiences extreme emotional distress. A testifies that when D began to shoot at him, D could see both B and C, but opened fire anyway. May any or all of A, B, and C recover damages on the basis of intentional tort theory?

2. D, driving his automobile, negligently runs down P, breaking his leg. While P is lying in the road, X drives by and also strikes P, breaking his arm. When P arrives at the hospital, X-rays determine that he has several cracked ribs, but it is not clear which of the accidents caused the injury to the ribs, although it is undisputed that one of them did. To what extent are D and X liable to P?

3. P was a passenger on D's ship, the "Palsgraf." The ship leaves port, apparently in seaworthy condition, for a day cruise in good weather conditions. The ship disappears without a trace. Assuming that there is a survival statute, may P's survivors succeed in an action against D? On what grounds?

4. Who said the following:

a. "The risk reasonably to be perceived defines the duty to be obeyed and the risk imports relation; it is risk to another or to others within the range of apprehension."

b. "Due care is a duty imposed on each one of us to protect society from unnecessary danger, not to protect A., B., or C. alone. . . . Unreasonable risk being taken, its consequences are not confined to those who might probably be hurt."

c. "[D]uty is a function of three variables: (1) The probability [P] that [the event will occur]; (2) The gravity of the resulting harm [L]; (3) The burden of adequate precautions [B] . . . in algebraic terms: liability depends on whether B is less than L multiplied by P."

How would each decide the following case? A is struck by D's negligently operated automobile. A is thrown at an odd angle through the air, and his body strikes the support for a scaffolding, causing it to collapse. P, a house painter working on the scaffolding, collapses with it, and is injured. P sues D.

5. P buys a television set at D's store. D's servant negligently leaves open the door on the loading dock. P, seeking directions to pick up his set, is told by X, another customer on his way out, "Turn left at the door to the loading dock." Actually, X meant to tell P to turn right. P, following X's directions, turns left, and falls through the door of the loading dock to the concrete below, cracking his skull. Will D be relieved of liability in a suit brought against him by P, because of X's instructions? Why or why not?

6. D is in the business of repossessing automobiles. He is sent to repossess a car at 425 Cardozo Court. He finds a car fitting the

description of the auto to be repossessed across the street from 425. He takes the car, and discovers one hour later that it belongs to P, who lives at 426 Cardozo Court, across the street from 425. D returns the car. What action, if any, does P have against D? Will P prevail? Why or why not?

7. D is a manufacturer of automobiles. The 1984 Leymon, one of its products, contains a defective hood latch that comes loose at speeds in excess of 65 mph in one out of 20,000 cars. When this happens, the hood will fly up, obscuring the driver's ability to see. The defect was not discovered until 200,000 Leymons were sold and on the road. It would cost $50 per automobile to recall and replace the latches, but D takes no action to do so. P is injured while riding in X's new Leymon when the latch comes loose, the hood flies up, and X loses control of the car and hits a telephone pole. P's damages are estimated by his attorneys to be $300,000. May P recover from D? Why or why not?

8. D, who is a lawyer, enters into a fee agreement with P to represent P in a personal injury matter. The agreement contains the following clause: "P agrees that D shall take such steps as necessary to effectuate settlement of this matter." After negotiations with the other party, D recommends to P acceptance of a settlement offer of $10,000, which P accepts. Later, at a party, P tells X, another lawyer, about the case. X says, "I can't believe it; that case should never have been settled. A first year law student could have gotten a minimum of $50,000 in a jury trial." P checks with other lawyers, all of whom agree that the case should have gone to trial. Does P have any recourse against D? On what theory? Will he prevail?

9. In the cases <u>In re Polemis</u>, <u>Wagon Mound 1</u>, and <u>Wagon Mound 2</u>, the British courts wrestled with the question of reasonably forseeable risks and consequences in cases where the damage that results may be different from the damage reasonably to be anticipated. What are the policy considerations underlying the rules that evolved from these cases? Do you agree with the position of the British courts? Why and why not?

10. D, who is fourteen years old, mows lawns during the summer to earn money. He operates a riding tractor lawn mower in his work. One day, while mowing P's yard, D observes Wanda Kissya (a girl in D's class at school) walking by in a scanty and revealing outfit. Temporarily distracted, D fails to notice P, Jr., P's toddler son, in the path

of the mower. Sparing the details, suffice it to say that P, Jr. is mowed and mulched. Is D responsible for P, Jr.'s death? What if P had been negligent in allowing P, Jr. out of the house while D was mowing?

11.   D invites P to come up to her place for a nightcap. P agrees. After one beer, P is still thirsty, and D directs him to the kitchen to get another beer. P gets the beer from the refrigerator and, while opening it, leans his hand against an exposed pipe. The pipe turns out to be an uninsulated hot water pipe, which D had been meaning to cover up, but had never gotten around to doing. P's hand is severely burned. Is D liable to P? What rationale?

Short Answer Question
(20 Minutes)

Marjorie Schoolgirl was driving without a valid driver's license at a speed of 39 miles per hour in a zone that had a legal limit of 35 miles per hour. Suddenly, Haddie Mayes darted out from between two cars parked on the right side of the street. She was struck by Marjorie's vehicle and severely injured. What would be the result if Haddie sued Marjorie for her injuries?

Short Answer Question

A city ordinance states: "It shall be a violation of the law for any person to use city property without the permission of the city." D and several friends used a parcel of land belonging to the city as a park without permission. P fell and was injured while walking in the park. P sued D, citing violation of the statute as the basis of civil liability. Will a court hold D liable, and why?

Short Answers
(15 Minutes)

One of your clients, Dr. Hatchett, has come to see you for advice. His practice is limited to OB-GYN patients, and has been very successful. Unfortunately, he just received a notice from his malpractice insurance carrier increasing his annual premiums from $15,000.00 to

$50,000.00. The letter from the company pointed out that although he had never been sued, doctors in his specialty faced a 70 percent chance of being sued for malpractice during their careers. Dr. Hatchett is outraged that his premiums should be so high in spite of his own unblemished record. He is considering canceling his insurance, and taking his chances. He is also interested in the recent articles about legislation that would modify the tort recovery system by limiting pain and suffering and punitive damage awards, forcing arbitration, placing a cap on attorney's fees, and providing for periodic payments of damage awards for the life of the victim. He would like you to advise him what he should do about the malpractice insurance, and about the impact of these alternative compensation systems on his practice, and his legal rights.

(15 Minutes)

The neighborhood children always teased Buster Brown's pet bull terrier. Over the July 4 holiday, they kept throwing firecrackers over the fence into the yard where the dog was kept. The terrified animal bolted through the gate, breaking it down, and rushed across the street where it seriously mauled little Brian Dailey who had not been throwing firecrackers (only) because he was attending a party for his aunt. Brown also kept a number of hogs on the premises, and these animals followed through the breach and stampeded Esta Clock's daisies, petunias, and other flora. Meanwhile, little Tommy Greed (who also was not one of the children throwing firecrackers) wandered into the yard, fell into the pond Brown had made to water his hogs, and drowned.

What tort actions may be brought? On what basis will plaintiffs argue for recovery? What defense might be presented by defendants?

(15 Minutes)

Larry Liar brought a silver teapot to an auction being conducted to raise money for a local charity [proceeds were to be split between charity and seller]. Liar told the auctioneer that the teapot had been crafted by Paul Revere, a famous eighteenth century silversmith. Indeed, although the teapot was heavily tarnished, the word

"Revere" was visible. The teapot was set on display with other items for inspection by prospective bidders. At auction time, the auctioneer described the pot as "a genuine Revere." Ima Sucker, a collector of Paul Revere crafted silver, immediately recognized that the bidders and auctioneer did not appreciate the value of such a piece. He was the successful bidder, having offered $75.00, but he knew that it was worth at least twice that amount. Sucker was especially pleased as he now had a complete Revere tea service and the value of the entire set was $1,000.00 more than the value of the individual pieces. When Sucker began to polish the pot at home, he discovered that the name "Charlie" proceeded the word Revere. Research disclosed that Charlie Revere was a twentieth century insurance salesman for whom silversmithing was a hobby. The teapot's only value was its silver content of $50.00.

Does Sucker have any legal recourse against Liar? For what? Do you anticipate any problems?

(15 Minutes)

A Roman Catholic nun, Sister Candida, was depicted on a greeting card produced by California Dreamers, Inc., and sold throughout the United States. The card bore a black and white photograph of Sister Candida seated in a chair, with a caption, "It's all right if you kiss me." Inside the card, the caption added, "So long as you don't get in the habit."

California Dreamers had obtained the photograph when it purchased the portfolio of a deceased photographer, and assumed that this photo was of a model in nun's clothing. At no time did Sister Candida consent to publication of her picture.

When Sister Candida learned about the card from her niece in Iowa, she was extremely upset and sought the advice of an attorney. She considers the depiction to impute to her a vile and suggestive remark, and the words on the card to constitute filthy, seamy, and degrading verse.

Sister Candida comes to you for advice. She would like to know whether the publication of this card is actionable and whether she might succeed in a suit against California Dreamers, Inc. What is your advice?

Questions 1 and 2 deal with the problem below.

Annie B. Still brought her three-year-old daughter Vanna to the home of Ira Insurer when she came by to drop off her insurance premiums. Isador Insurer, the twelve-year-old son of Ira, was mowing the lawn using his father's lawn tractor. When Annie went inside, at Ira's invitation, for a cup of coffee, she left Vanna on the front steps. Vanna soon wandered onto the lawn, sat down and began to play. Unfortunately, Isador did not notice Vanna playing in the grass and in the course of mowing the lawn, he ran over her foot and seriously injured it.

1. (15 Minutes)   Discuss the potential liability of Ira for the injuries sustained by Vanna.

2. (15 Minutes)   Discuss the potential liability of Isador for the injuries sustained by Vanna.

Questions 3, 4, and 5 deal with the problem below.

M. B. McManymen owned a restaurant called the "MacAttack." Because she was one of the best customers of Fisch's Fish Market, Dave Fisch, the owner, allowed her into the area normally reserved for employees to inspect the fish. One day, while looking at fish, McManymen slipped and fell on a banana peel that was on the floor and fractured her left arm. This injury put an end to McManymen's aspirations of becoming a concert violinist. Several years later, McManymen was in an automobile accident. Because of the weakened condition of her left arm, it broke (although had the arm not been weakened by the prior fracture, it would not have broken).

3. (15 Minutes)   Discuss whether McManymen can recover from Fisch for negligence and, if so, for what injuries.

4. (15 Minutes)   Would your answer regarding Fisch's liability change if Fisch had told his employees, prior to McManymen's fall, that it was a violation of company policy to bring food onto the work floor?

5. (15 Minutes)   How would your answer regarding the extent of liability be changed if McManymen were (seven) 7 months pregnant at the time of the fall and the following day gave birth to a stillborn baby?

Questions 6 and 7 deal with the problem below.

On April Fool's Day, Jack Jokes put on a bandit's mask, took the starter's pistol that he used when he officiated at track meets (loaded with blanks and incapable of firing bullets), and set out to trick his friends who were playing poker at the home of Garfield D. Katt. Jack burst into the kitchen, while pointing the pistol, and ordered the gamblers to put up their hands and hand over their money. Garfield, believing the robbery to be genuine, was so frightened that he fainted, fell, and died due to the concussion he sustained in the fall. Jack was secretly glad as he had never liked Garfield. Pattie Melt suspected the robber's identity and that the robbery was a practical joke, but was uncertain, so she cooperated. Jack took Pattie's money and that night wrote a note to Pattie telling her about the joke, that he had the money, and that it would be returned promptly.

6. (15 Minutes)   Discuss Jack's liability, if any, for Garfield's losses.

7. (15 Minutes)   Discuss Jack's liability, if any, for Pattie's losses.

Questions 8, 9, 10, and 11 deal with the problem below.

Paul S. Graff was attacked by a gang of young hoodlums (who were members of a gang called Daley's Dogs) as he walked down the street. One of the assailants struck him with a tire iron, while two others held him. A fourth took Graff's wallet; the leader, Brian Daley, kept watch while the muggings took place. Graff, badly bruised but conscious, went to the Mother of Mercy Hospital to be checked out. Mark Thyme, the resident on duty, bandaged Graff's head and sent him home. Although Graff complained of some dizziness, Dr. Thyme did not conduct any special tests or order Graff to remain in the hospital for observation. The next day, Graff got up and, feeling

better, went out to play touch football. During the game, while playing quarterback, Graff was tackled by his friend Willy "Icebox" Parry,
who forgot that they were playing touch. Graff collapsed, and died
the next day, although before he died he signed the following note:
"In consideration of $10,000 paid to me, I release Icebox Parry from
liability for my injuries in the football game. /s/Paul S. Graff." An
autopsy disclosed that an artery in Graff's brain was congenitally
weak; the artery was weakened further in the beating; it ruptured following the football injury, causing Graff's death.

8. (15 Minutes)   May Graff's estate recover in tort against
    some or all of the gang members? On what theories? What
    defenses, if any, are available?

9. (15 Minutes)   May Graff's estate recover in tort against Dr.
    Thyme? On what theories? What defenses, if any, are available?

10. (15 Minutes)   May Graff's estate recover in tort against
    Parry? On what theories? What defenses, if any, are available?

11. (15 Minutes)   Graff sued and obtained a judgment against
    Brian Daley's gang and Dr. Mark Thyme in the amount of
    $300,000. The jury found that the gang was 30 percent
    responsible, Dr. Thyme 30 percent responsible, Parry 30 per-
    cent responsible, and Graff 10 percent responsible. Dr. Thyme
    had liability insurance; Graff carried his own accident insur-
    ance, which will pay up to $200,000. The gang members were
    destitute, impecunious, and otherwise judgment-proof. Parry
    was independently wealthy. In a comparative negligence juris-
    diction, who will be required to contribute to satisfy the judg-
    ment and what will each contribution be? What if the
    jurisdiction has not adopted comparative negligence? Explain
    your answers.

Index

A

Absences, 34, 153
Academic overkill, 70
Academics, 152–155
Accreditation, 9
Admissions Office, 12
After class review, 66–67
Aggravations, 141
Alcohol, 145–146
American Bar
    Association, 9, 138,
    159
Americans with
    Disabilities Act
    (ADA), 151
Announcements, 31
Anxiety, 56, 112–113
Assignments
    help with, 26
    posting of, 13, 31
Assumptions, 106
Attendance in class, 34,
    153–154

B

Bar review course
    selection, 154
Bar review outlines, 69
*Barron's Guide to Law
    Schools,* 139, 160
*Barron's Guide to the
    LSAT,* 89
Big picture, focus on,
    76–77
Black Letter Law Series
    (West's), 69
Book briefing, 49
Breaks, 18, 32–33
Briefing of cases, 48–54
    note taking, 52,
    63–66
Budgeting, 139

C

Calendar for law school,
    12–13
Canned briefs, 49

Careers in Law, 148
Case
    description, 50
    reading of, 35–47
Characteristics of school,
    8–11
Checklists, 76
Choosing a law school,
    7–11
Civil procedure, 22
Class preparation,
    34–47, 57
Class rank, 152–153
Classroom experience,
    34–66, 153–154
Classroom participation,
    54, 56–57
Classroom routine,
    54–58
Clerkships, 160
Clinical education, 159
Codes, 30–31
Commercial outlines,
    69
Commitment, 140–141,
    165
Competitiveness, 27,
    33
Computers, 130–131,
    134
Concurring opinions, 52
Constitutional law, 22
Constructive notice
    concept, 31
Contracts, 21–22
Coping, 142–143
Courses, 20–23
    selection of, 154–155
Cramming, 80
Criminal law, 23
Culture of law school
    breaks, 18, 32–33
    competition, 27, 33
    rules and procedures,
    30–31
    socializing, 27, 32–33
Curriculum, 11, 160

D

Daily list, 135
Databases, 78, 129
Diet, 143
Disposition of case,
    51–52
Dissenting opinions,
    52
Diverse students,
    149–151
Drugs, 145–146
Due process, 31

E

Electronic databases,
    78, 129
E-mail, 129
Emotional involvement,
    28
Encyclopedias, 78
*Erie Railroad v.
    Tompkins,* 22
Essay examinations,
    83–86
Ethnic students,
    150–151
Evening school, 10
Examinations
    anxiety, 112–113
    beforehand prepara-
    tions for, 93
    description of, 92–93
    essay, 83–86,
    205–216
    evaluations, 120,
    123–124
    final, 18–20
    instructions, 93–94
    IRAC, 103–105
    logic, 105–107. *See
    also* Logic
    multiple-choice,
    88–90
    ongoing study for,
    80–81
    organizational steps,
    95–103

practice questions and
answers, 83,
113–127
preparing for, 93
reading of questions,
94–95
short answer, 86–88,
218–227
taking of, 80–127
time management,
108, 110–112
types of, 83–92
writing, 107–110
See also Writing
examinations
Exercise, 143

F
Facilities, 13
Facts of case, 50–51
Falling behind, 19
Federal Rules of Civil
Procedure, 22
Financial aid, 136–137
Financial planning,
136
First classes, 13, 15–16
First year, 152–153,
161–162
Foreign study, 160
Full-time student, 133,
136–138

G
Garratt v. Dailey,
35–44, 52, 63, 69,
186–187
Grades, posting of, 19

H
Henslee, William D.,
148
"Hitting the wall," 17
Holding of case, 51
Hornbooks, 68–69

I
"Independent" law
school, 30
Intent, 36–44, 58–63,
69

resource materials on,
170–192
Intentional torts, 21
Internet, 128–130
Issue of case, 51

J
January blues, 19
Job market, 146–148
Joint degree program,
160

K
Katko v. Briney, 96–103,
105

L
Laroux, Gaston, 28
Law review, 155–156
Learning, 3, 128–129
Legal Career Guide,
147–148
Legal encyclopedias,
78
Legal research, 129–130
Legal writing, 23
Legalines, 69
LEXIS, 78
Library, 78–79, 83
Logic, 105–107

M
Malpractice, 146
Marbury v. Madison,
22
McGuire v. Almy,
44–47, 54, 69
Meditation, 144
Memorization, 76–77
Mentor, 29
Microfiche, 78
Mnemonic devices, 76
Money management,
136–139
Moot court, 156
Multistate Bar Exam,
89, 111

N
Negligent torts, 21
Nonlaw courses, 158

*Nonlegal Careers for
Lawyers*, 148
Note taking, 52, 65–66
Nutshells, 69

O
One L, 15
Ongoing study, 80–81
Orientation, 12–14
Outlines, 71–76

P
Panic, 18, 110
Paper Chase, The, 15,
24
Part-time student,
133–134, 137–138
Peer pressure, 27
Personal digital assistant,
131
Physically challenged
students, 151
Pitfalls, 145–146
Posting of assignments,
13, 31
Pressures, 16–17, 26–28
Prestige, 8–9
Private schools, 137
Procedures, 30–31
Professional
responsibility, 23
Professors, 24–26
control by, 54
grilling by, 62–63
review for
examinations
by, 81
talking to, 67–68
Property, 21
*Prosser and Keeton on
Torts*, 68, 170–180

R
Ranson v. Kitner, 189
Rationale of case, 51
Reading
of cases, 35–47
of examination
questions and
instructions, 93–95
outside, 68–70

suggested types of, 167–168
"Red herrings," 104
Research, 129–130
Research assistants, 158
Responsibility
  for stress-related effects, 140
Rest and relaxation, 32–33, 143
Restatement of Torts, 41, 62, 68, 178–180
Restatements, 68
Review
  after-class, 66–67
  for examination, 81–83
Routine, 16–17
  classroom, 54–58
Rules, 30–31

S
Scholarly writing, 158
Scholarships, 138–139
Second semester, 19
Self-fulfilling prophecy, 162
Self-review, 81–82
Semester breaks, 18, 32–33
Short answer
  examinations, 86–88
  questions, 218–227
Shorthand symbols, 65–66
Silence of the Lambs, The, 29
Skills training, 159
Socializing, 27, 32–33
Socratic system, 12, 24, 54, 56, 130

Special interest groups, 157
Specialization, 160
Spelling, 107–108
Spivey v. Battaglia, 58–63, 67, 187–188
State schools, 137
Stoicism, 142
Stress, 140–145
Strict liability torts, 21
Students
  classmates, 26–28
  full-time, 133, 136–138
  getting acquainted with, 15
  grapevine of, 31
  part-time, 133–134, 137–138
  second career, 151
  transfer, 8
  upperclass, 16, 29–30
Student activities, 155–157
Student Bar Association (SBA), 156
Study groups
  description of, 26, 77
  outlining by, 74
  review for examinations with, 82–83
Substantive course selection, 154
Success, 1–6, 163–165
Suggested reading, 167–168
Summer school, 159–160
Syllogism, 105
Symbols for note-taking, 65–66
Synthesizing, 70–71

T
Technology
  electronic learning, 128–129
  Internet, 128–130
Terkel, Studs, 164
Tests. *See* Examinations
Tickler system, 135
Time management, 132–135
  examinations, 110–112
Torts, 21, 190–192
  case study analysis and questions, 194–203
  hornbook, 68–69
Tour of facilities, 13
Transfers from different schools, 8
Tuition. *See* Money management
"Type A" personalities, 146

U
Uniform Commercial Code, 22
Upperclass mentor, 29

W
Waning interest, 161
Weekly schedule, 134–135
WESTLAW, 78
White, Robert Bruce, 164–165
Women, 149–150
Working, 137–138, 160–161
Working, 164
Writing examinations, 107–110
  legal, 23
  scholarly, 158